EN PLEIN AIR

Watercolor

Expert techniques and simple step-by-step projects for creating dynamic landscapes in the open air with watercolor

Ron Stocke

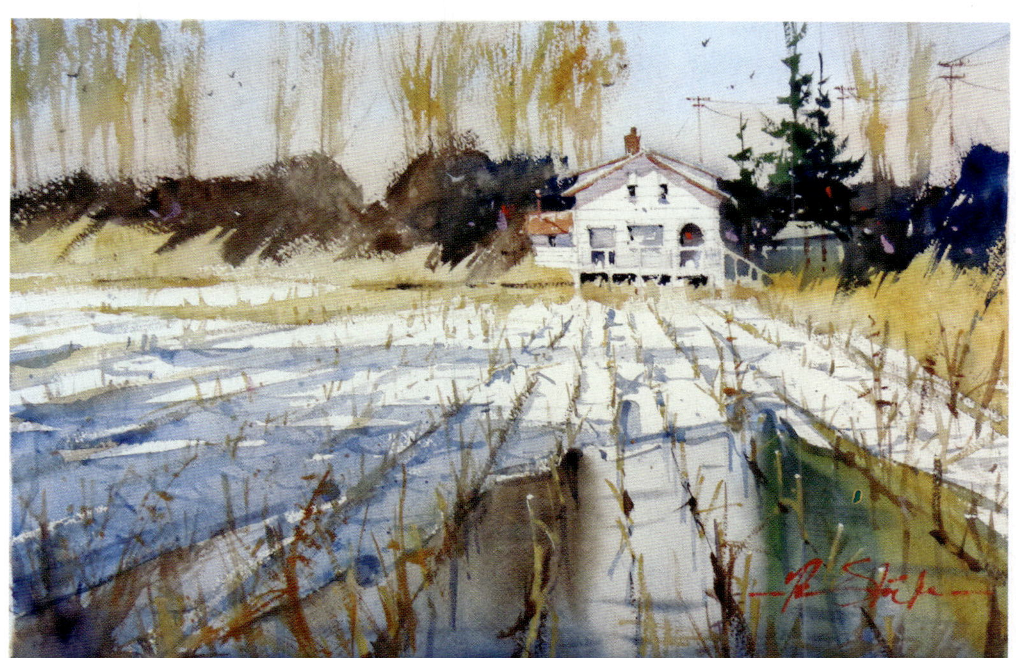

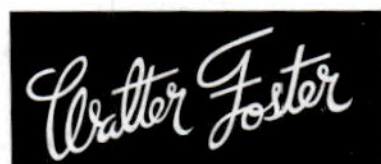

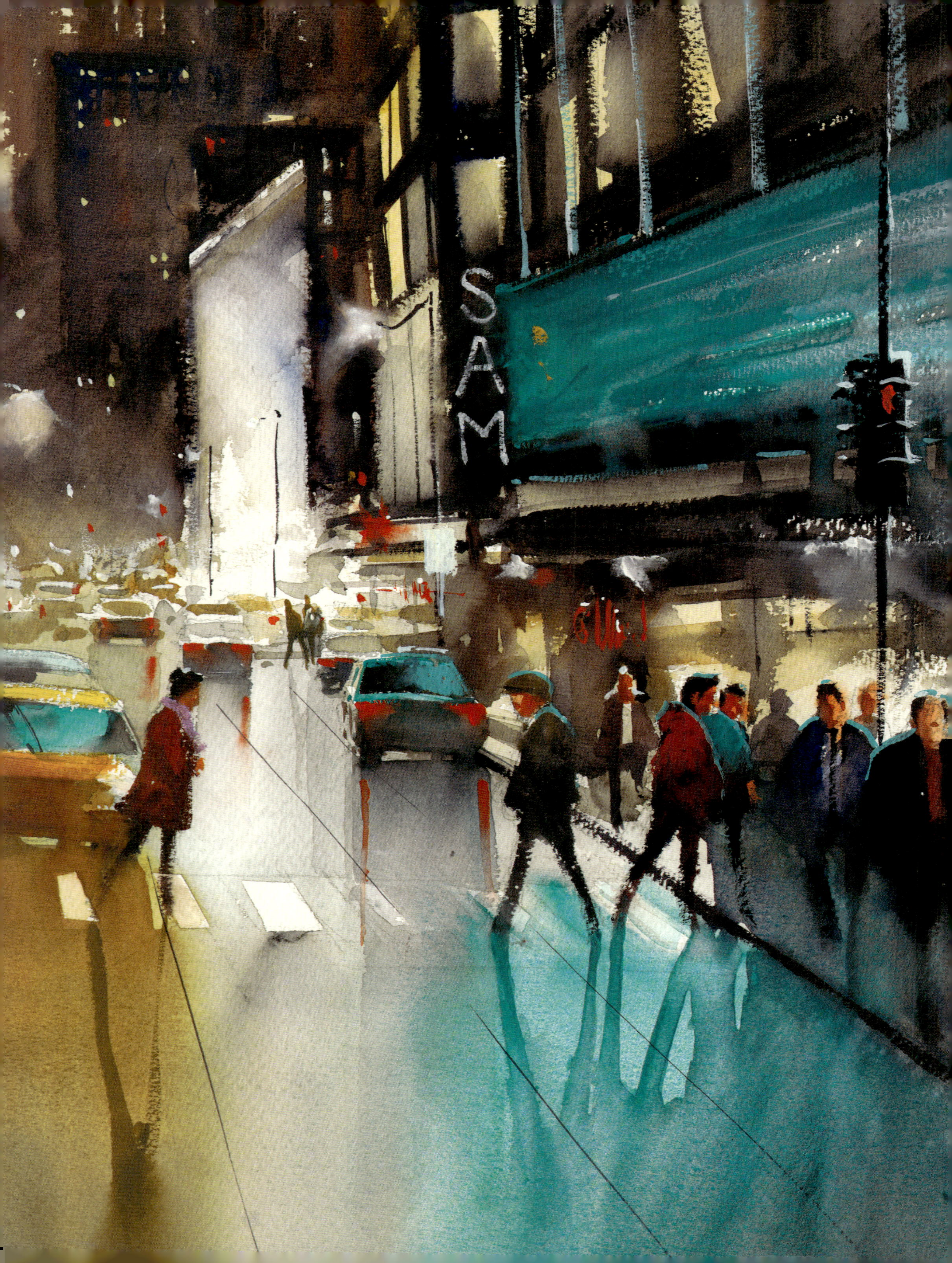
SAM

EN PLEIN AIR

Watercolor

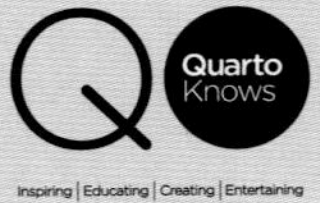

First Published in 2018 by Walter Foster Publishing, an imprint of The Quarto Group.
26391 Crown Valley Parkway, Suite 220, Mission Viejo, CA 92691, USA.
T (949) 380-7510 **F** (949) 380-7575 **www.QuartoKnows.com**

ISBN: 978-1-63322-616-6

Digital edition published in 2018
eISBN: 978-1-63322-617-3

Text and artwork by Ron Stocke
Editorial and design by BlueRed Press Ltd.

Printed in China
10 9 8 7 6 5 4 3 2

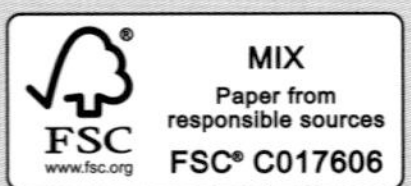

Page 1, *No One Home for the Holidays*
Page 2, *Seattle Art Museum at Night*
Page 6, *English Village Reflections*

Contents

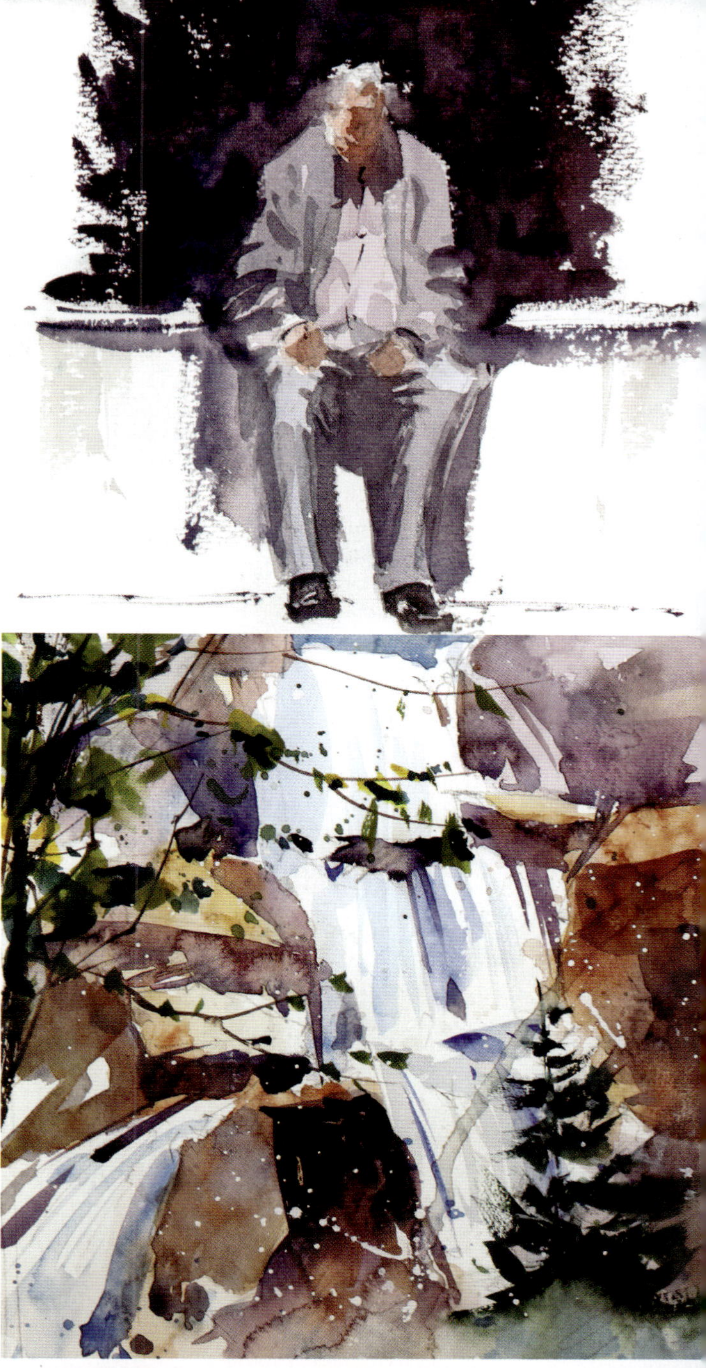

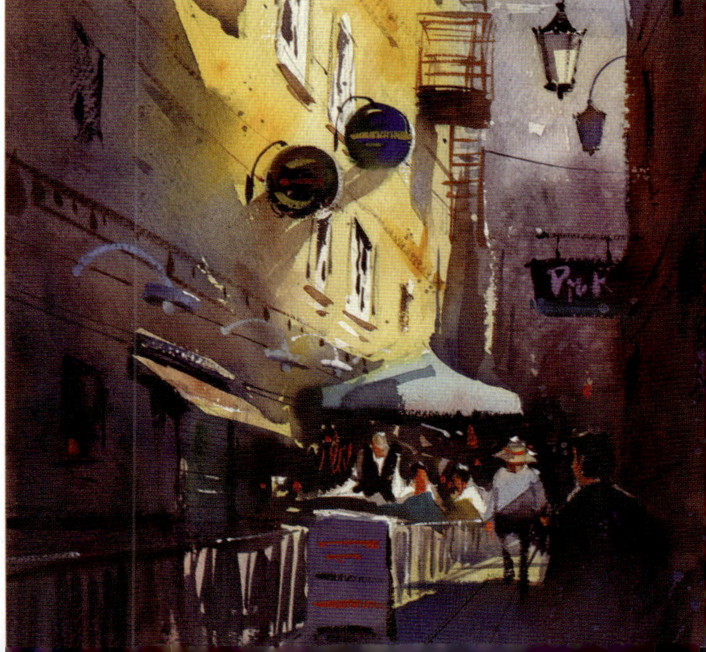

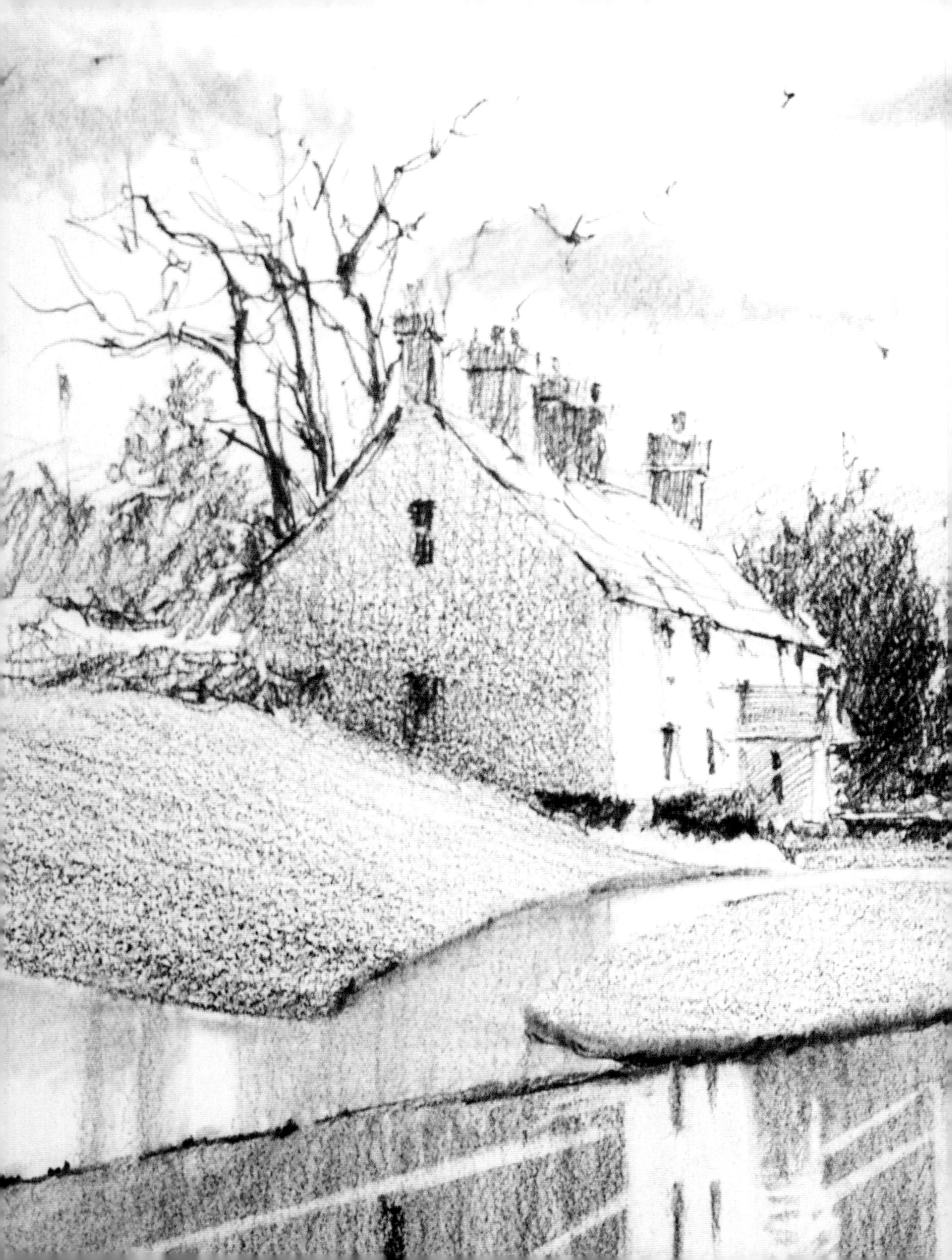

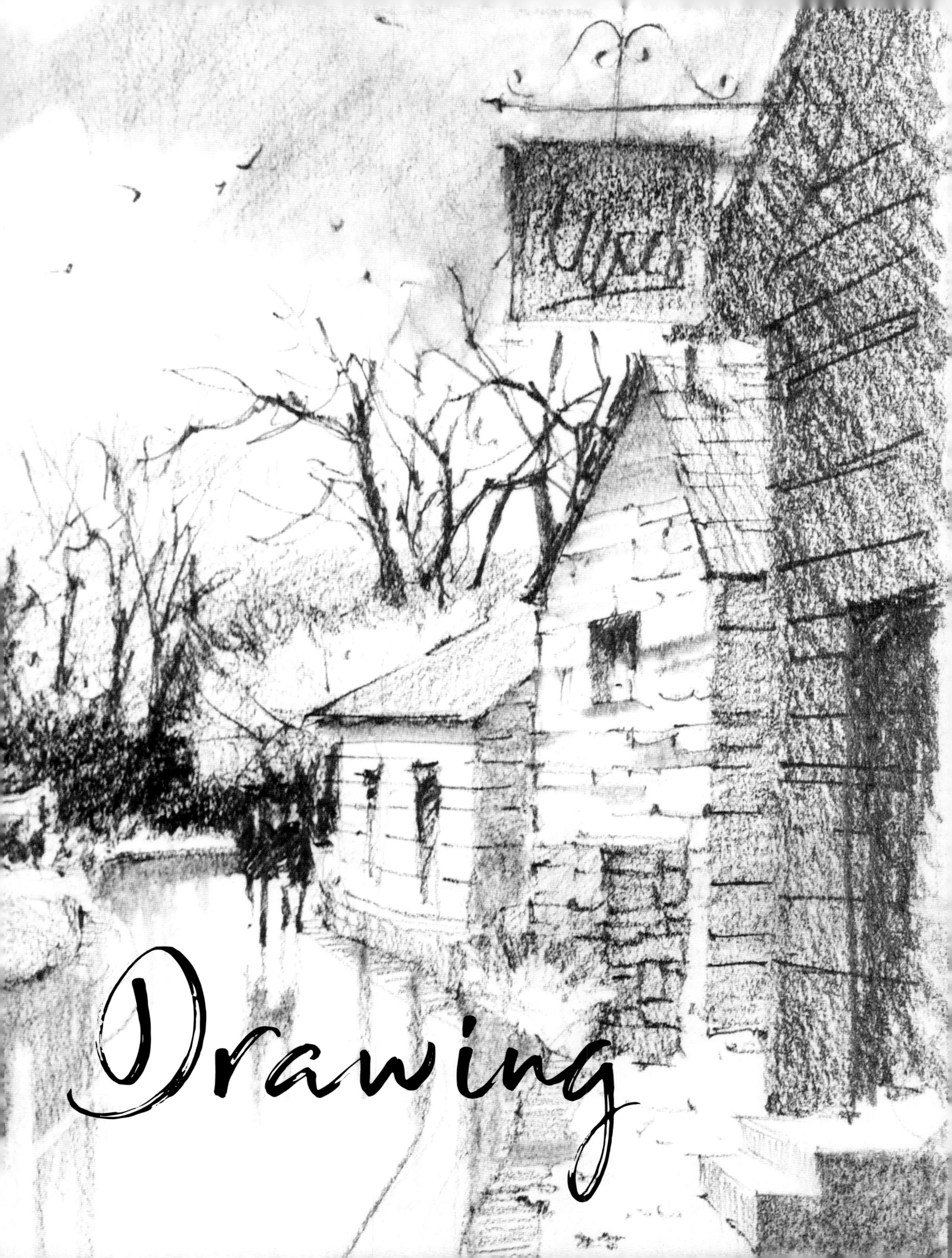

Drawing

Drawing Philosophy

Draw all you want, but paint only what you need.

Drawing is the foundation of your paintings. It is the act of observing your three-dimensional subject, and then trying to visually recreate it on a two-dimensional plane using shape, value, and perspective. It is the one thing that can derail your painting from the start, and it is perhaps the most important exercise you will take from this book. I discuss drawing on almost every page—reinforcing the old saying, “You can’t hide a bad drawing with a good painting.”

In this section, I will show you a few pieces to the puzzle that have helped me see drawing as part of the painting, rather than a hurdle I need to overcome before I put brush to paper.

There is one rule in painting that I have learned to be especially true: “If you want to learn to paint, learn to draw.” I am simply carrying on a tradition from the many artists who came before me, particularly those whom I admire and have given me this sage advice.

Drawing is one element that I’m always working on. I consider my sketchbook to be my most valuable tool. The work you do today in your sketchbook will pay dividends later in your finished work. In today’s busy world, it is often difficult to find time to complete a painting every day; it’s easier to open up your sketchbook and do a quick thumbnail drawing or value study. Spend your time drawing different subjects in different styles and with different media. Learn the fundamentals of basic perspective and how to see your subject well enough that you can recreate its likeness in a sketch. Remember, these are your lines, and they can never be duplicated; and if they originate from a strong foundation, they can never be challenged. This will soon become one of your favorite pastimes. As you develop your ability, you are also developing your artistic fingerprint. This, to me, is perhaps the best reason to be a creative person and should give you the permission to draw your own way. It’s what inspires me every time I go to my easel.

Madrid Fountain

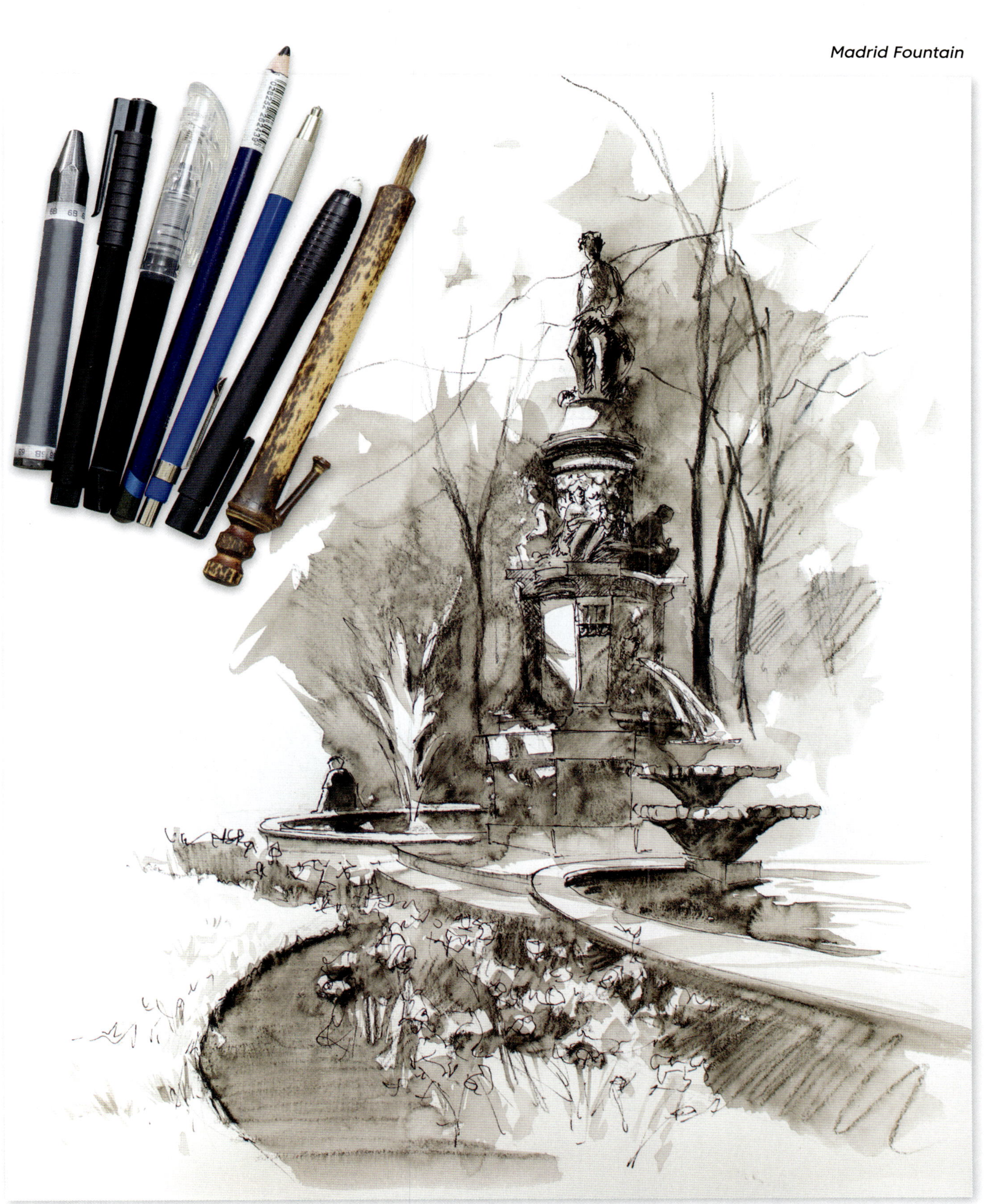

Drawing Styles

There are many drawing styles to practice—crosshatching, pointillism, scribbles, etc. My preferred technique is a modified contour drawing. I call this a "controlled scribble." Contour drawing is a technique in which you draw your subject with one continuous line without lifting the pencil from the surface of the paper. This technique is a wonderful way to help soften edges, loosen up, and connect your shapes. In most of my work, my first concern is connecting shapes. With contour drawing you can achieve this easily—it just takes practice.

Start by making a simple shape, say a circle. Now keep your pencil moving and don't lift it off the paper. Move to the side of the circle and draw a square, the whole time never lifting your pencil from the surface. Think of it as a controlled scribble.

What you have done is draw two shapes with a connected the pencil line—but more importantly, you have connected the two shapes in your mind. So when you paint them, you won't hesitate to connect them with a brushstroke, a wash, or by some other means. The reason connecting shapes is so vital in watercolor is because, unlike other media, it is very easy to get caught up in the work and accidentally establish unattended hard edges. This is known as tension. Most artists tend to paint all of their shapes separately, but this can be the kiss of death in watercolor. By connecting these shapes in your drawing, you've created a path to paint.

Hashmark This consists of straight intersecting lines that build form and value.

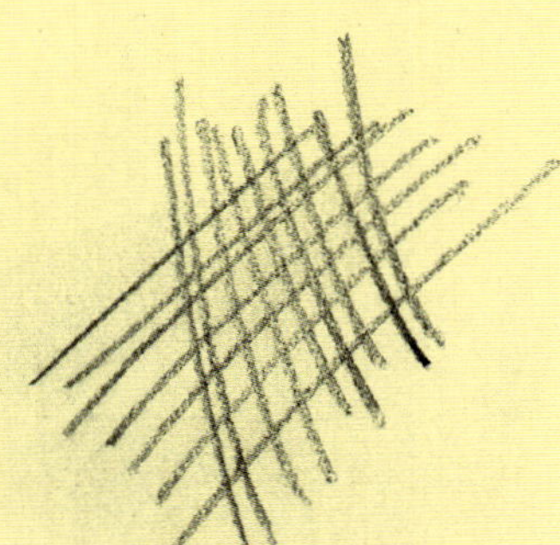

Contour This exercise is great for drawing organic lines.

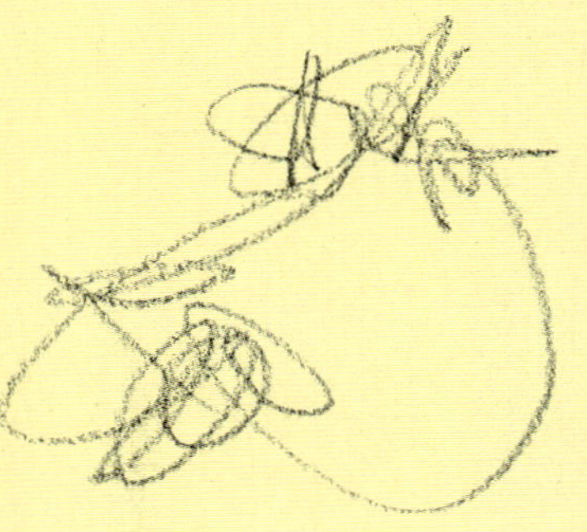

Combination Combining both styles takes advantage of both line strengths and frees up your mind so that you can draw in a loose and unpredictable way.

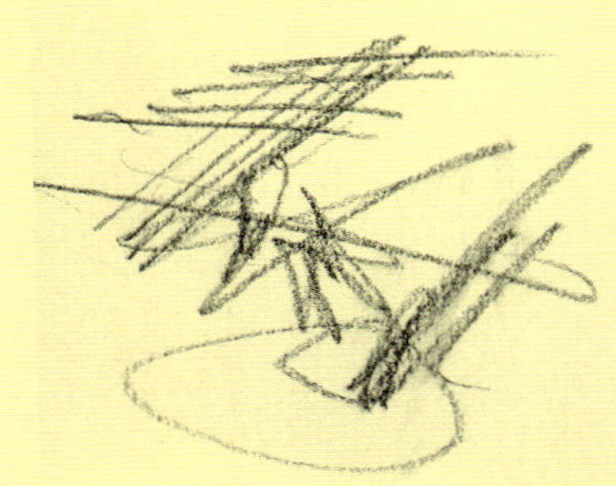

Washington Square Park, NYC

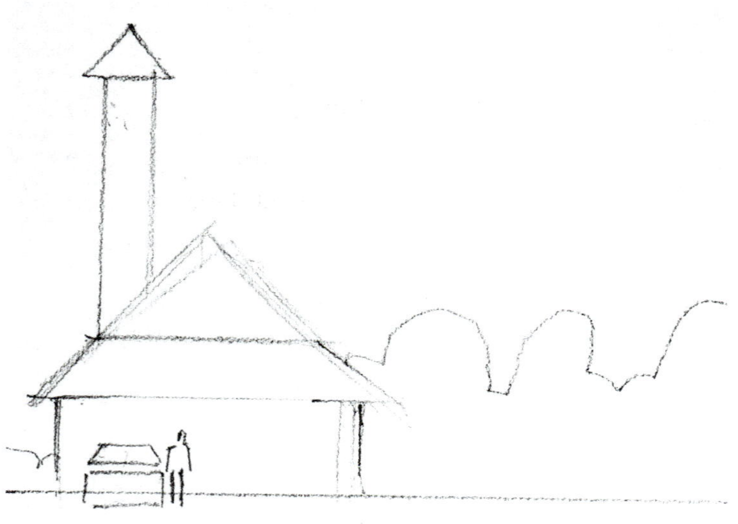

On Location

When on location, you rarely need to render a finished drawing, because chances are you are just sketching. However, back in the studio, it is tempting to tighten things up and begin to draw more detail than needed. Don't do this! The line quality of a quickly drawn gesture drawing can have unique energy that will help you in your paintings. It is your artistic fingerprint.

The examples on these pages demonstrate what I mean. I have drawn the same composition twice. On this page, at left, each element is drawn separately, as if cut and pasted. On the opposite page, I've drawn the same group of shapes with one continuous series of lines, not hesitating to draw through shapes or even taking the time to complete some shapes. When these lines are filled in, the finished result gives a looser, more intuitive composition.

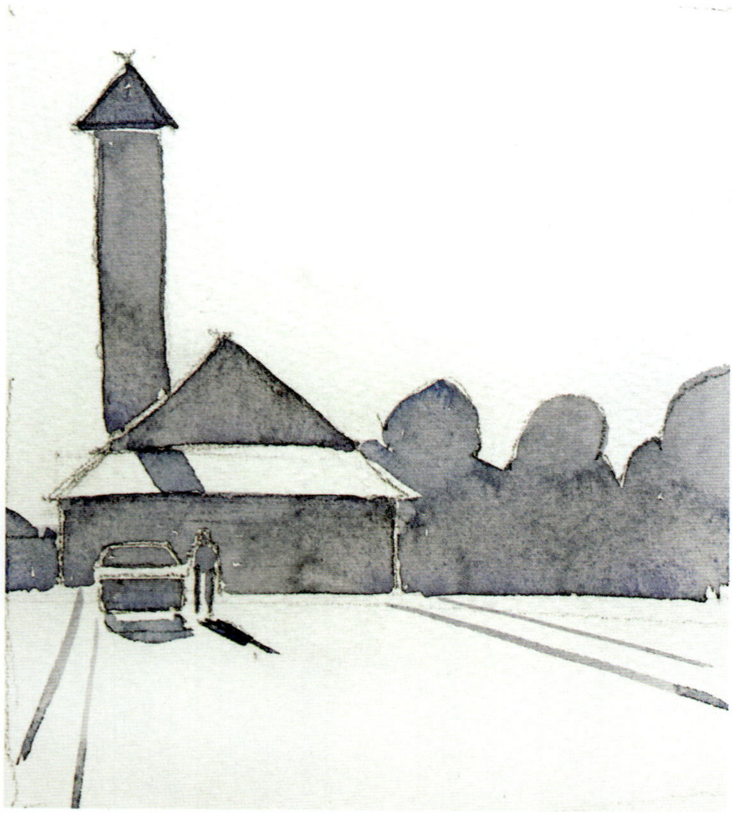

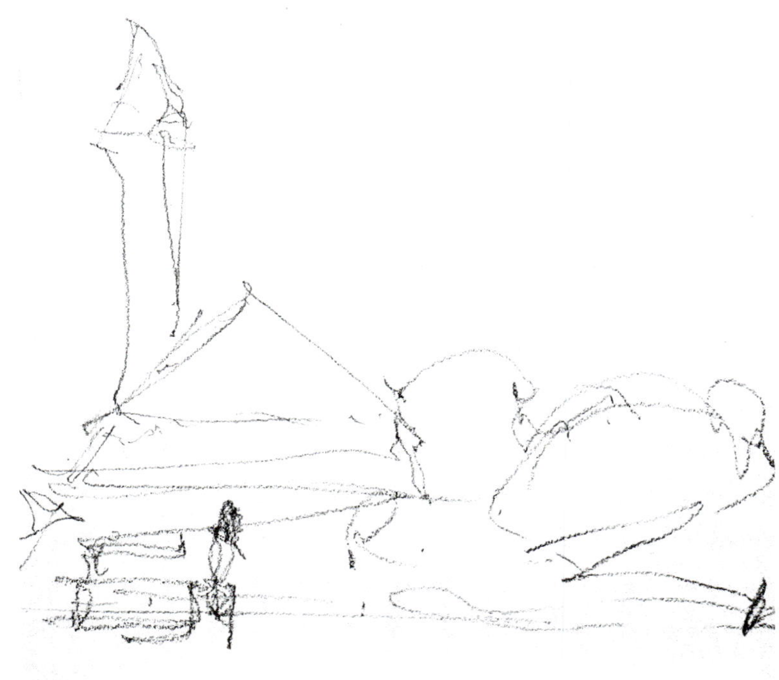

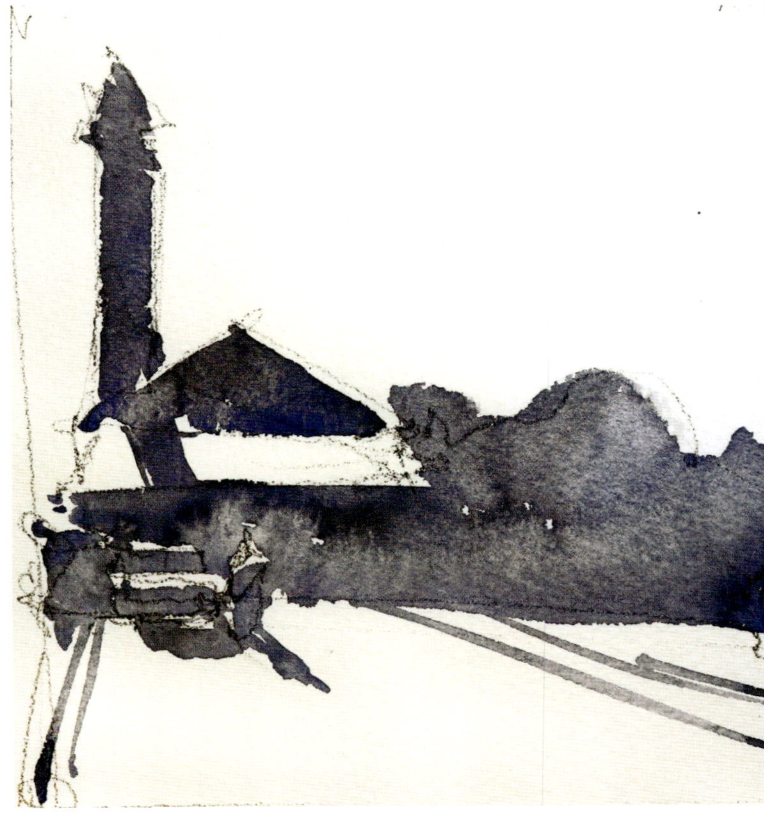

Loosening Up

All lines are not created equal. When I approach my subject, I ask how I can recreate it with as few brushstrokes as possible. This is also how I approach a drawing. My focus is not the inner detail of my subject, but rather its outside edges. As you spend time drawing, think of how you can create your subject with as few lines and shapes as possible.

By drawing in this way, you are doing several things, including setting the stage for how the painting will feel. Connecting your shapes with one continuous line creates an image with less negative tension, and therefore, when you apply paint it will flow more easily and give a fresher feel. This is the beginning of loosening up and creating exciting watercolors!

Simplify Your Subject

Say I'm painting on location. I've set up and I'm ready to go. I evaluate my subject, sketch my composition, and then finish my drawing. Just before I start painting, a car either parks in front of my subject, or the car that was prominently placed in my composition drives away! These events happen often. My remedy is to simplify the car shape so that I can place one in the composition whenever or wherever I want.

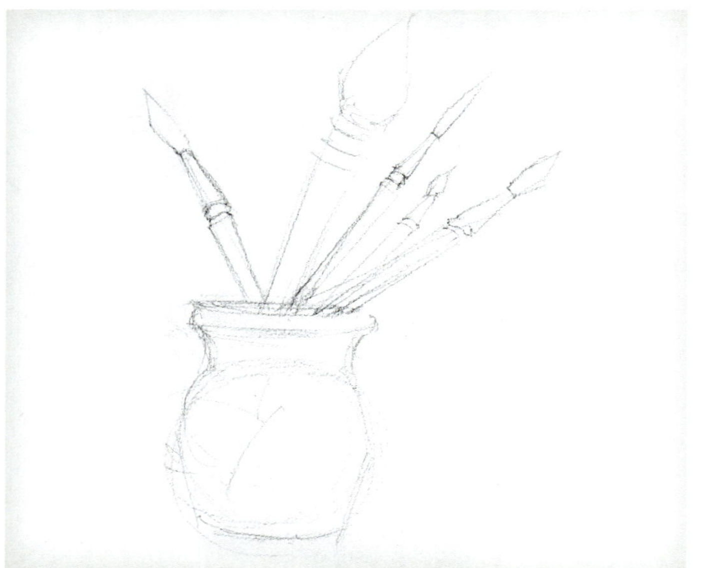

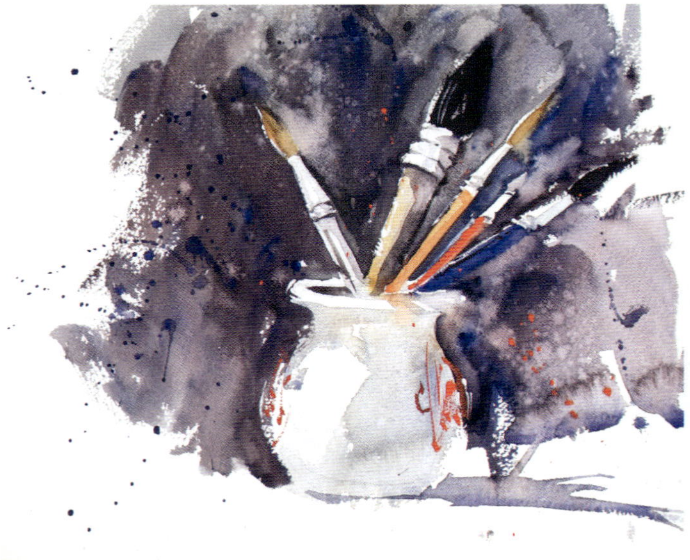

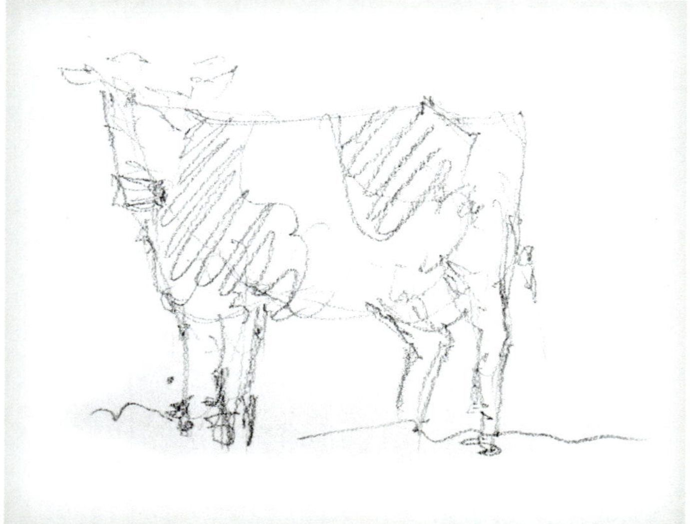

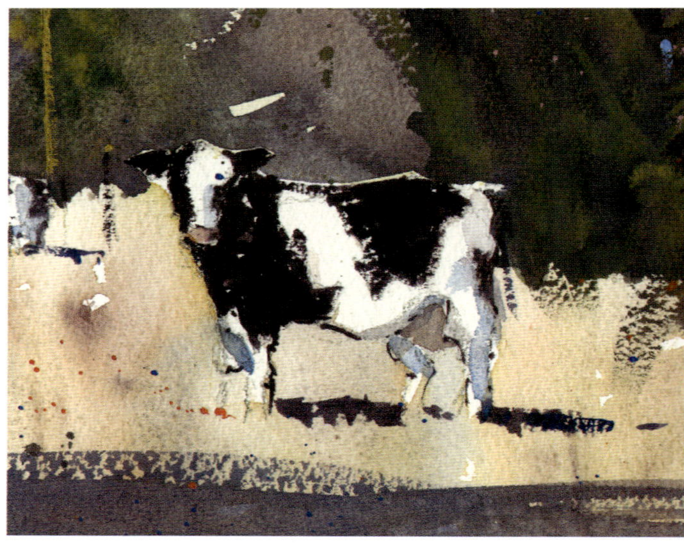

Above are two more examples of how to draw a subject, leaving out unnecessary details, so that it has more interest and a looser, spontaneous feel.

Breaking down and simplifying your subject into as few shapes as possible can help save time on location. It also helps to remember that you really only need to inform the viewer once. If they believe that they are looking at three boats, then you need only be accurate with one. The other boat shapes can be rendered freely. This will not only loosen up your painting style, but it will help add a unique quality to your work.

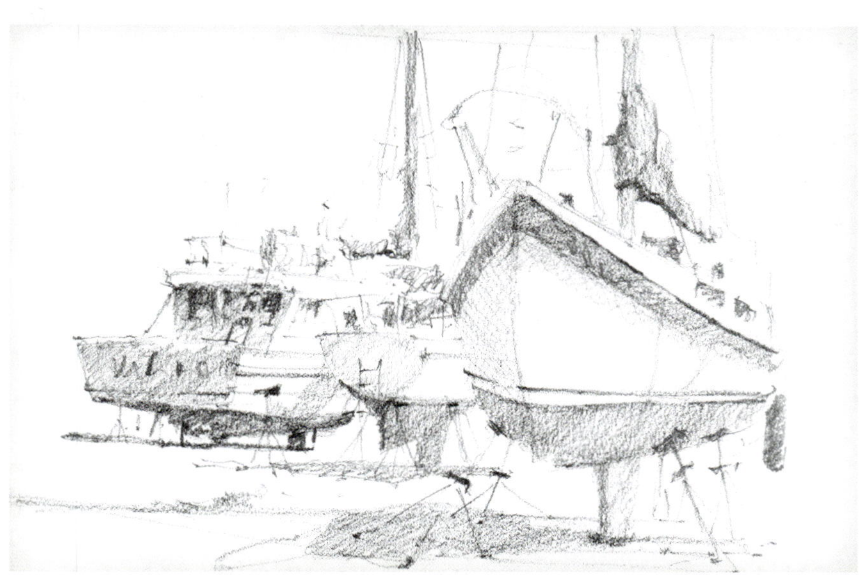

Dry Dock

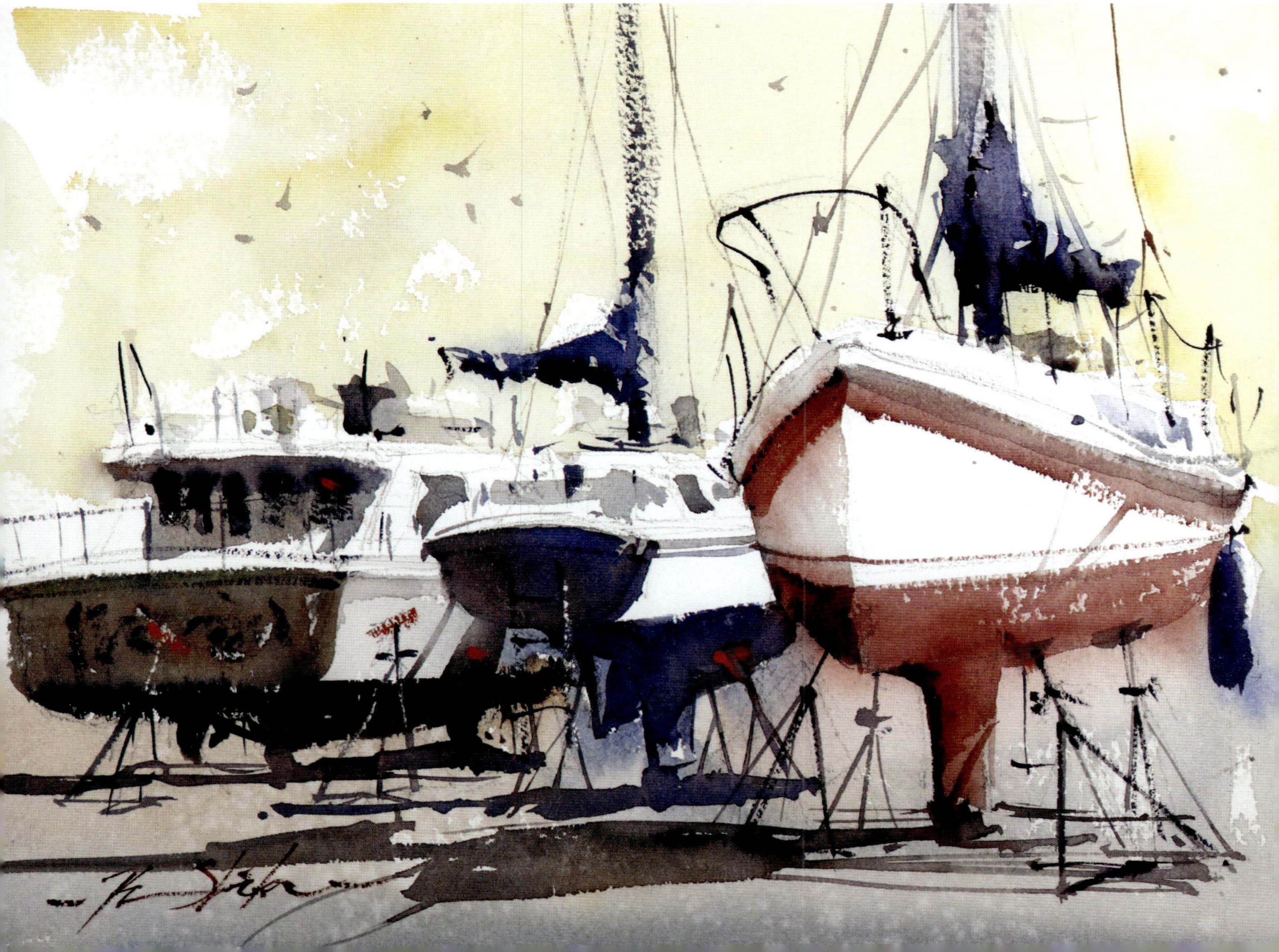

Perspective & Architecture

Perspective can be confusing at first, but once you have grasped the basic principles, your drawings and paintings will begin to look and feel more authentic. To understand perspective, you have to start with the horizon line, and accept the paradox that it presents when moving from a drawing to a painting (see "Breaking the Horizon" on page 62). The horizon line is not just a line that separates the sky and earth; it is the foundation from and to which everything is either physically or visually connected. It should be placed before attempting to draw anything else.

Artists have one major choice that is completely theirs: the placement or angle of the horizon line. Note that this choice can change the viewer's position. I encourage you to explore the possibilities—they can add drama and excitement to your work. The horizon line should be the first thing you place on your imagined plane when you start a new drawing.

A simple rule for perspective is to trust what you see. If you establish your horizon line and find your vanishing points (VPs), then most of the job is already done. The VP is a point on the horizon where all lines converge. You only need to connect these lines from your structure to the VP or vice versa—whichever way works best for you. Starting from your structure makes more sense, simply because you are originating from the window, door, roofline, etc. But don't worry. Once you get the hang of it, this will become a natural part of your drawing process.

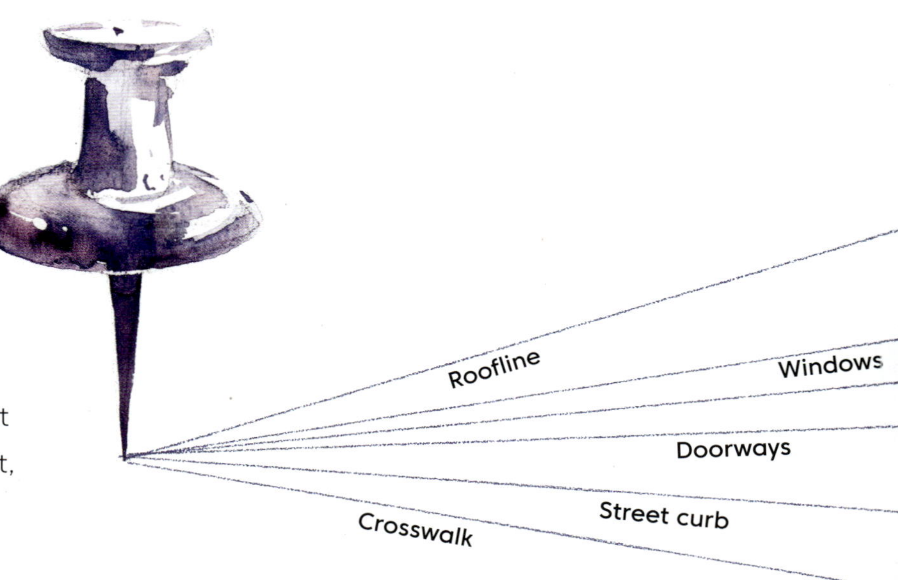

Say you are trying to establish the perspective of a building or any parallel horizontal lines within the structure. First you want to find the vanishing points. In this example, we will concentrate only on single-point perspective. Look at one side of the building (the front or left-side view shown below). Think of your VP as a giant pushpin, where all of your perspective lines are strings tied to the point of the pin.

After establishing the horizon line, I like to start at the roofline because it normally has a large value shift between the building and the sky. Value shift is defined as the range of light and dark of two opposing objects. This helps me place the object into my composition. Use a pencil or the handle of your brush to help you follow this line from the top edge of the roof to the horizon. Where these two lines meet is your vanishing point. This line also represents the angle of your roofline. Use this VP to find the angle for your windows, doors or any other architectural detail on the building, but don't stop there. Your VP dictates the lines above and below the horizon. Street curbs, crosswalks, and even cars will be affected by the same VP.

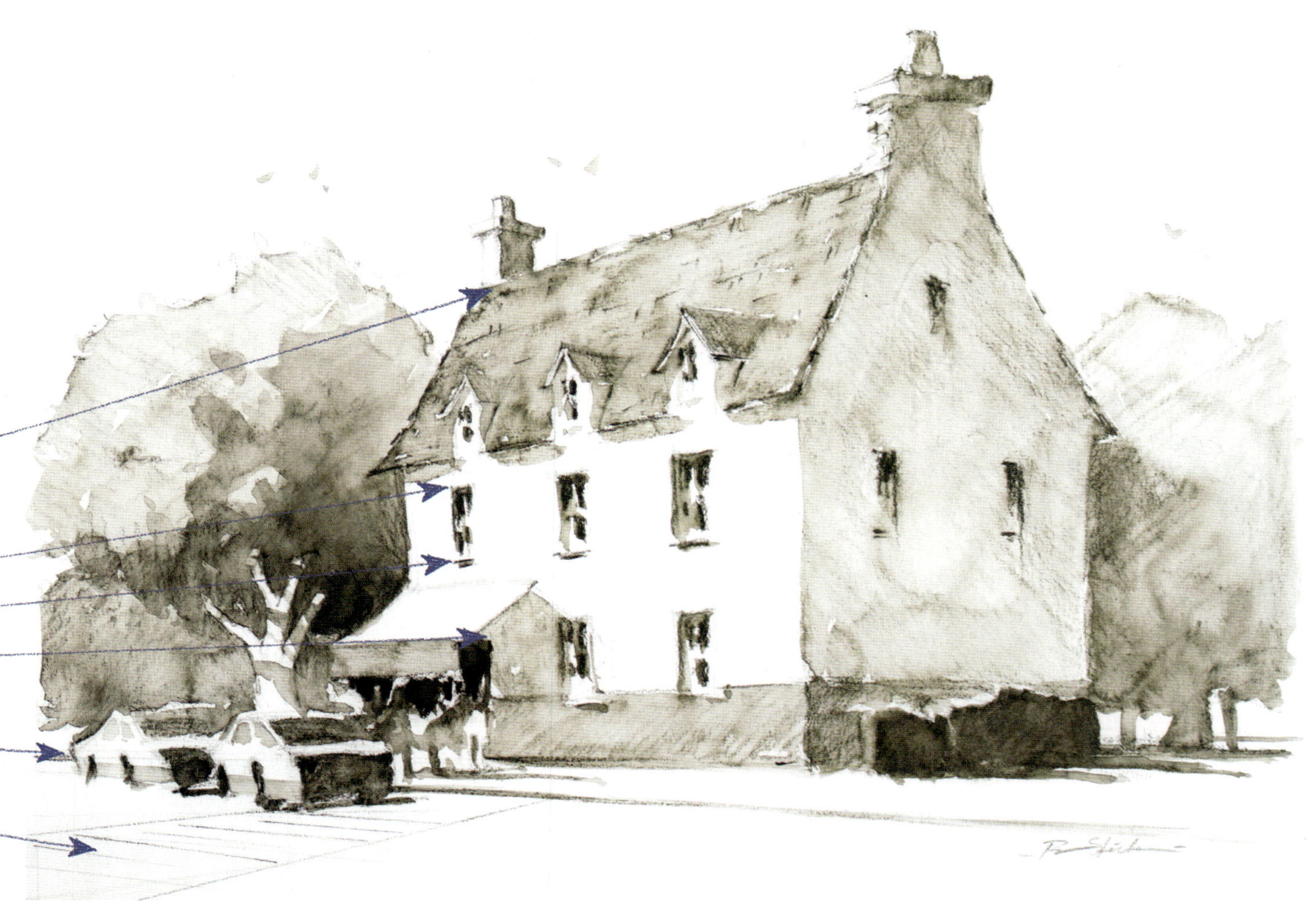

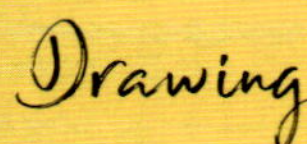

An Overview of Perspective

In real-life, your drawings and paintings will commonly have multiple VPs. It's safe to say that each side of a building, cube, or box will have one. The exception is when you are facing the building straight on. See how the two blue parallel lines will never meet in the single-point perspective figures below.

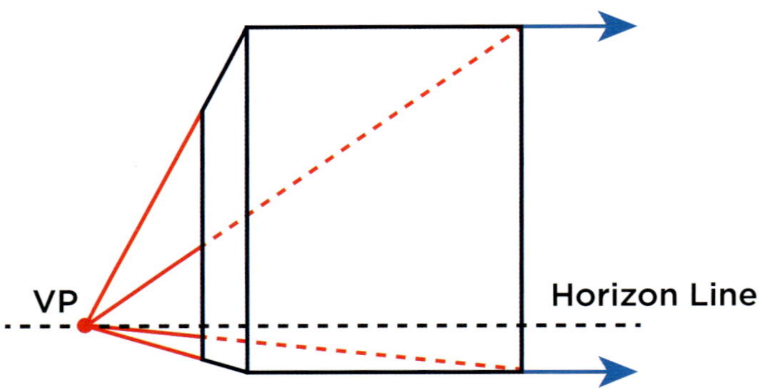

VP

Horizon Line

SINGLE-POINT PERSPECTIVE

The two red lines converge to the same point. The two blue lines never meet.

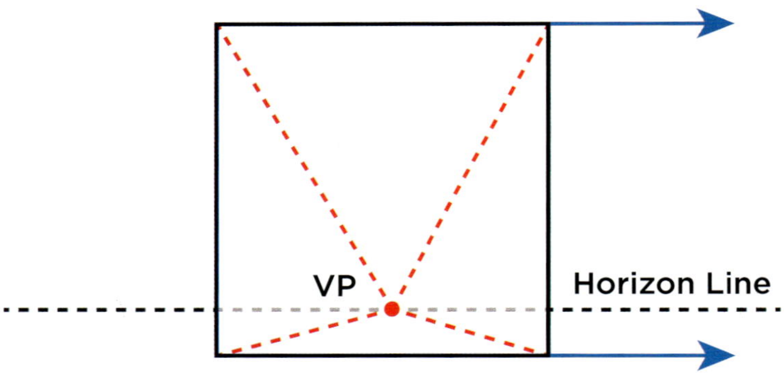

VP

Horizon Line

This shows the VP located behind the cube out of view; however, the same rules apply.

TWO-POINT PERSPECTIVE

Both the red and the blue lines converge to separate vanishing points, thus giving the cube its form.

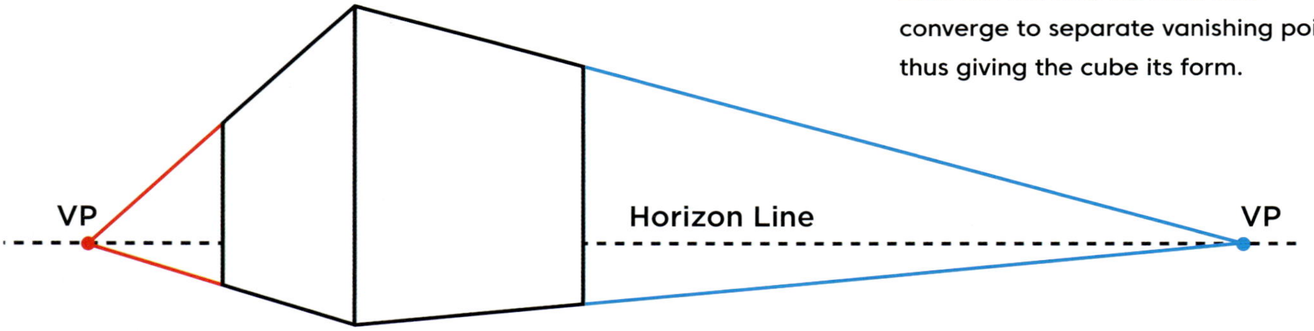

VP

Horizon Line

VP

Vanishing Points in Practice

Here I've simplified the concept by illustrating how all the major lines of the buildings eventually end at one point. I would like to say that this is an absolute with all man-made structures, but I have been proven wrong with creative architecture (think of Frank Gehry) and where buildings have aged and settled over time. That said, use this as a general rule to avoid the major issues you will otherwise experience.

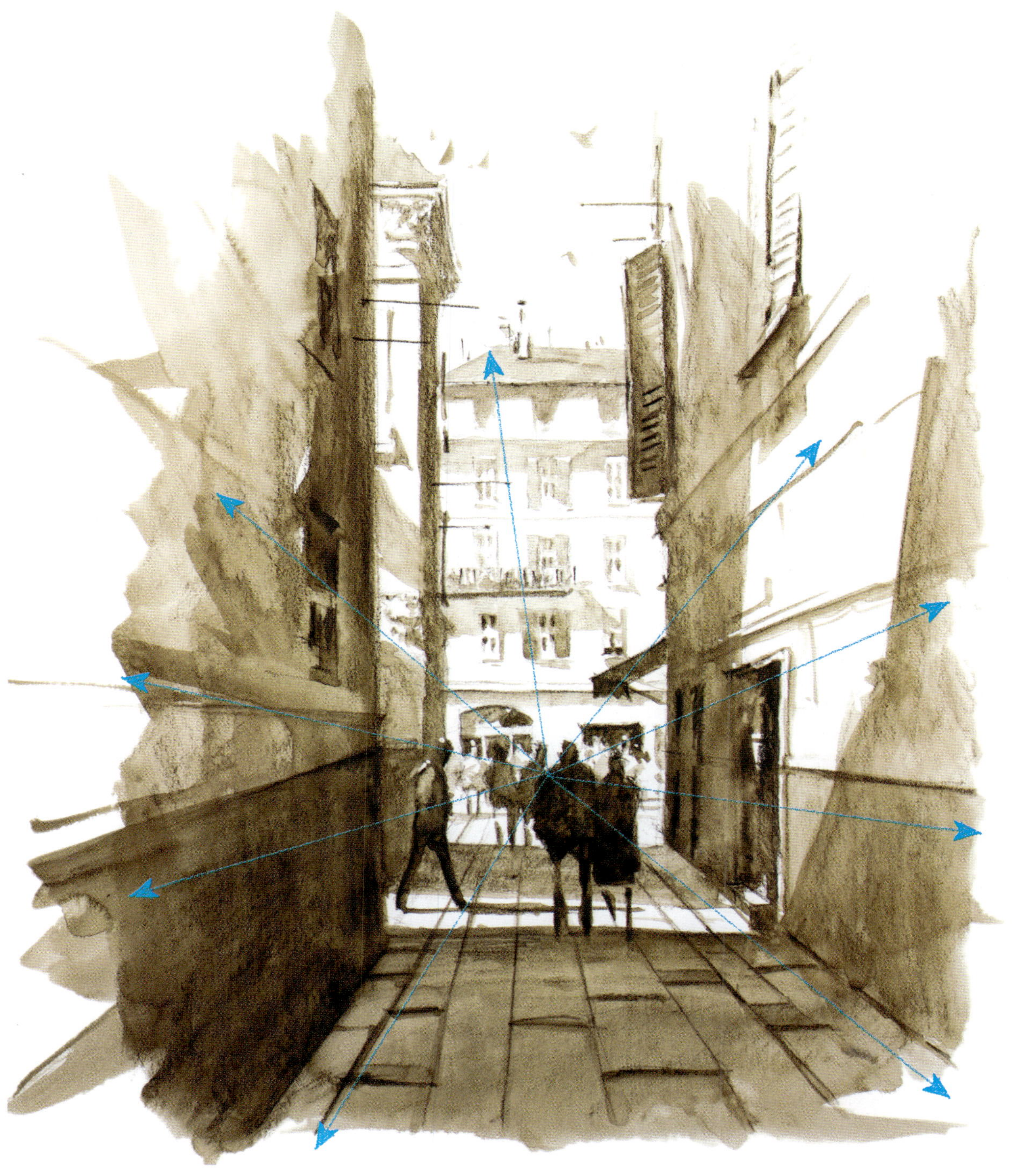

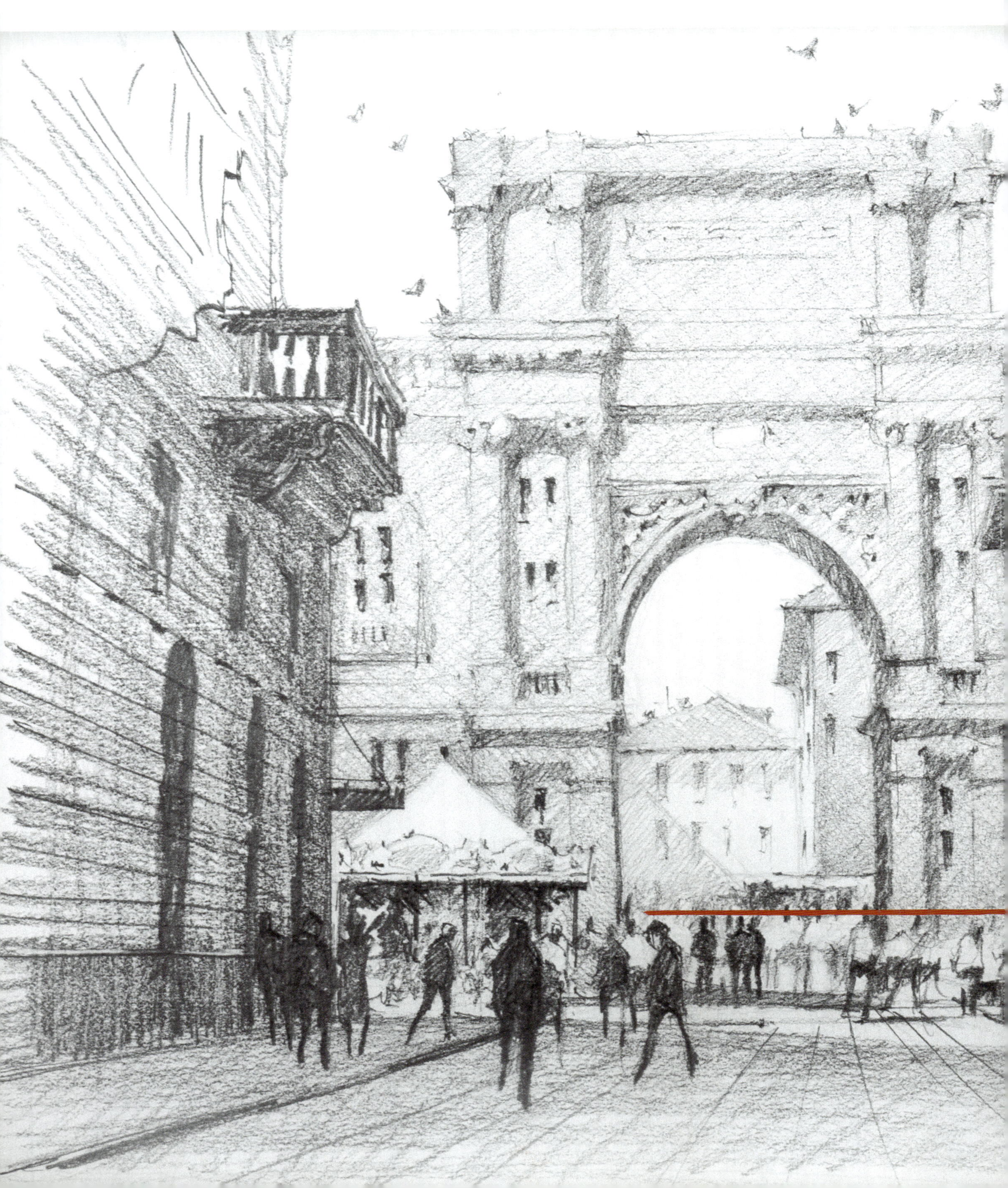

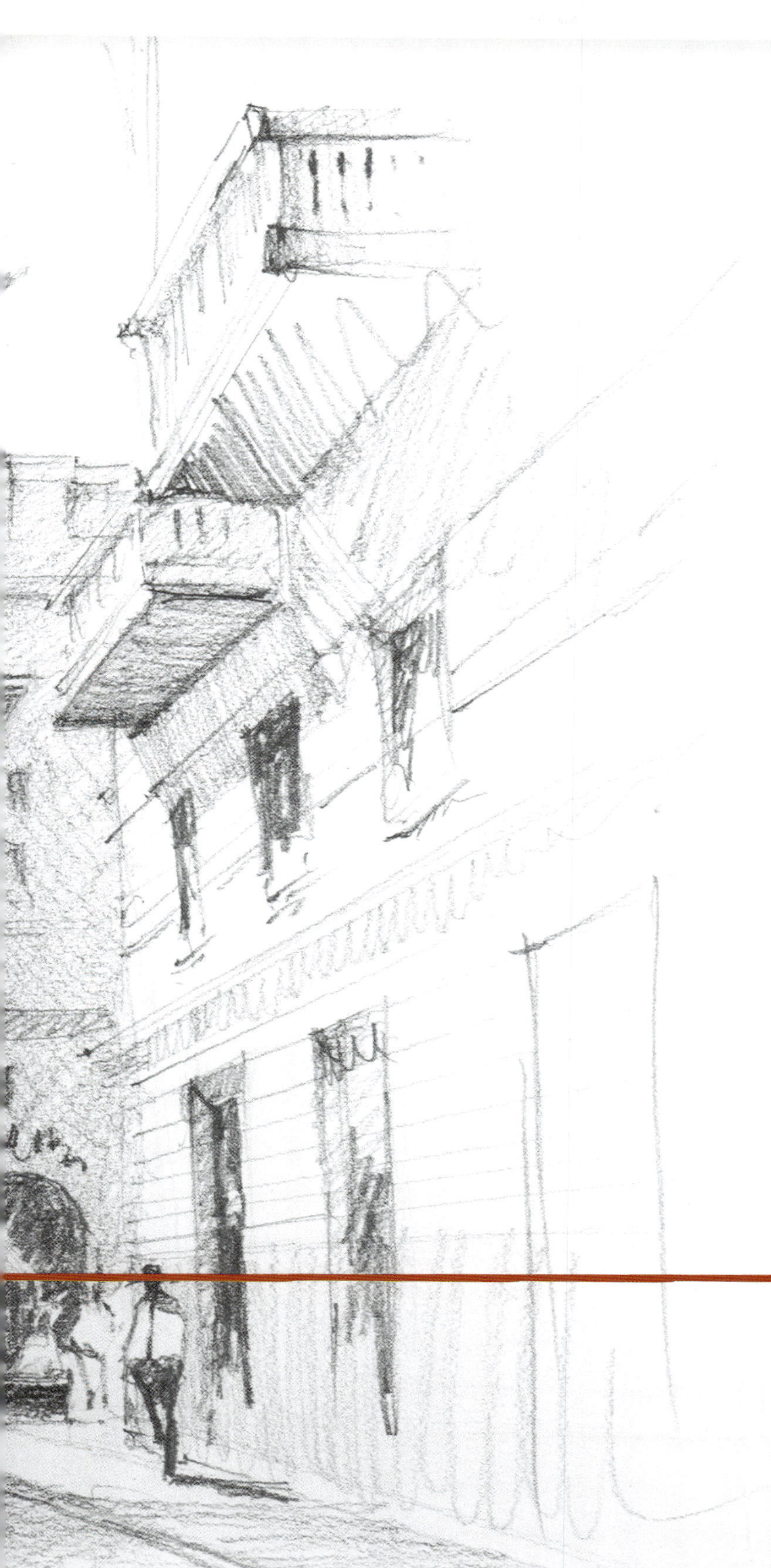

I did this sketch in Florence, Italy, at what is normally a very busy Piazza. I wanted to capture the scale of the archway next to the carnival that was taking place in the far lefthand corner. It is also an example of how perspective and value can work together to draw the viewer's eye to the focal point.

Many times, the best way to draw a viewer's eye to a focal point is to place the darkest darks next to the lightest lights, creating the highest contrast in that area. This is done with my use of the dark figures and shadow next to the bright triangle of light capturing the top of the carousel.

Piazza della Repubblica, Florence

Scale

It is important to know what size an object is in relation to its surroundings. Here are a few examples to keep in mind, so that your proportions look correct in your work.

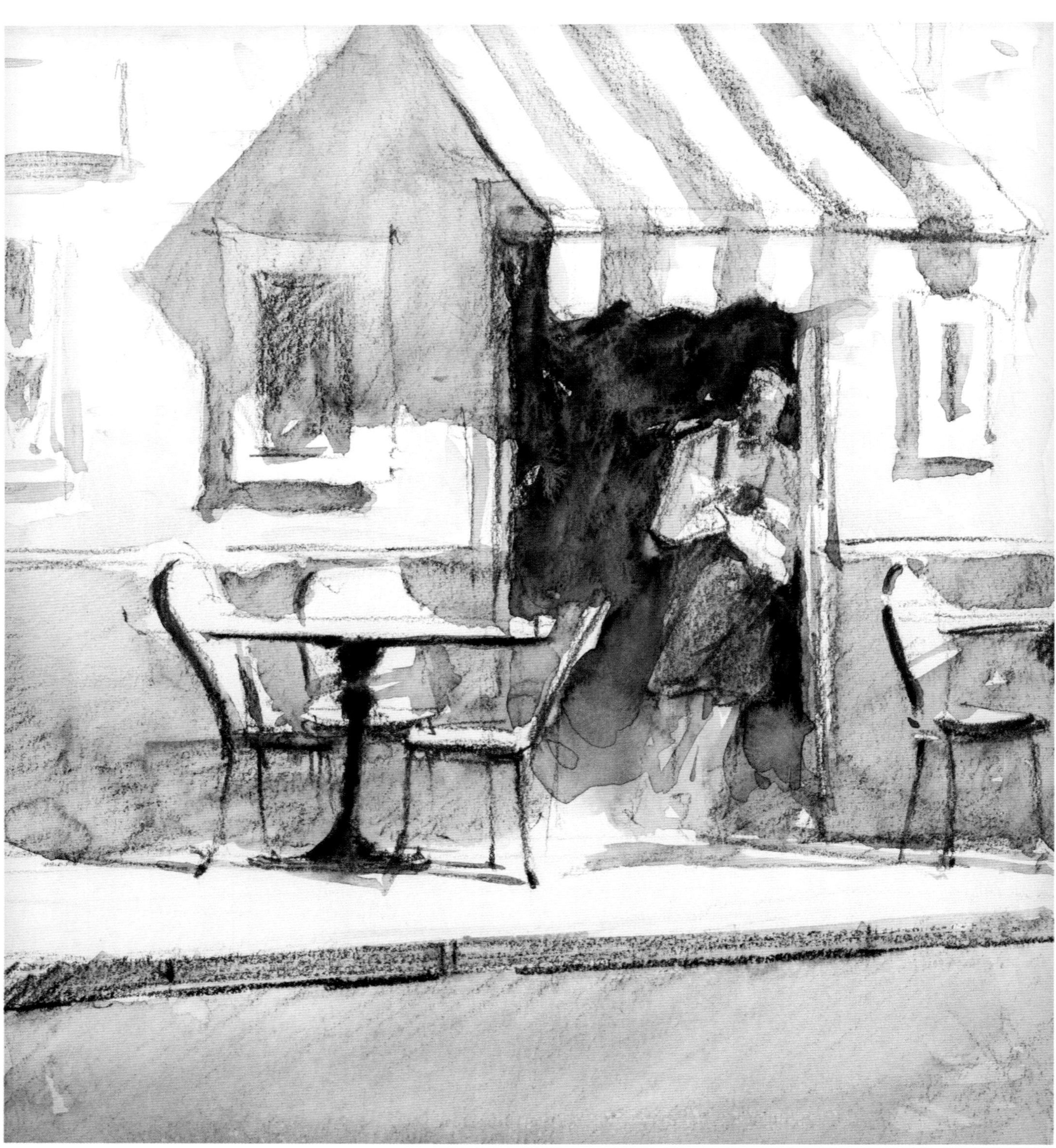

The average height of a man is 5 feet, 10 inches; the average woman is 5 feet, 4 inches; and the average height of a car is 5 feet. These measurements won't do you much good in the field, so look for other ways to scale objects so they look correct in your paintings. For example, the average car rests under the outstretched arm of an adult male. The seat of a café chair rests at about the same height as your knee, and the height of a table is at about mid thigh of a standing figure. If the figure is sitting, then the table height sits just below the rib cage. The standard doorway is around 7 feet, 6 inches tall, but windows can vary widely in height and width. Find other ways of relating the size of objects in your paintings to avoid issues with scale.

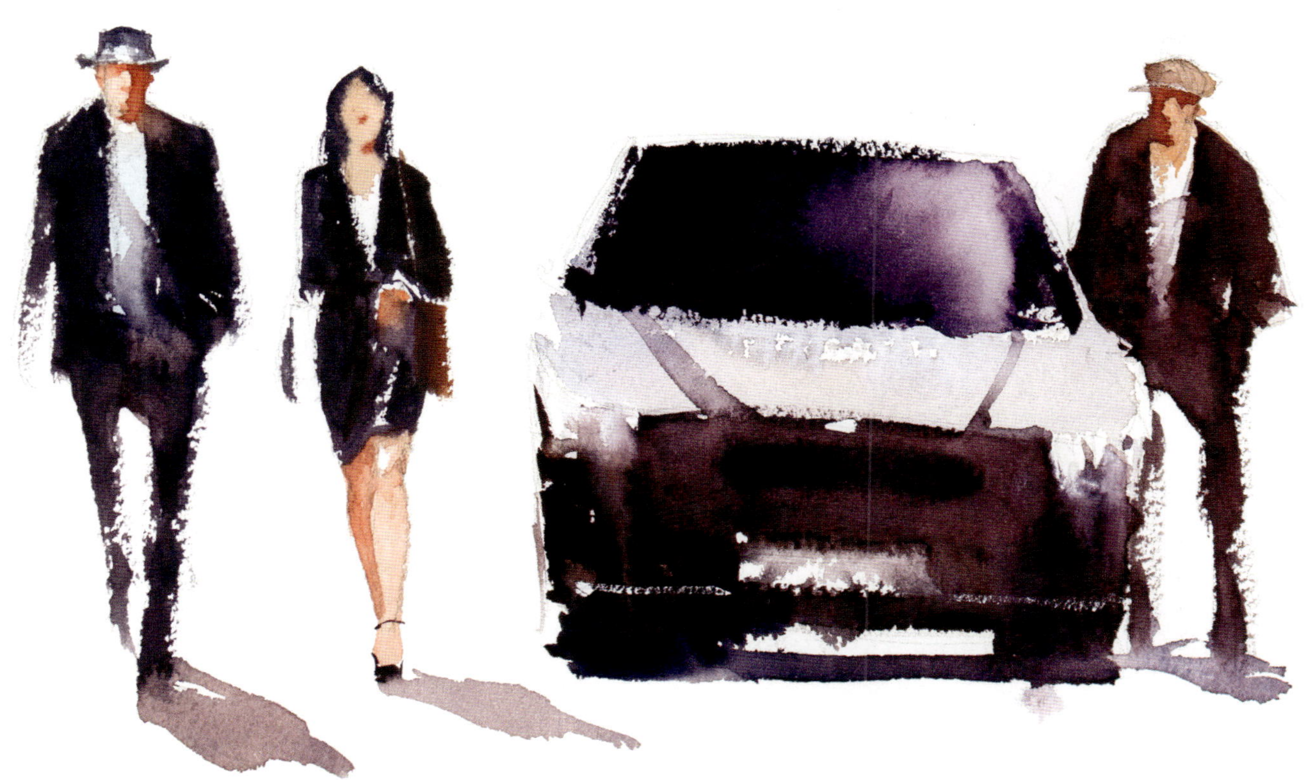

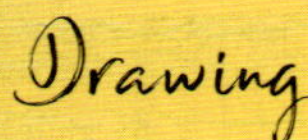

Knowing how to judge the size of your subjects in comparison to their surroundings is important when making those first notes on paper. I like to use a pencil as a quick measuring device. It helps me with the key elements of my drawing, such as figures, cars, café umbrellas, etc.

I hold out my pencil at arms length. Starting at the top of the pencil (eraser end), I find the top of the object and with my thumbnail make a mark on the pencil. I can then easily transfer this to my paper.

Understanding general rules will help the process go much faster. For example, it will help you get the scale correct if you know that a person riding a bicycle and a person standing next to a bicycle are roughly the same height.

These small but important details will help you draw objects so they don't look out of scale. You'll pick them up as you become more experienced.

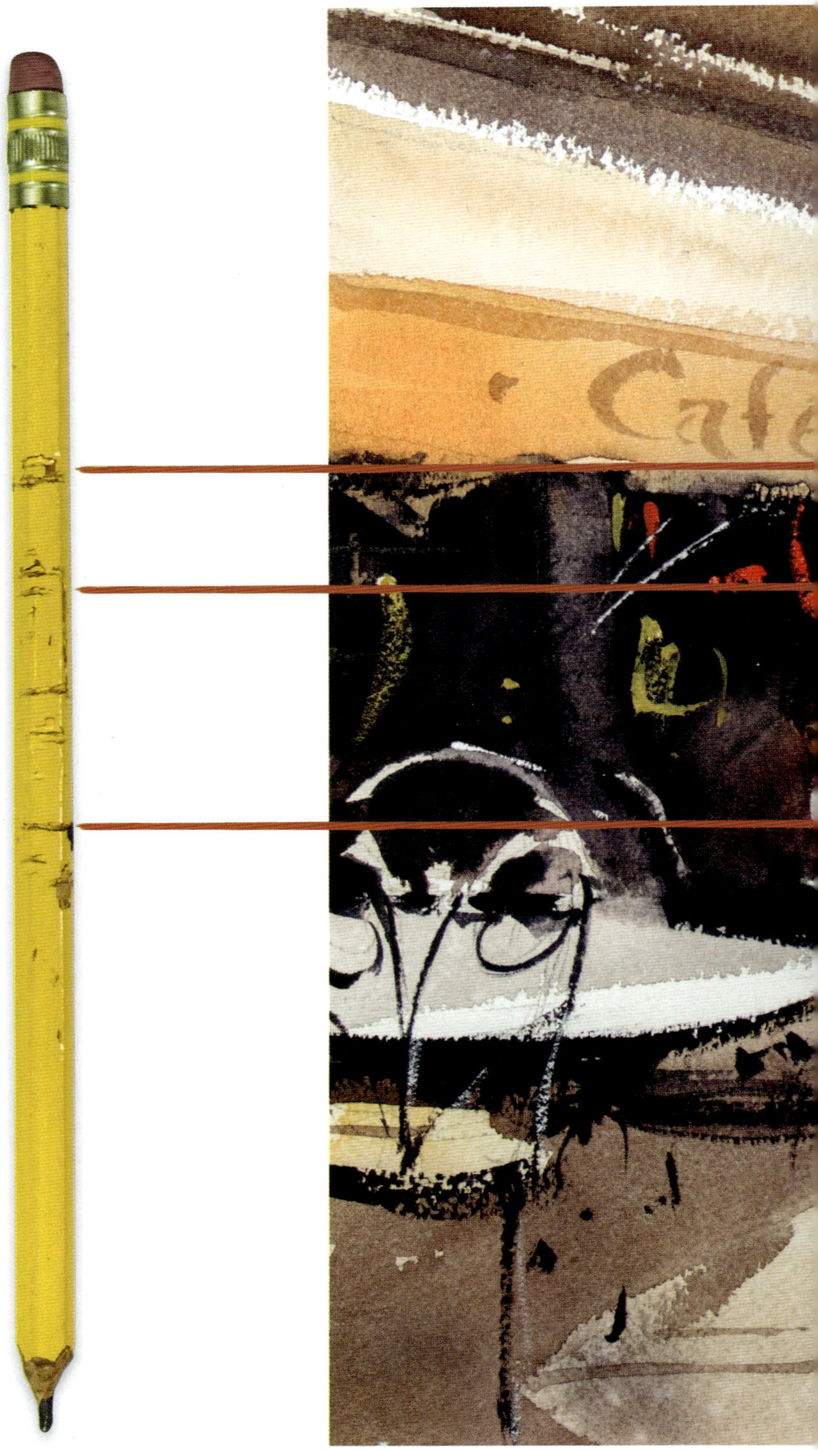

Market Café, Nice, France

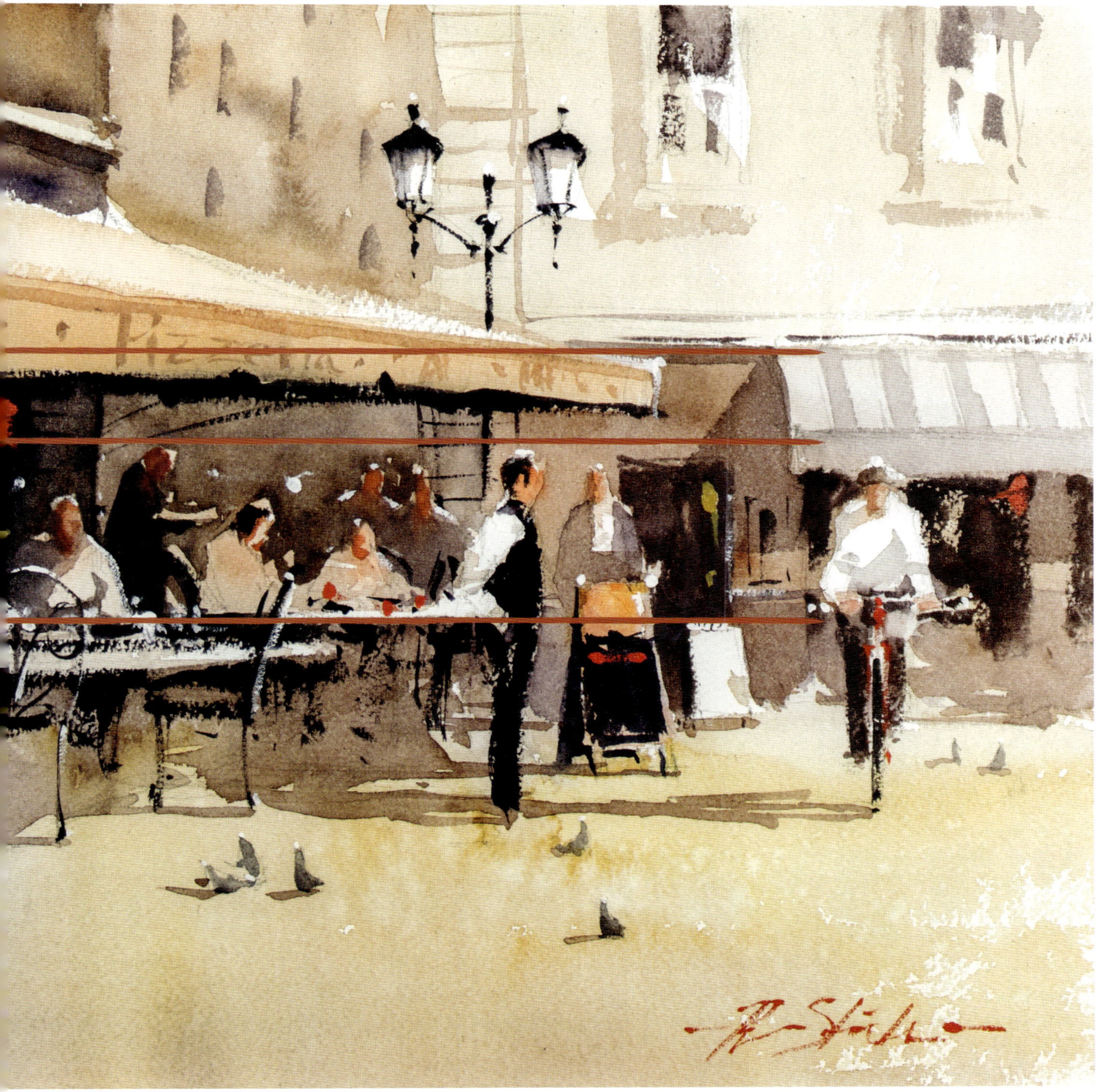

Cars

It is hard to imagine not seeing a car in your everyday life. The automobile is a shape that most of us will see hundreds, if not thousands, of times a day. In some situations, vehicles will outnumber humans two to one. I'm referring to parking lots, sporting events, and freeways. Unlike the human figure, automobiles are much easier shapes to draw.

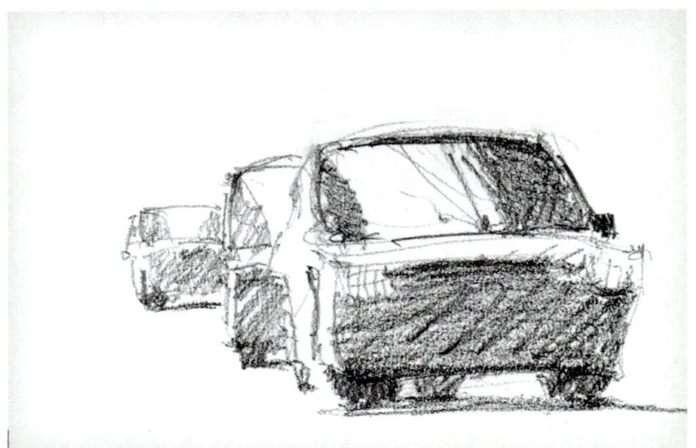

BASIC SKETCH This is a basic sketch of cars parked on the side of the street. Remember, I'm only trying to depict one. If I do that successfully, your eyes will understand and "fill in" the others.

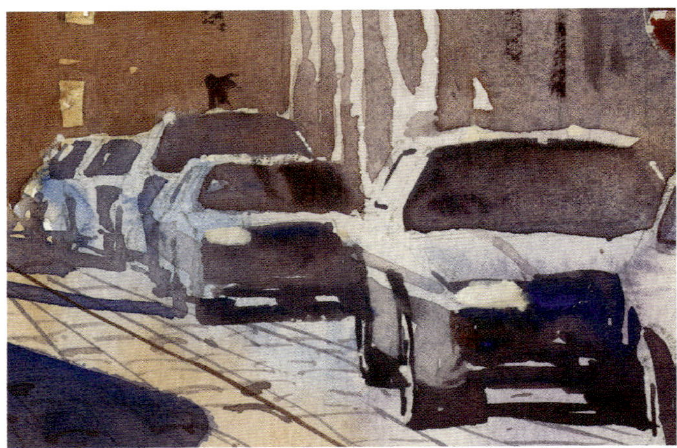

ATMOSPHERE A row of cars is a perfect example of how to create atmosphere using these shapes.

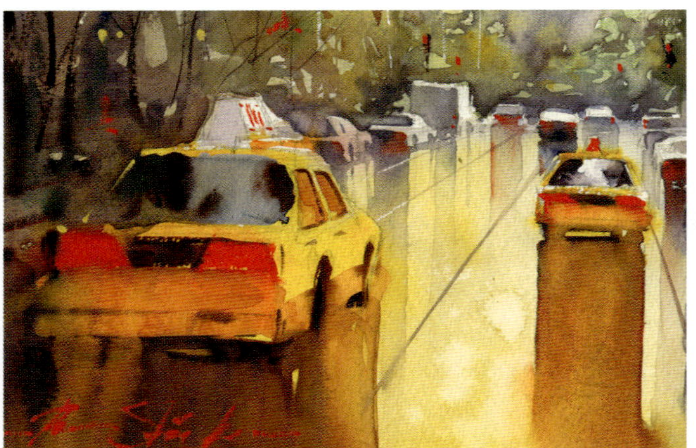

CARS WITH REFLECTIONS This is not only a great way to depict a reflective surface, but the reflections and shadows also help ground your shapes.

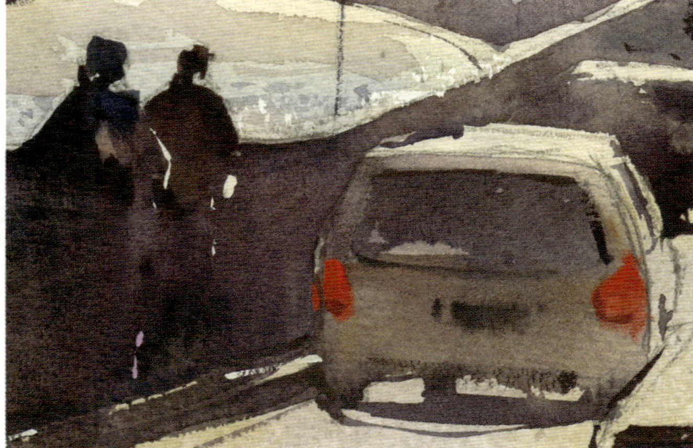

CARS TO SCALE Pay attention to the scale of your shapes in relation to each other. Here, note the height of the people next to the car.

In most of my compositions, cars are usually placed to fill in space, create atmosphere, and to break up tension. Here are some examples of vehicles that have been cropped out of their original paintings, so that you can view them in isolation.

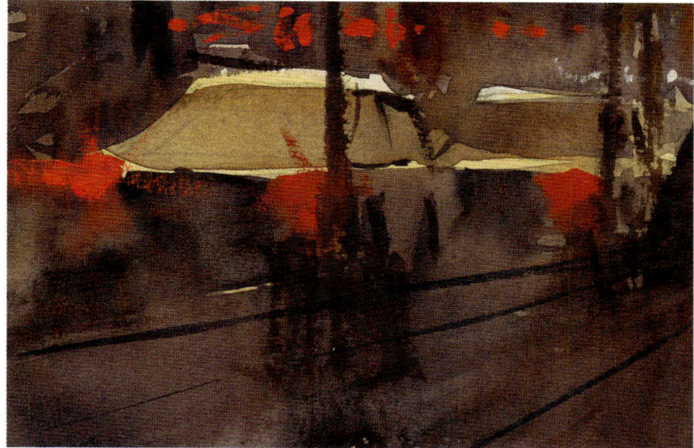

CARS IN SHADOW The simplicity of a few lost-and-found lines may be all you need to convince the viewer.

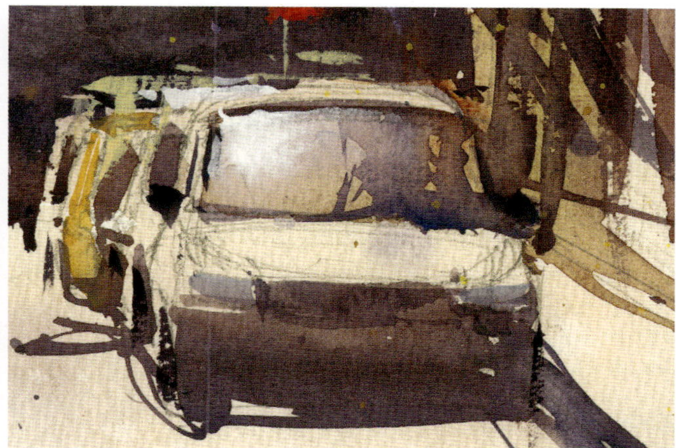

CARS LIT FROM ABOVE One of the more effective ways to create mood and light is to highlight the top and shadow the base.

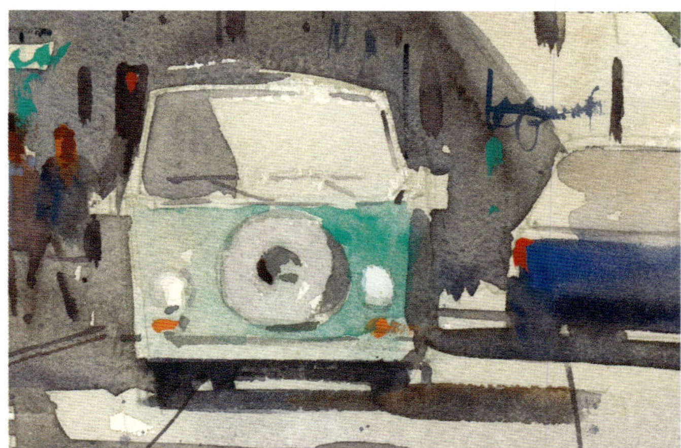

CARS EMERGING FROM SHADOWS It can be effective to grab a portion of the vehicle to help connect it to its surroundings.

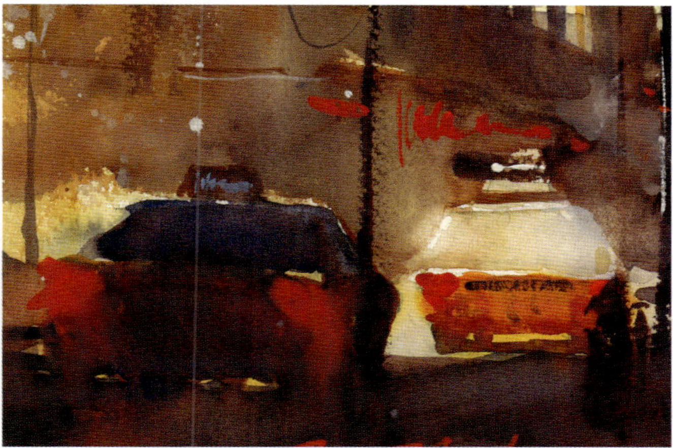

ONE IN SHADOW Having one shape connected to a large shadow creates an interesting tension point between the large shadow and the smaller shape grabbing the light.

Drawing Figures

No subject is more challenging in drawing and painting than the human figure. Unless the figures are sitting for long periods, you rarely have the time to capture the entire shape. Train yourself to draw quickly to emphasize the things you notice. For example, it might be how the legs are positioned when a figure is shifting weight. Remember, like any other object in your painting, the human figure is just a series of shapes.

Taking a life-drawing class is time well spent and can help you understand the human figure better. For now, here are some basic rules that you can use on location to help you create a believable gesture to fit into your paintings.

When the shoulder line moves up on one side, the waist line on the opposite side also moves up.

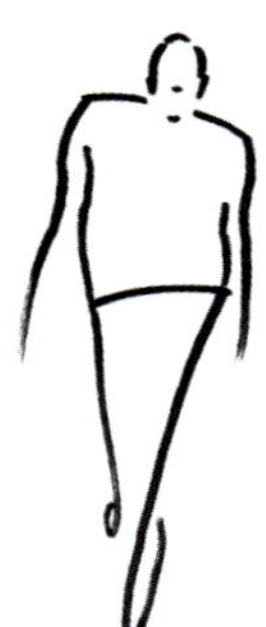

As the figure picks up speed, the arms become engaged.

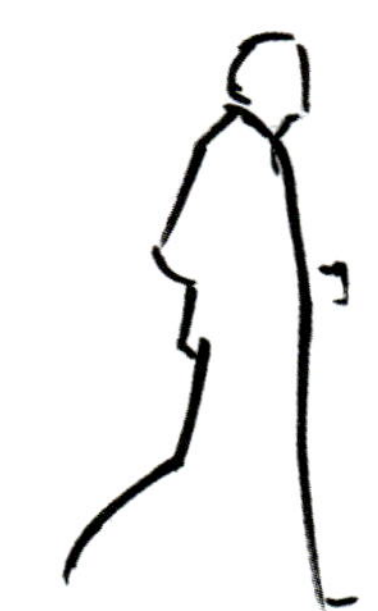

When the figure shifts weight to one leg, it shouldn't feel out of balance. The leg connected to the ground should be in line with the head.

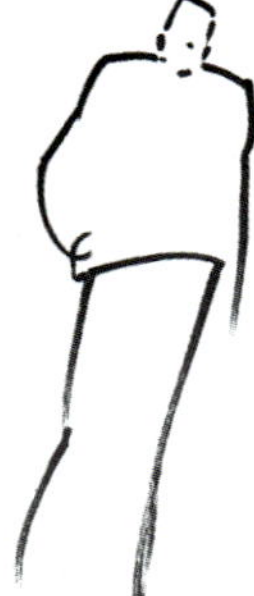

In the running pose, the figure's arms and legs separate from the body to give a greater sense of motion.

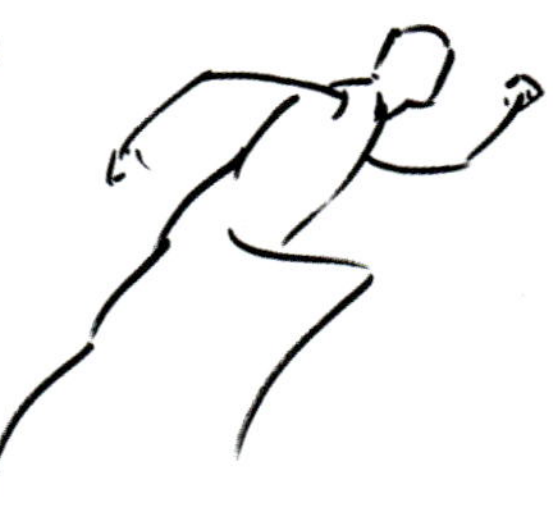

As the figure begins to walk, notice how the front leg stays straight and the back leg curves below the knee.

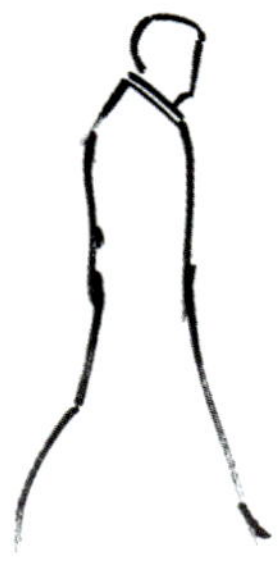

For the sitting pose, make sure you add gravity. We are constantly moving from one sitting position to another. To indicate this, drop the head into the shoulders and foreshorten the legs.

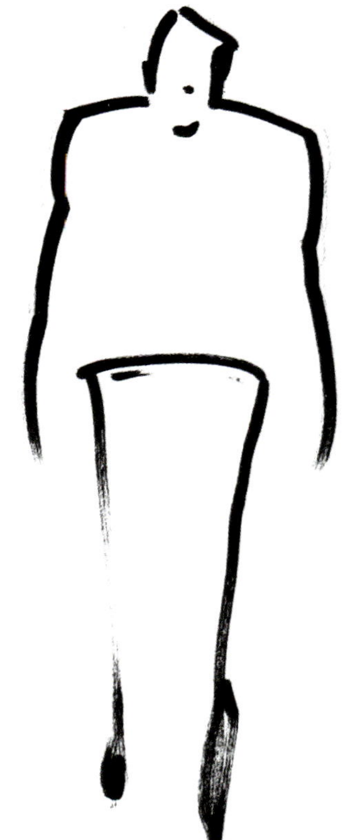

There are two common issues when drawing figures on location:

1. The figures aren't connected to the painting.
2. The drawing of the figure seems to be overworked and overdrawn.

This comes from insecurity about how to draw these shapes. Here's the basic rule of drawing the figure: The shoulders and the waist are connected! When the shoulders are drawn flat, the waist line also needs to be flat.

Now that you have a basic idea of how I draw figures, here is an example of a more finished drawing (below center) next to how I would draw the same figure for a painting (below left) and the painting of that figure (below right).

Notice that the simplified sketch has more gestural energy than the more finished drawing. This allows more artistic license to paint the figure my way. It keeps a likeness of the actual figure but has not become caught up in detail.

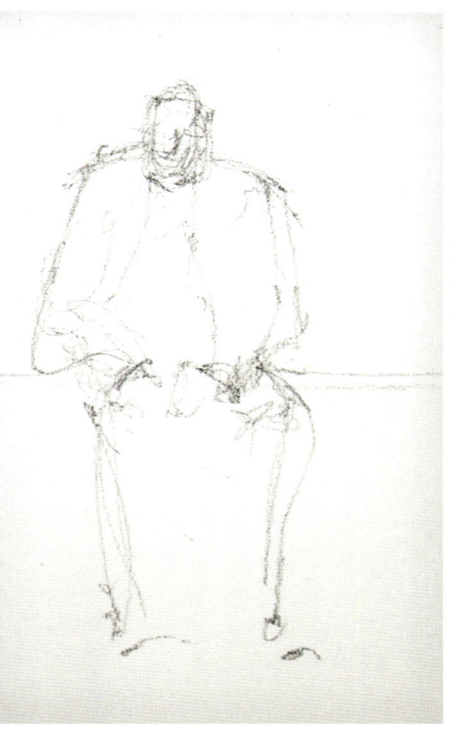

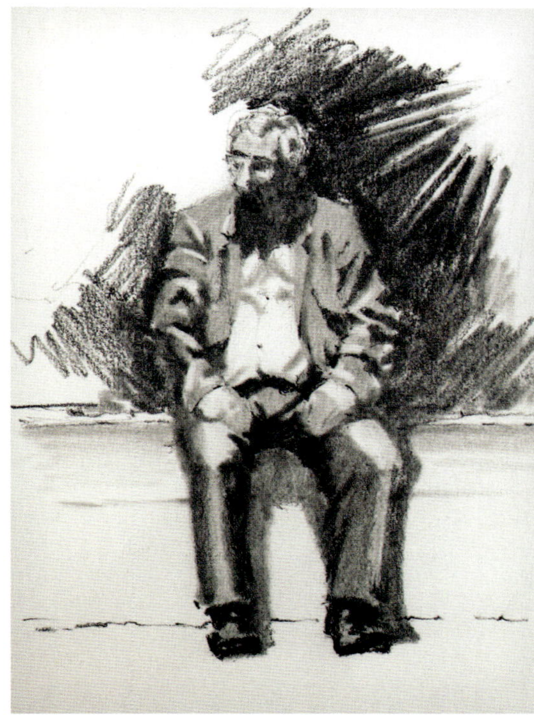

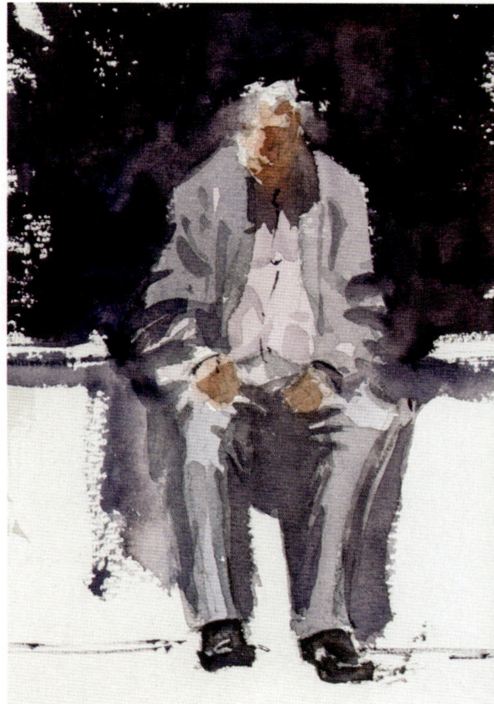

Connecting Figures to Your Painting

No more cut-and-paste figures! When painting figures, cars, buildings, or other objects, you don't want to be too cautious around the edges. If you isolate them, you'll be left with hard, white edges that give the figure an unintentional outline, separating it from everything else in the painting, and bringing unintended tension. Here, in my painting *A Hot Day in Nice,* notice how the figures come in and out of the shadows—yet they are all connected.

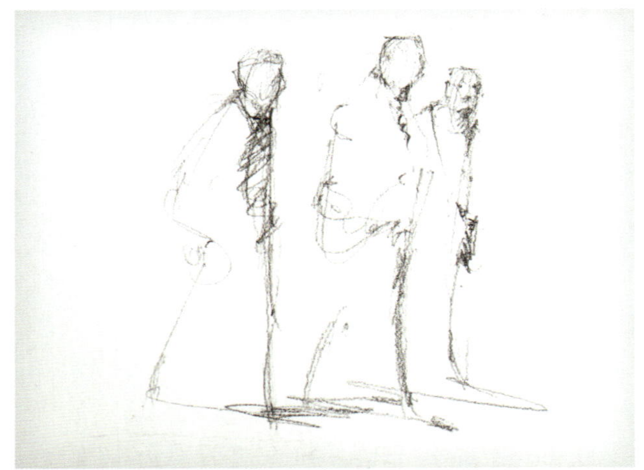

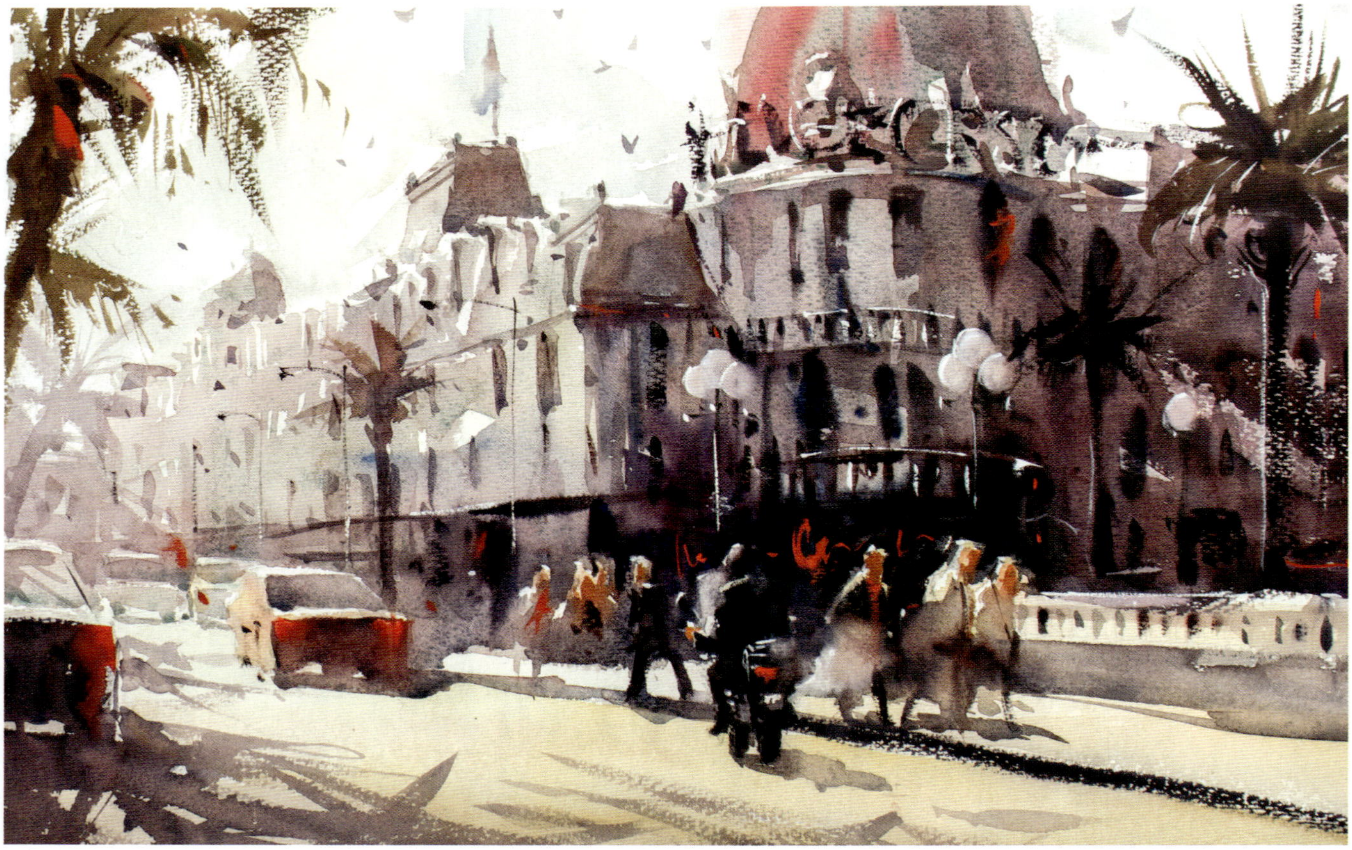

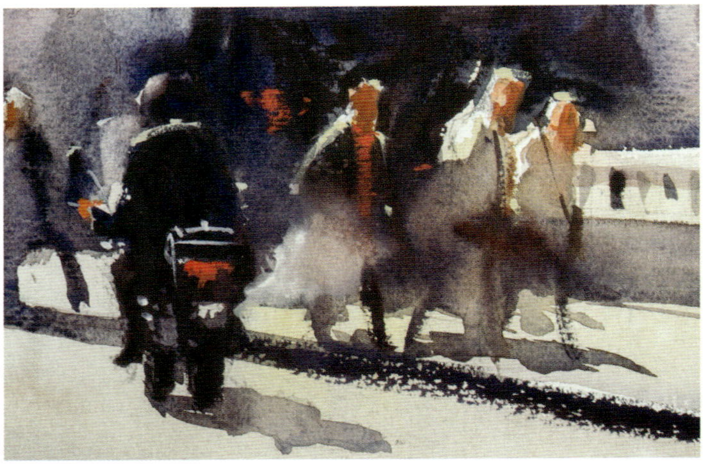

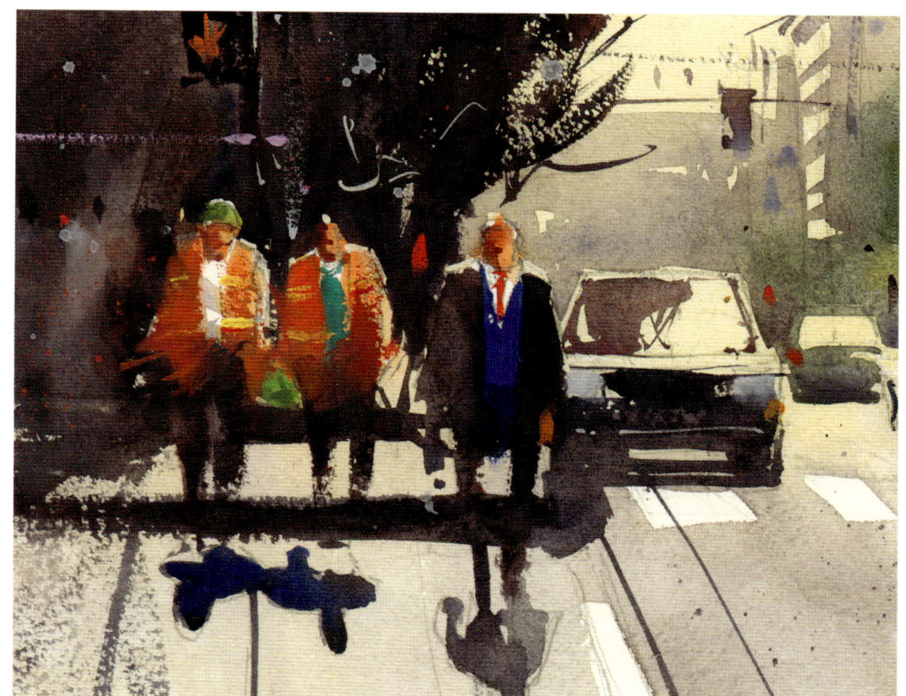

1st Avenue, Seattle

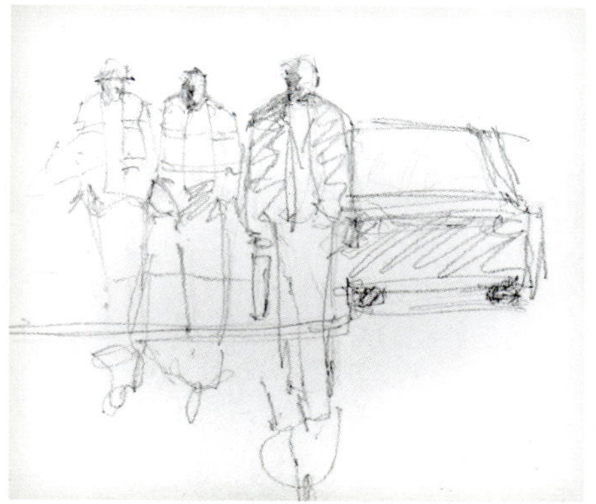

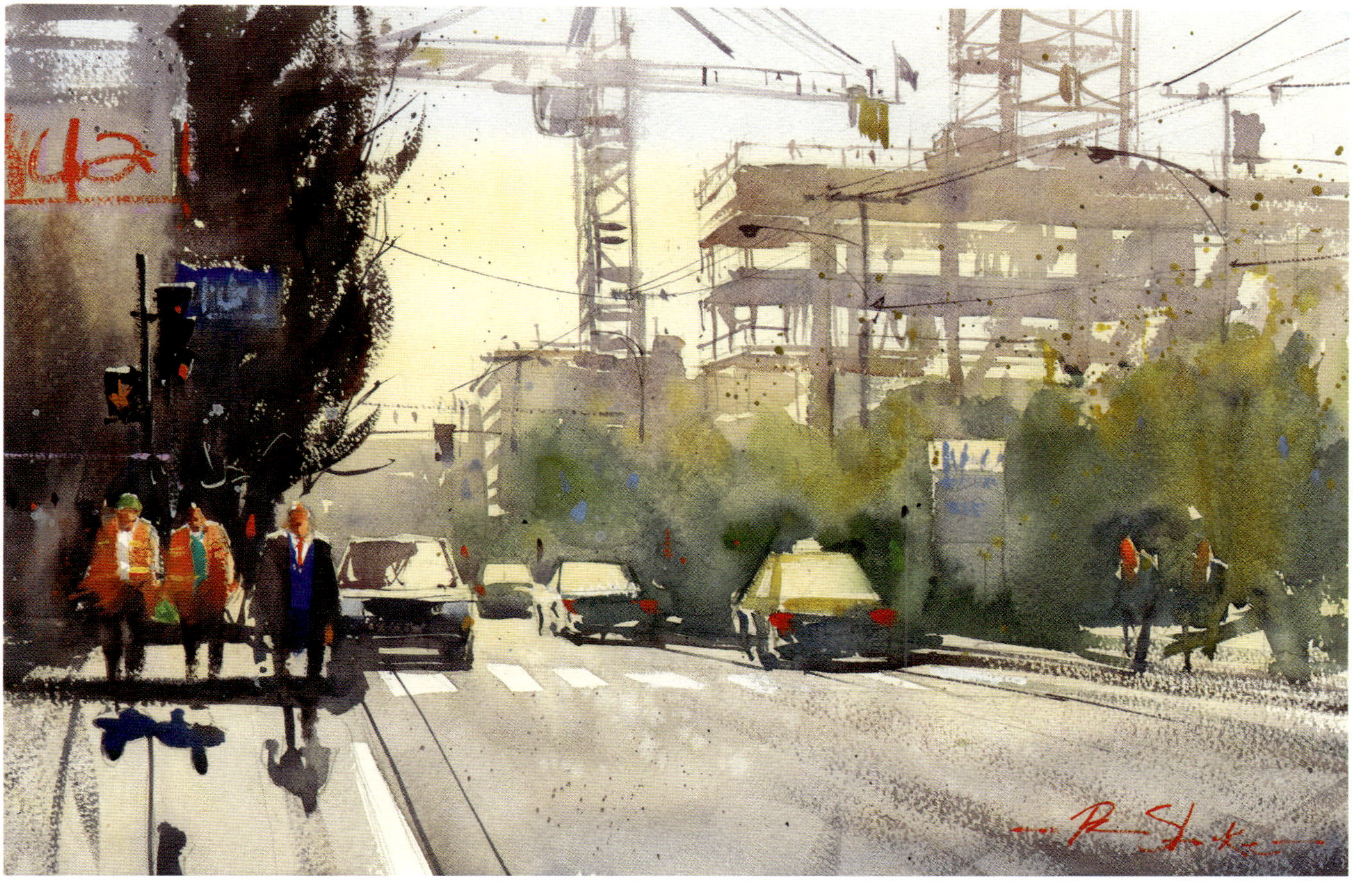

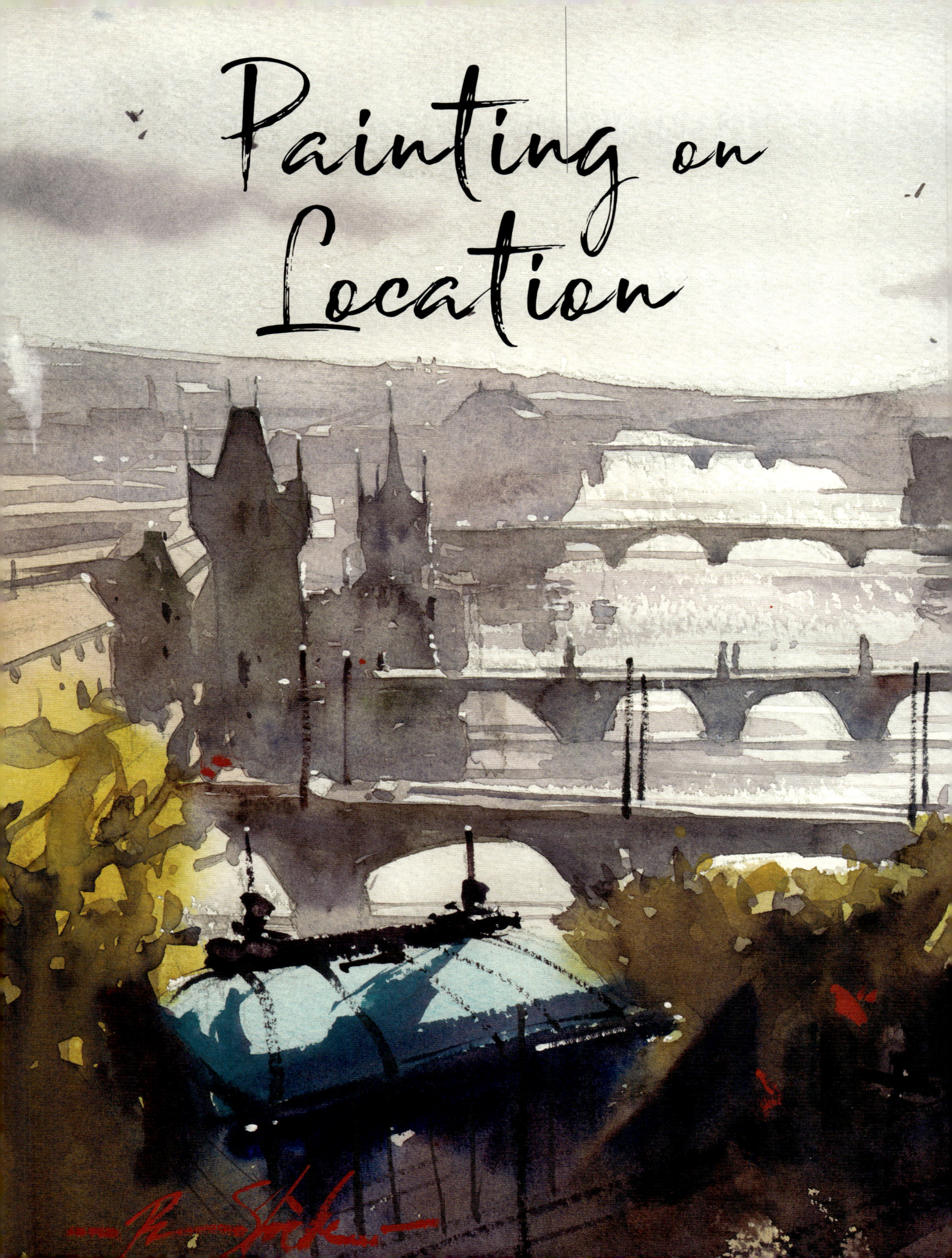
Painting on Location

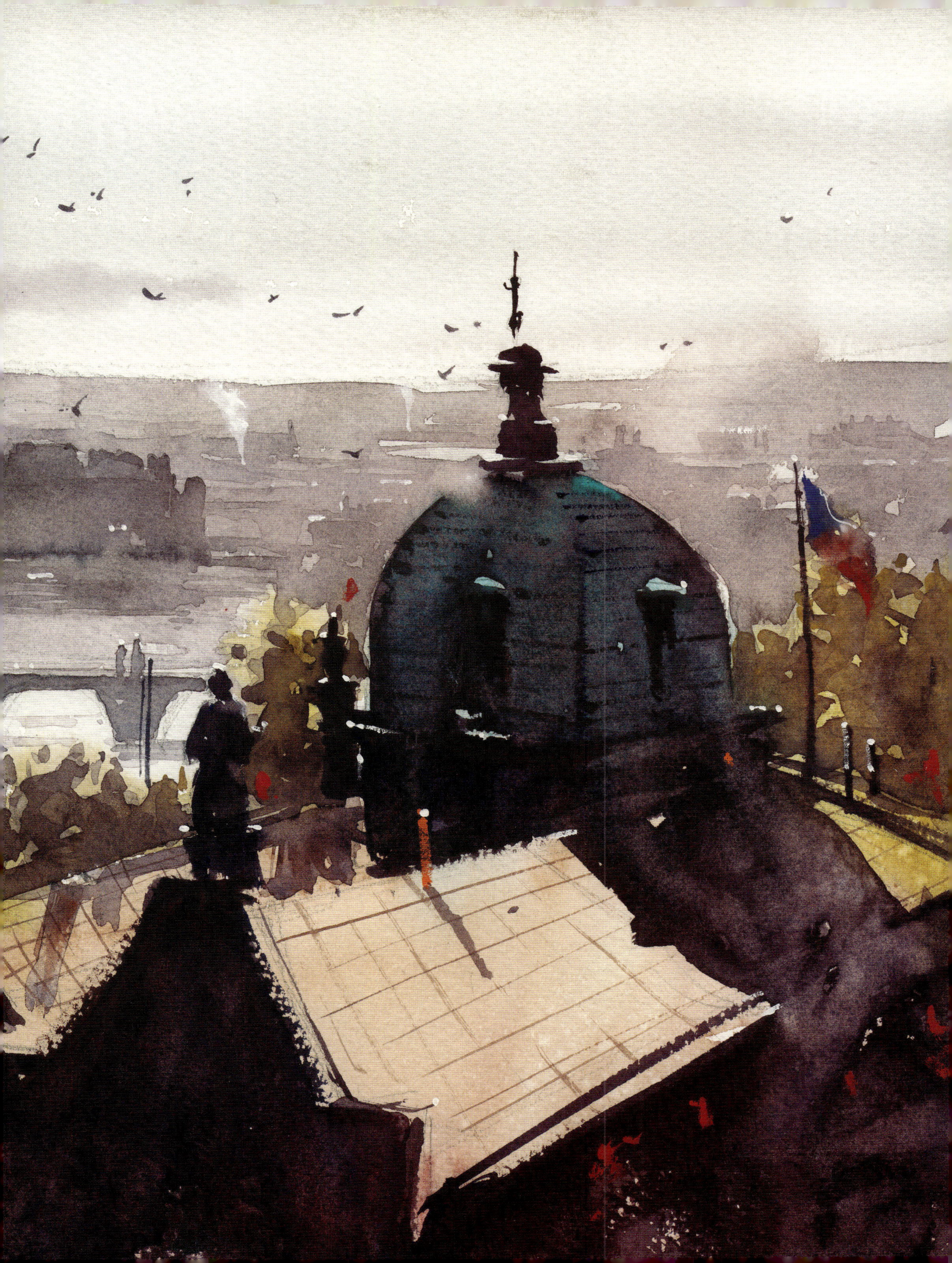

Getting Started

Painting on location has benefited me in many different ways throughout my career. Although it has its challenges, it is most often rewarding. It will help you simplify shapes, understand values, and develop brushstrokes that are full of energy. Here are a few lessons I've learned that can help in your process.

Scope out your location. Get a feeling of where the best spot is to set up your gear. Remember you may be there for a while, so try to anticipate where your light source will be an hour or two from the time you start. It's very difficult to judge your values in direct sunlight, so if you have the option, pick a shaded location.

Pick your spot. This will depend on what you really want to say in your painting. Too far away and you might not get the information you need. Too close and you may not have the atmosphere for a really good design.

In this picture, the subject is in the background.

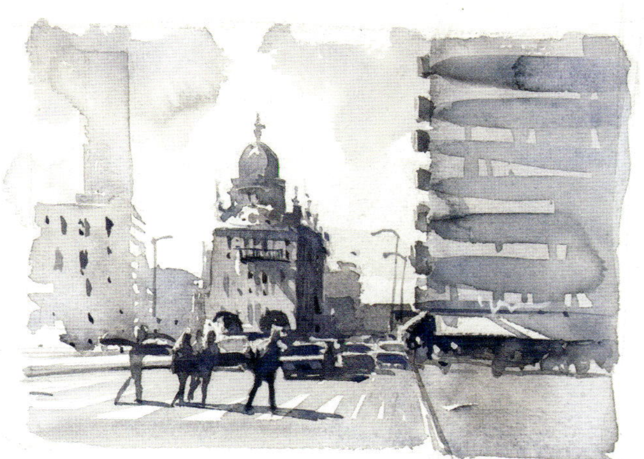

Here the subject is in the middle ground.

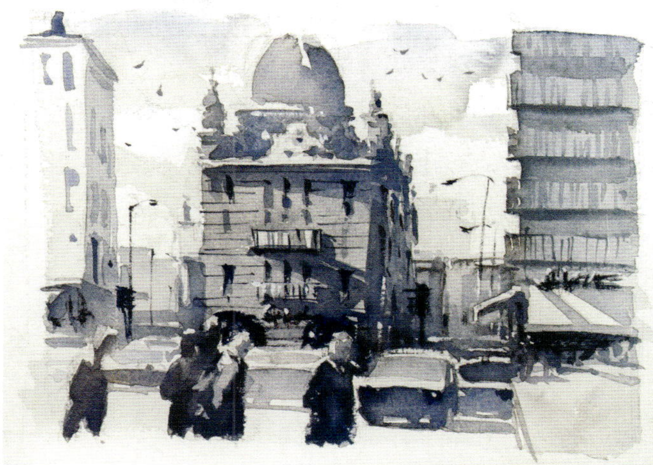

Now the subject is in the foreground.

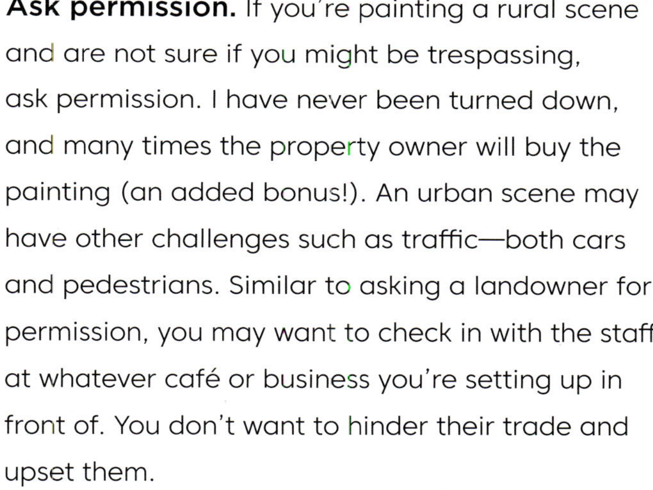

Ask permission. If you're painting a rural scene and are not sure if you might be trespassing, ask permission. I have never been turned down, and many times the property owner will buy the painting (an added bonus!). An urban scene may have other challenges such as traffic—both cars and pedestrians. Similar to asking a landowner for permission, you may want to check in with the staff at whatever café or business you're setting up in front of. You don't want to hinder their trade and upset them.

Draw out your image. A common mistake is to draw too small. This usually creates negative tension and can lead the viewer's eye to the wrong part of the picture. Think of your image as a puzzle, where there are large, medium, and small interlocking pieces supporting one another. Missing some will only make the puzzle incomplete.

Set goals for the session. If your only goal is to paint a masterpiece, then chances are you'll be frustrated by the end of the day. You'll leave not remembering the time spent in the environment, or ≥the interactions you may have had with other artists, and you'll have a poor painting as a reminder. If you are a beginner, have a plan before you put pencil to paper. Maybe you want to improve your compositions, work on values, or experiment with the ratio of water to paint. Make these your goals, and the paintings will follow.

Page 32, ***Prague Vista***

Equipment

The equipment I use on location are the same brushes, palette, and boards I use in the studio. This way I'm familiar with the equipment and don't have to adjust in the field.

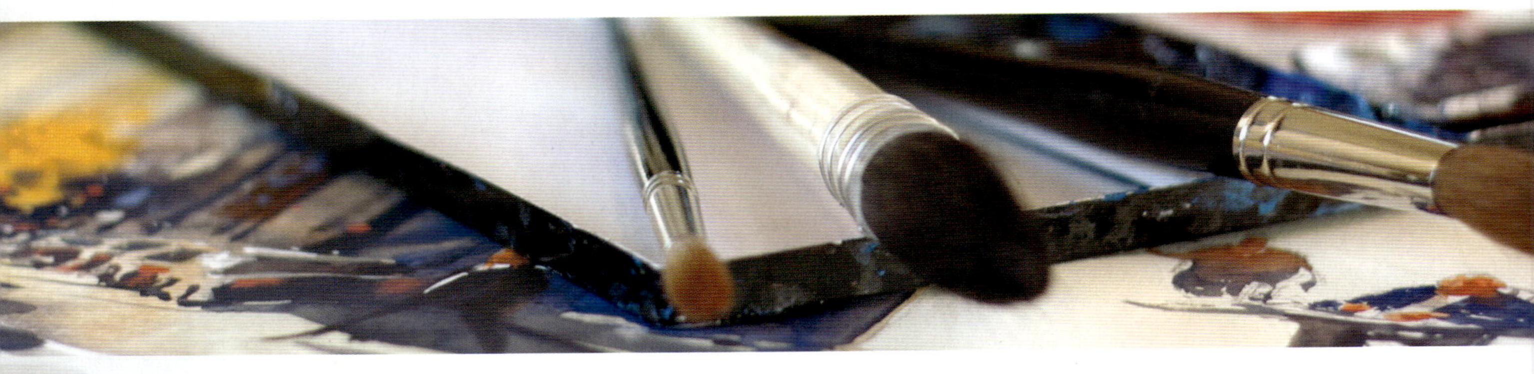

Brushes

When it comes to brushes, you'll eventually find your favorite shapes and styles. My best advice is to purchase the largest size brushes you can afford. You can cover an area with fewer brushstrokes when you use a larger brush. What might take you ten brushstrokes with a small brush may only take you three with a large brush. Also, it's easier to make more mistakes with a size 10 (small brush) than with a size 3 (large brush).

Papers

I predominantly use three paper types:

Aquabee Super Deluxe, American; 93 Lb sketch, slight texture, bright white. This is my primary sketchbook. This paper takes all kinds of multimedia and is sized well, giving it a durable characteristic. The hard cover helps protect the paper when I travel. Available in pads, sheets, and rolls.

Saunders watercolor, English; 140 Lb Cp (cold press), medium to rough texture, natural white. I prefer the natural white tone and unique painting quality. Available in blocks and sheets.

Arches watercolor, French; 140 Lb Cp (cold press), medium texture, bright white. Probably the most widely used paper on the market. It has a brighter tone that helps certain colors really pop. Consistent and available in most art stores. Available in blocks, sheets, pads, and rolls.

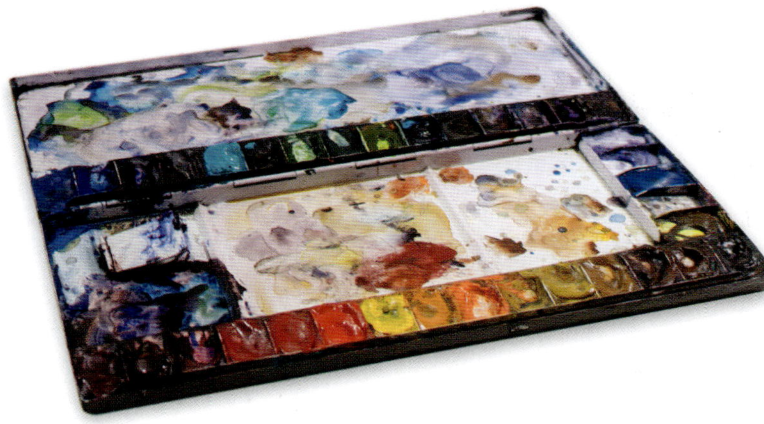

Palette

I use a metal palette. This palette is sturdy and convenient, and the honey-based watercolor I use adheres to the metal surface well. It is the same palette I use in my studio, so I don't have to readjust in the field.

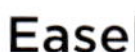

Easel

Easels should be lightweight but sturdy, collapsible but functional. I have used the same basic setup for years, but I'm constantly searching for ways to reduce weight.

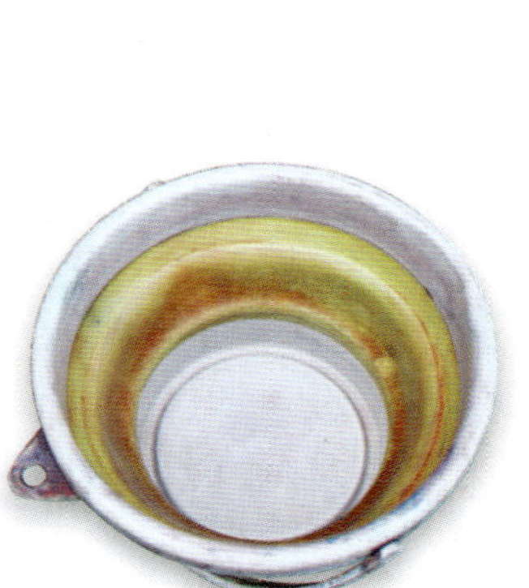

Accessories to Take with You

You will also need watercolors, board and paper, a water container, a spray bottle, and tape. Everything above can fit easily into the portfolio bag I purchased for the field and also fits into the overhead compartment of most major airlines.

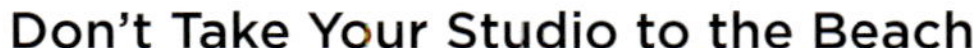

Don't Take Your Studio to the Beach

When it comes to equipment, I think a natural reaction is to bring more than you'll need. I use one simple rule: If I don't think I'll touch it, I don't bring it. Carrying around too much equipment can ruin your day.

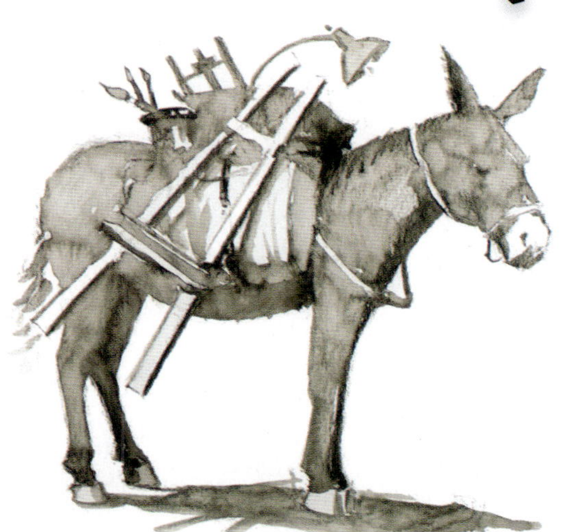

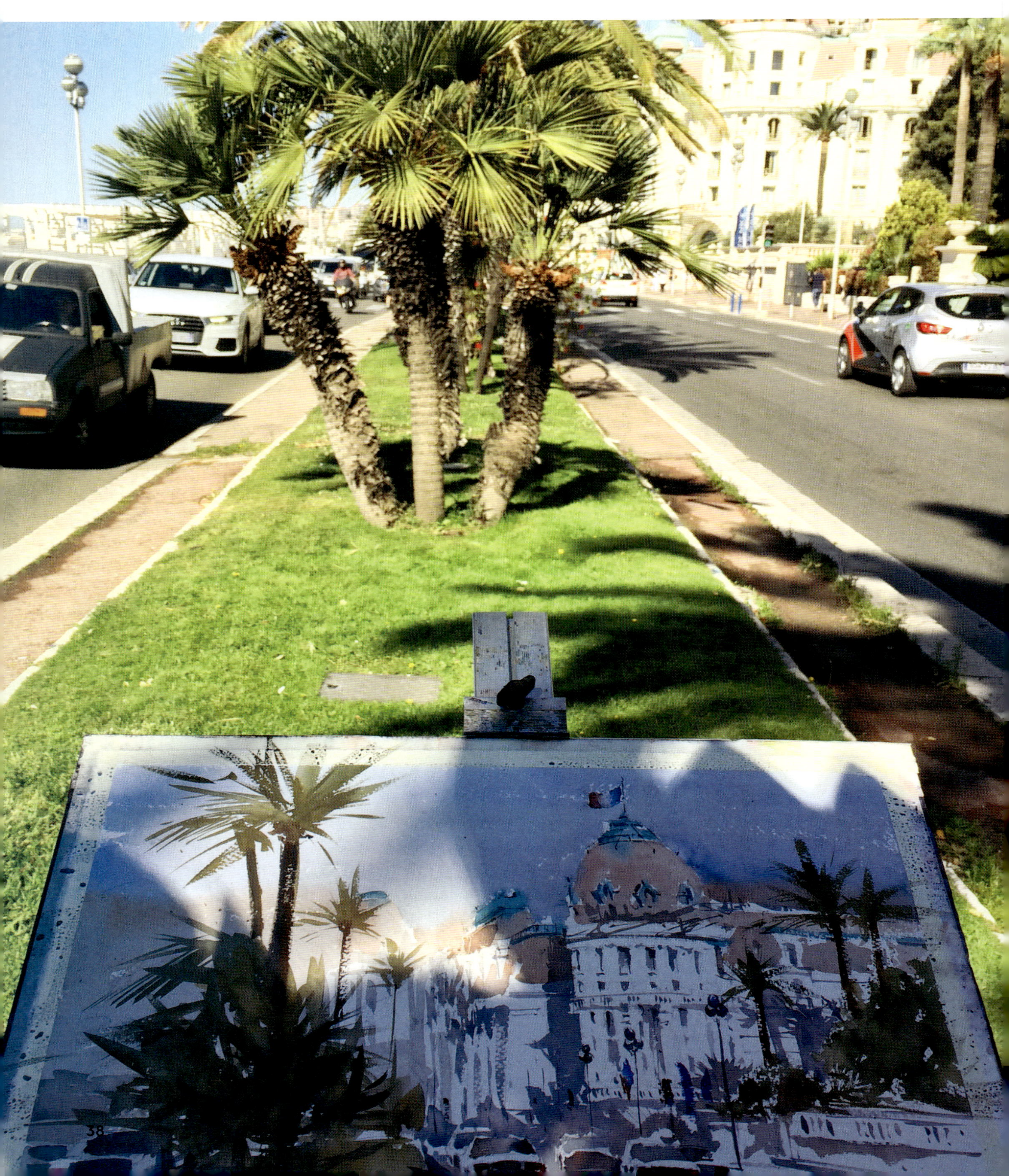

Setting Up

Throughout history, *plein air* painters have been inspired by painting the natural light. The effects of light can change the mood and appearance of a subject in a matter of minutes. My suggestion is not to chase the light. It is easy to want to paint the subject you are seeing now, but it can change dramatically in a quarter of an hour and be altogether different in an hour. If you chase the light, you'll get lost. It's important to try to freeze the moment on your surface while also painting in the moment.

Here are my steps:

1. I like to set up my gear as soon as possible: fill my water container, adjust the easel, and apply bug spray. I try to avoid direct sunlight because it makes it difficult to judge values properly and will only bleach out your colors. Remember, you may be there for a while, so take note of where the sun will be halfway through your painting.
2. Take a photo. Even though the goal is to paint on location from life, it's always nice to have a reference of where the light and shadows were if you need it.
3. Start your value thumbnail sketch. This should be no larger than 3 to 4 inches, and allows you to find your values and simplify your shapes. It is the blueprint of your painting. This will also help you loosen up and keep you from drawing too many unnecessary details.
4. Get your brushes ready. I like to soak mine for a minute before I start to paint. This allows the hair of the brush to relax and soften and gets them ready to accept paint.
5. For this first wash it's always a good idea to mix more than you think you'll need. Chances are you'll need more to finish the sheet.
6. The first wash should be the easiest; be bold and free. Don't hesitate—when in doubt, keep your brush moving.
7. Your focal point should rule the painting from start to finish. Unless you are leaving areas of the paper exposed, paint through the other shapes. They will eventually be covered by additional washes. Let the paper dry!
8. Think about what you are looking at as one large shape consisting of several small, medium, and large shapes that are all connected, and paint them that way.
9. Squint to see your values. Try to achieve at least three values and make sure one is dark. Let your paper dry!
10. Don't feel you must finish the painting in one go. If you gather all the information while on location, you can finish back in the studio.

Adapting to the Conditions

The most considered equipment and best-laid plans can fall apart if Mother Nature has her say. An umbrella can be helpful both in sun and rain. Comfortable shoes and dressing in layers can also make your experience more pleasant. Depending on the conditions, your paper might dry faster or slower than in your studio. If it is particularly warm out, you may want to have a spray bottle with you to keep the paper wet enough so that your washes don't dry at a crucial stage. If it is a cooler day, your paper may stay wet much longer than in the studio.

A common mistake I see is artists rushing the process, not allowing the washes to set up (dry) properly, and then ending up with muddy unpleasant edges. Adding some opaque color to your wash can help, but just be patient. This can give you time to plan out the next stages of the painting, talk to fellow artists, or just enjoy your surroundings.

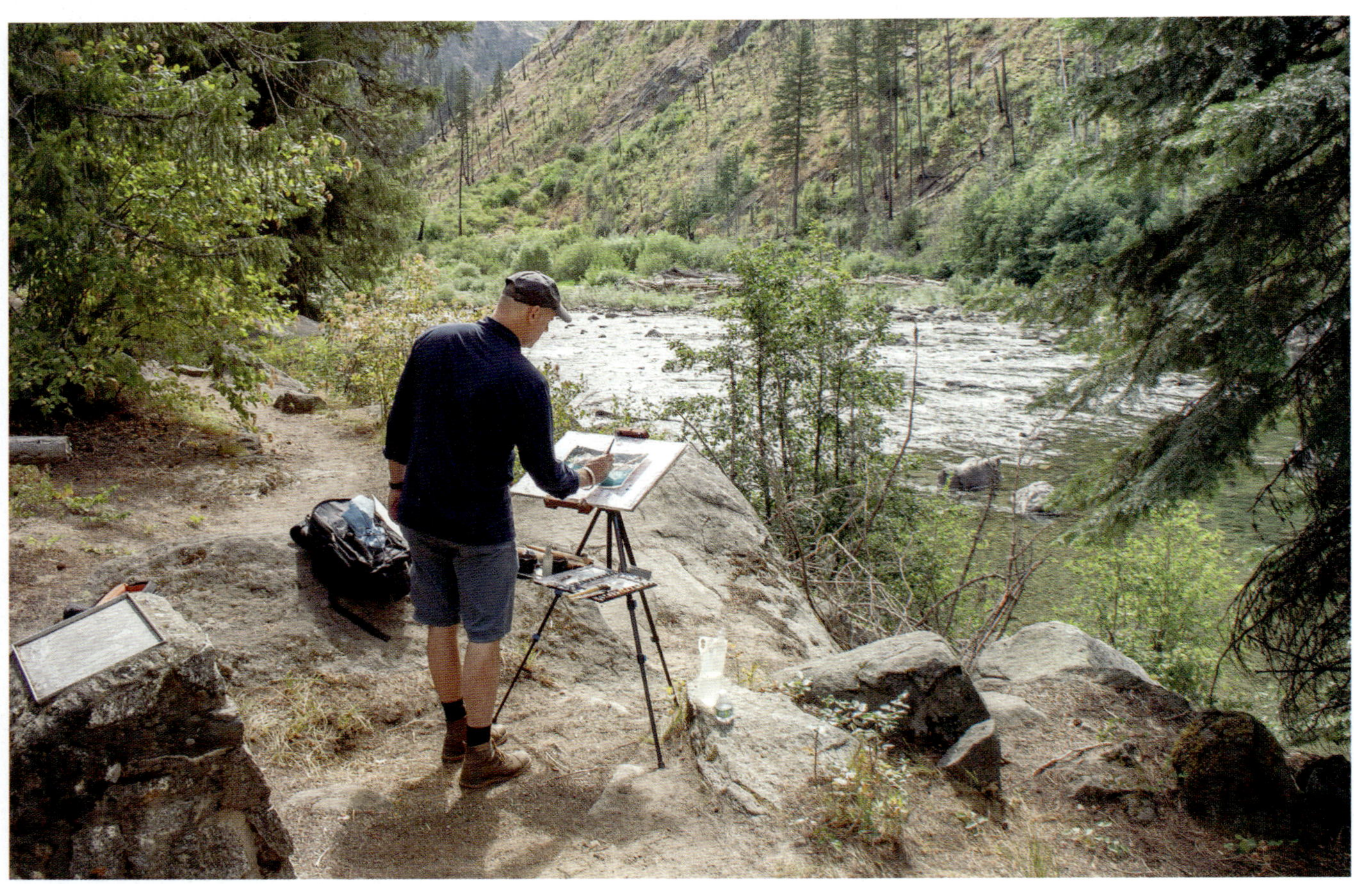

Painting from Photographs

We can't avoid painting from photographs sometimes. With all of the technology at our fingertips it's hard to imagine not using it, but technology has its limitations. This is why painting on location is so important.

I can't tell you how many times I've been on location and so inspired by the scene in front of me, only to get home and be really disappointed at the photographs I took. For one, painters are not the best photographers. We usually take photographs for reference rather than designing a well-thought-out composition. Second, the human eye sees its subject differently than a camera. Yes, the camera picks up details and color, but by being present, your other senses are engaged. Not only can you see the subtleties of color and value, but you can feel temperature, see form, and more importantly, see life as it's happening. This is my goal: to depict the energy and split-second happenings of daily life as if it has just happened in front of me.

Église Sainte-Rita, Nice

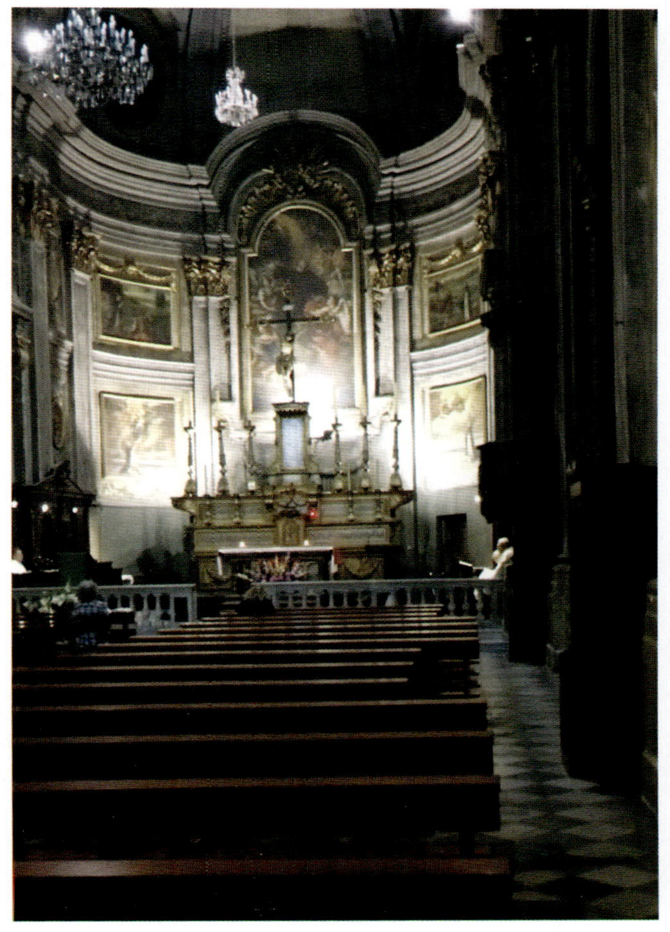

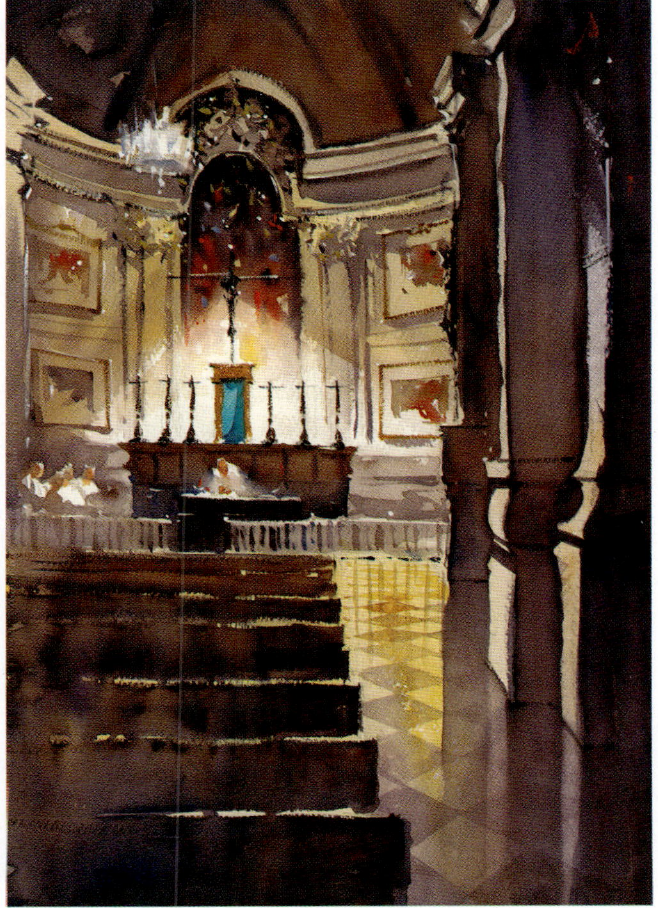

Brushes

You've probably heard this statement: "I have hundreds of brushes, but I really only use just five or six." I call this the watercolorist's curse. No matter how many we have, we are constantly looking for one more. I have friends in the construction industry who may have a few different hammers for specific jobs or for backups in case one is broken, but when was the last time you had a brush break on you? However, to justify our ailment, I offer you this: you will discover over the years that it is not the brush that improves the painting, but the time spent using these brushes. A brush you may dislike or be unable to control now, may become the brush you can't live without in a few years.

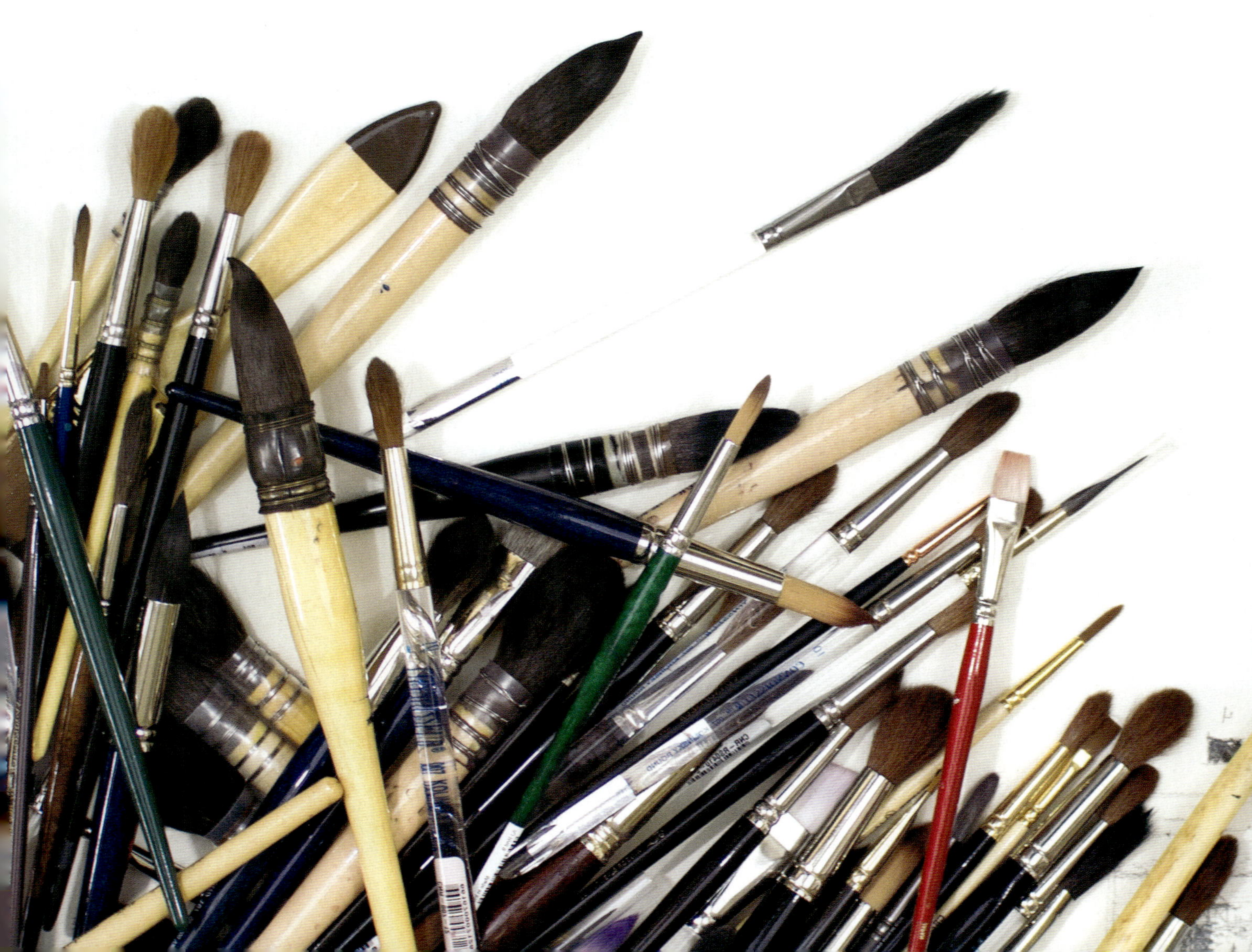

Try a multitude of brushes until you find a set you feel comfortable painting any subject with no matter the conditions.

Here are my personal favorites:

Large squirrel-quill brush

Hair: Although there are some good synthetics on the market, I prefer natural squirrel hair.
Carrying capacity: Best
Snap/hair strength: Poor
Line quality: Good

The term "quill" originally came from the quill of a goose feather used as the ferrule of these brushes. Many brands have now replaced the ferrule with synthetic materials. This brush is my main workhorse. I paint 50 to 70 percent of my paintings with this brush alone. My philosophy is, if I can cover an area with as few brushstrokes as possible, fewer mistakes can happen. Sizes may vary between European and American brands.

Rounds

Hair: Synthetic, natural, and a combination of both. I prefer Kolinsky sable rounds, sizes 10–16.
Carrying capacity: Better
Snap/hair strength: Better
Line quality: Best

Round brushes are the stars of the show. You can complete a watercolor painting from start to finish with a good round brush. The round brush is probably the most common brush on the market. They are available in more sizes than any other brush shape.

Flats

Hair: Synthetic, natural, and a combination of both.
Carrying capacity: Good with synthetics; better with natural hair.
Snap/hair strength: Better (The shape of the brush also allows for better snap.)
Line quality: Good

Even though the flat brush is designed for big washes, if you turn it on its edge or just use the corner of the brush, the line quality can be good.

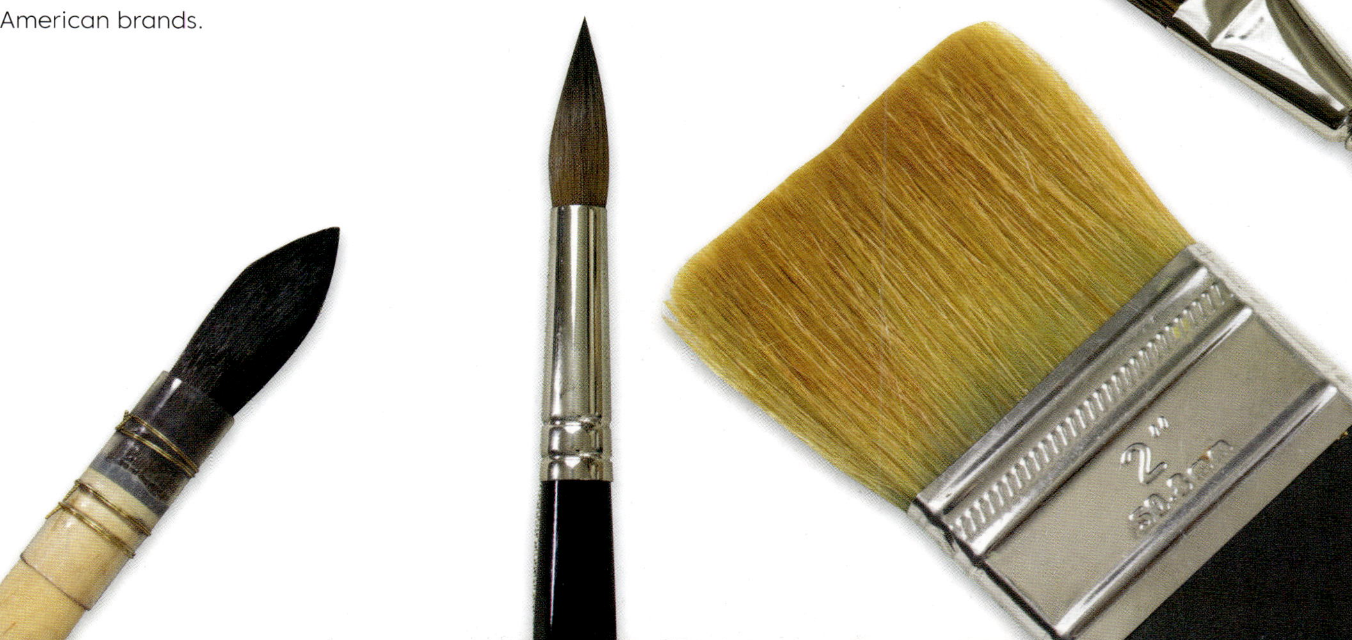

And here are a few specialty brushes that are also useful:

Dagger

Hair: Synthetic, natural, and a combination of both.
Carrying capacity: Good/better
Line quality: Best

The unique design of this brush lends itself to the watercolor medium. Its shape allows you to achieve a thick-thin line that no other brush can. Good for grasses, branches, and most foliage. It is also a good brush for floral painters.

Rigger

Hair: Synthetic, natural, and a combination of both.
Carrying capacity: Best—it is amazing how much water this brush can hold.
Line quality: Best

One of the more enjoyable brushes to use. You can achieve amazing things with this little brush. It is great for painting long, continuous lines such as branches, electrical lines, fence wire, etc.

Scrubber

For me, this brush has really only one function and that is to lift color from your paper.

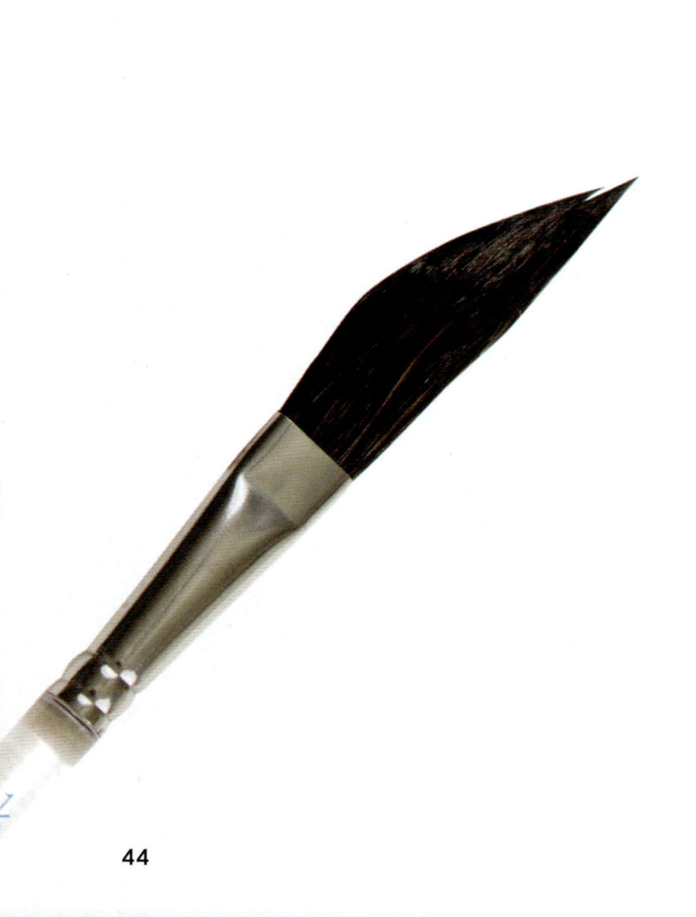

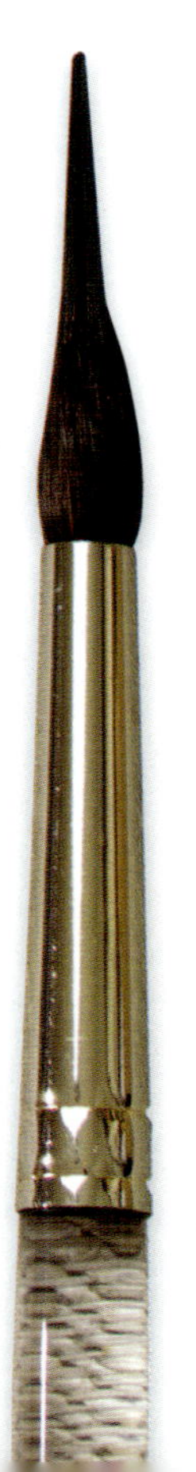

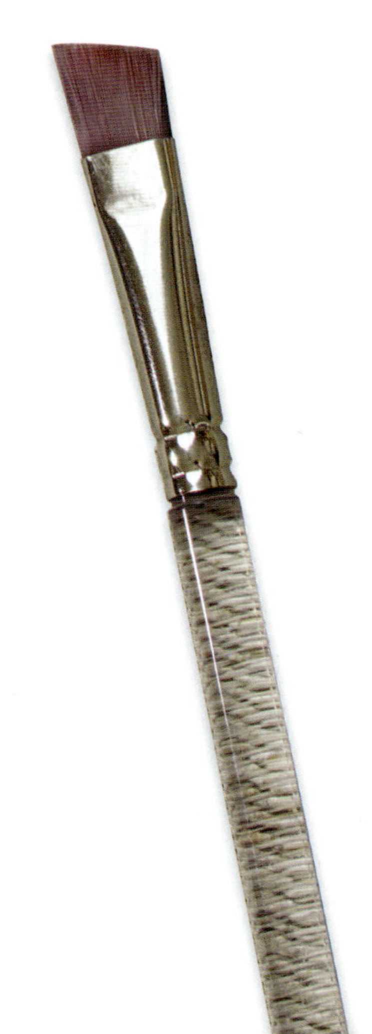

Paint

Like brushes, the colors you choose can make a big difference to the outcome of your work. If just starting out, my recommendation is to buy the primary colors from a good professional brand and learn to mix your own secondary and tertiary colors.

M. Graham

America

This company uses natural ingredients like honey in their watercolors. The honey gives the paint the ability to be reconstituted quickly while painting on location. It has a strong color intensity, with a good range of color. Most of the line is single-pigment colors.

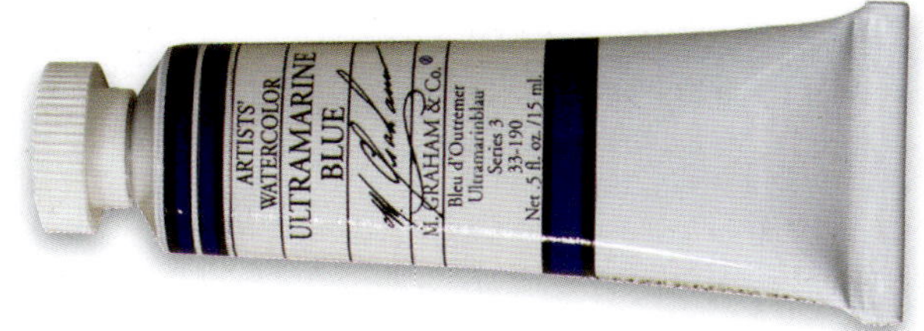

Daniel Smith

America

This company has the largest selection of colors, in particular some unique earth pigments that granulate well. It has a strong color intensity across most of the line.

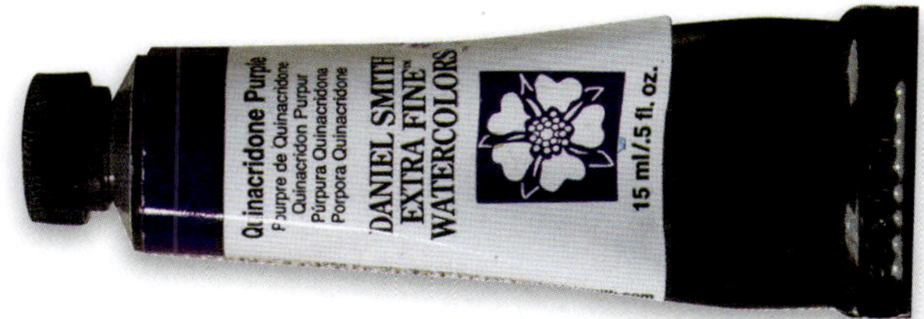

Holbein

Japan

It has a good range of color. Unique opaque and metallic colors offered.

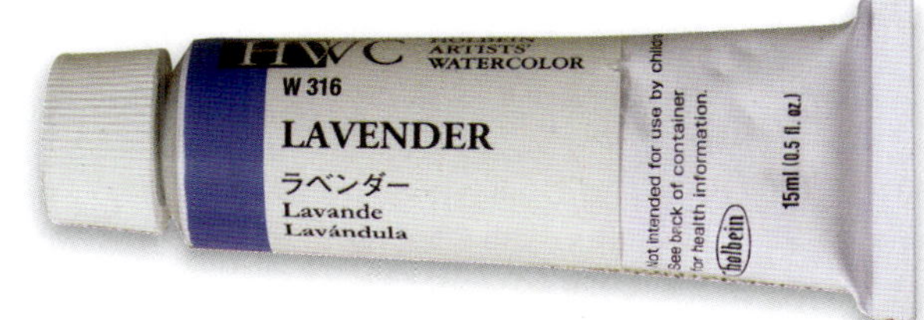

Winsor & Newton

England

Started in the 1800s, Winsor & Newton is by far the oldest paint company in the group. It has a large color range, with strong color intensity. Other watercolor products are also available.

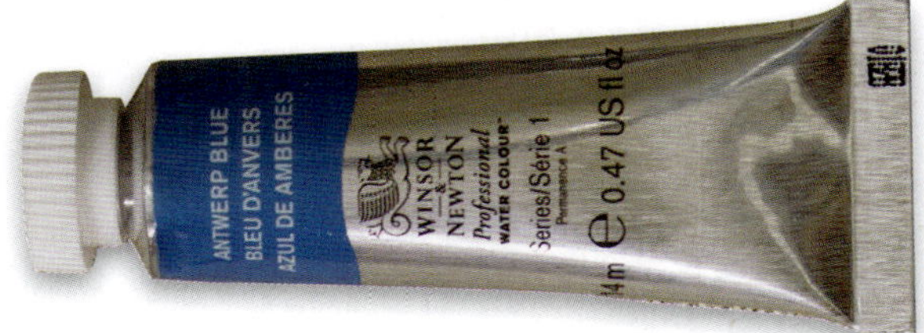

King Street Station Step-by-Step

Best plans can go awry when painting *en plein air*, so being flexible is key. Even though I had all of the materials I needed, a good spot picked out, and a familiar subject matter, Mother Nature had other plans.

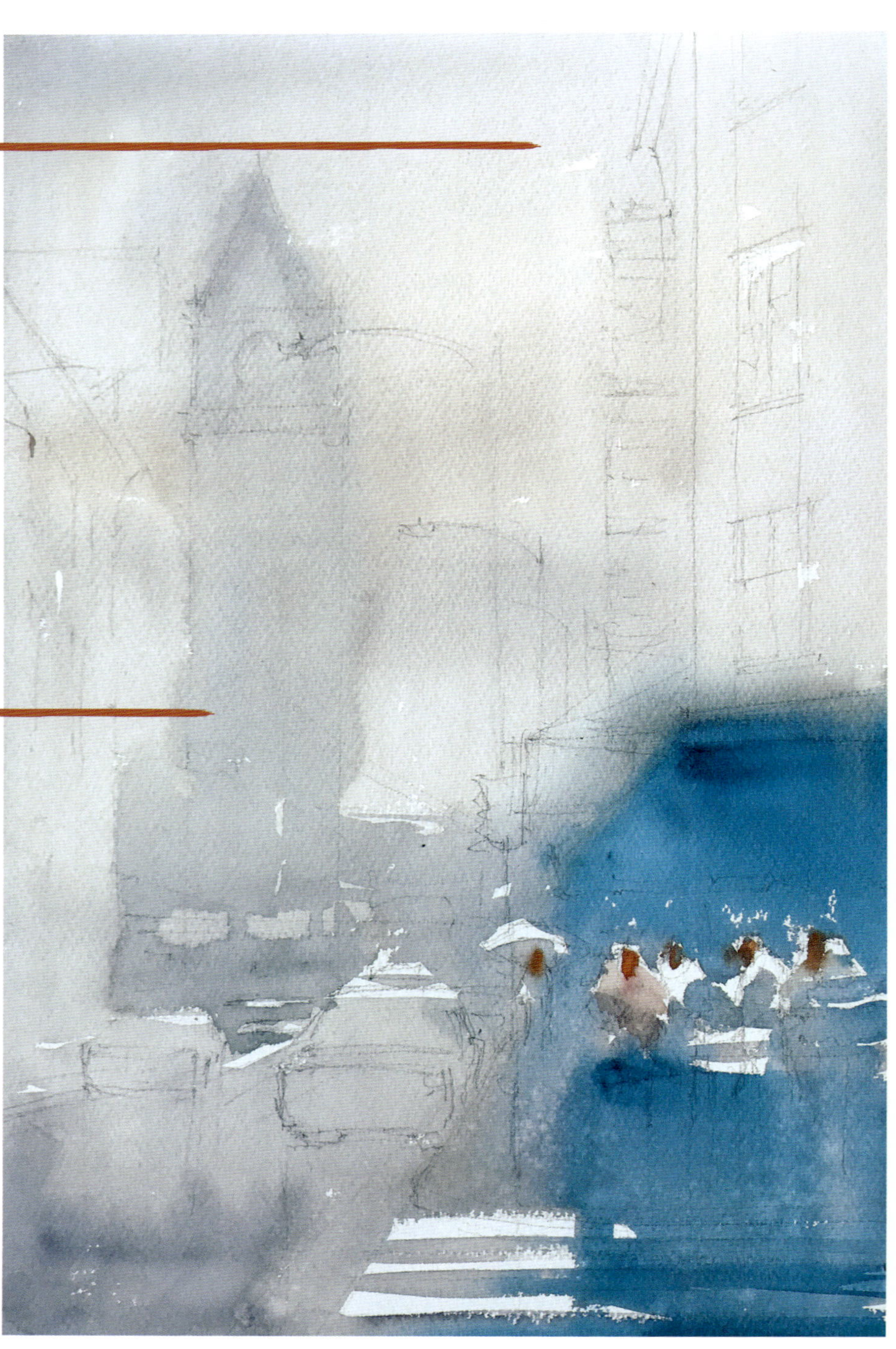

The first stage of this painting started with two main washes. The large gray wash that takes up two-thirds of the painting, followed by the turquoise wash in the bottom right-hand corner.

To define the clock tower, I waited for the background wash to set up, but not completely dry, before I laid in a second wash of gray so it would remain diffused and have a soft edge.

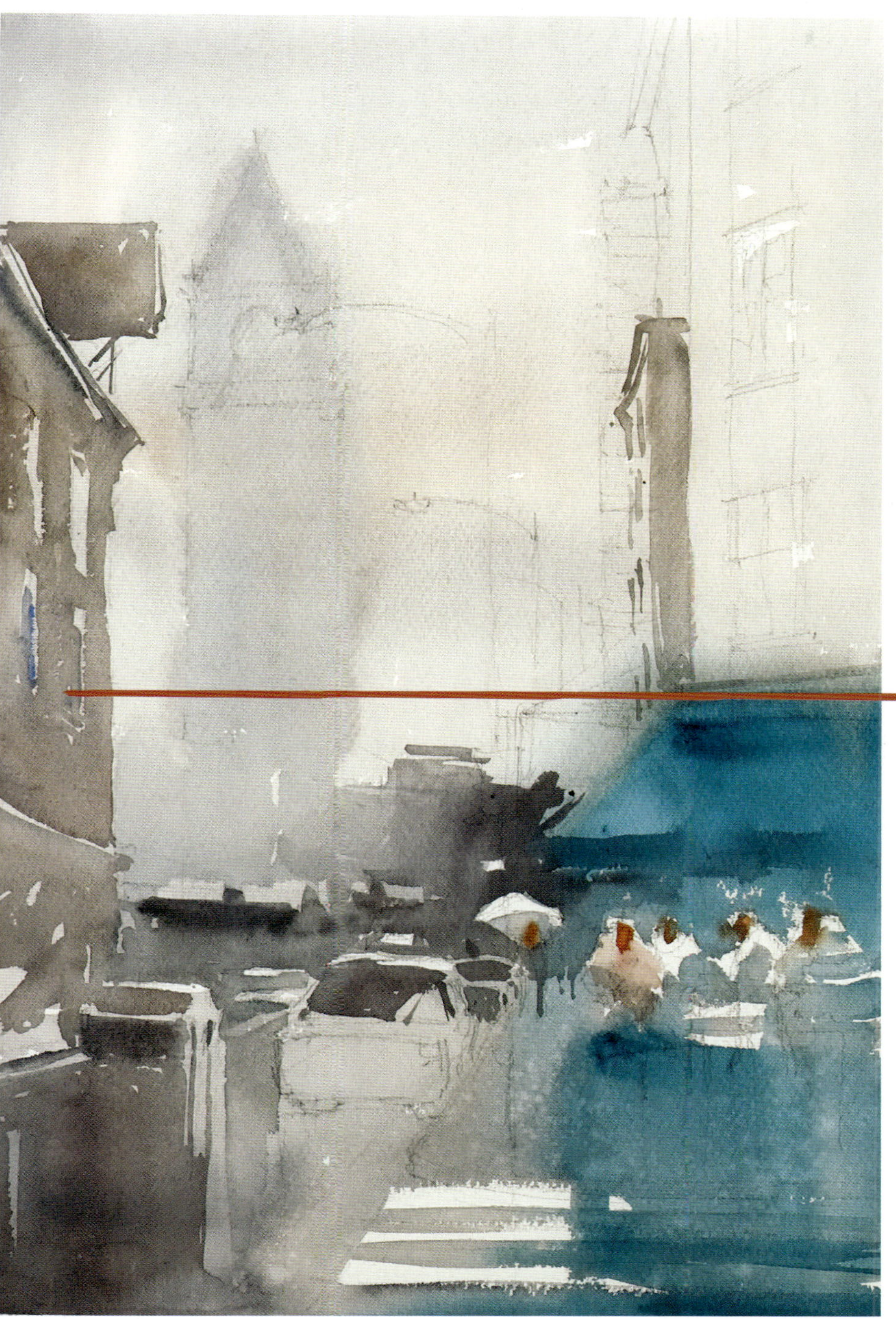

Since it was an overcast day, I didn't have the sun to dry my painting completely. This is common when painting *en plein air.* You have to go with the flow and continue on. I started painting the distant buildings with the same mixture of gray wash that I used for the background—but staying mindful that I needed to begin connecting many of the building and car shapes together.

Next I applied a warmer/darker value to the foreground building on the right, as well as a thick dark value for some of the details (signs, fire escapes, and so on).

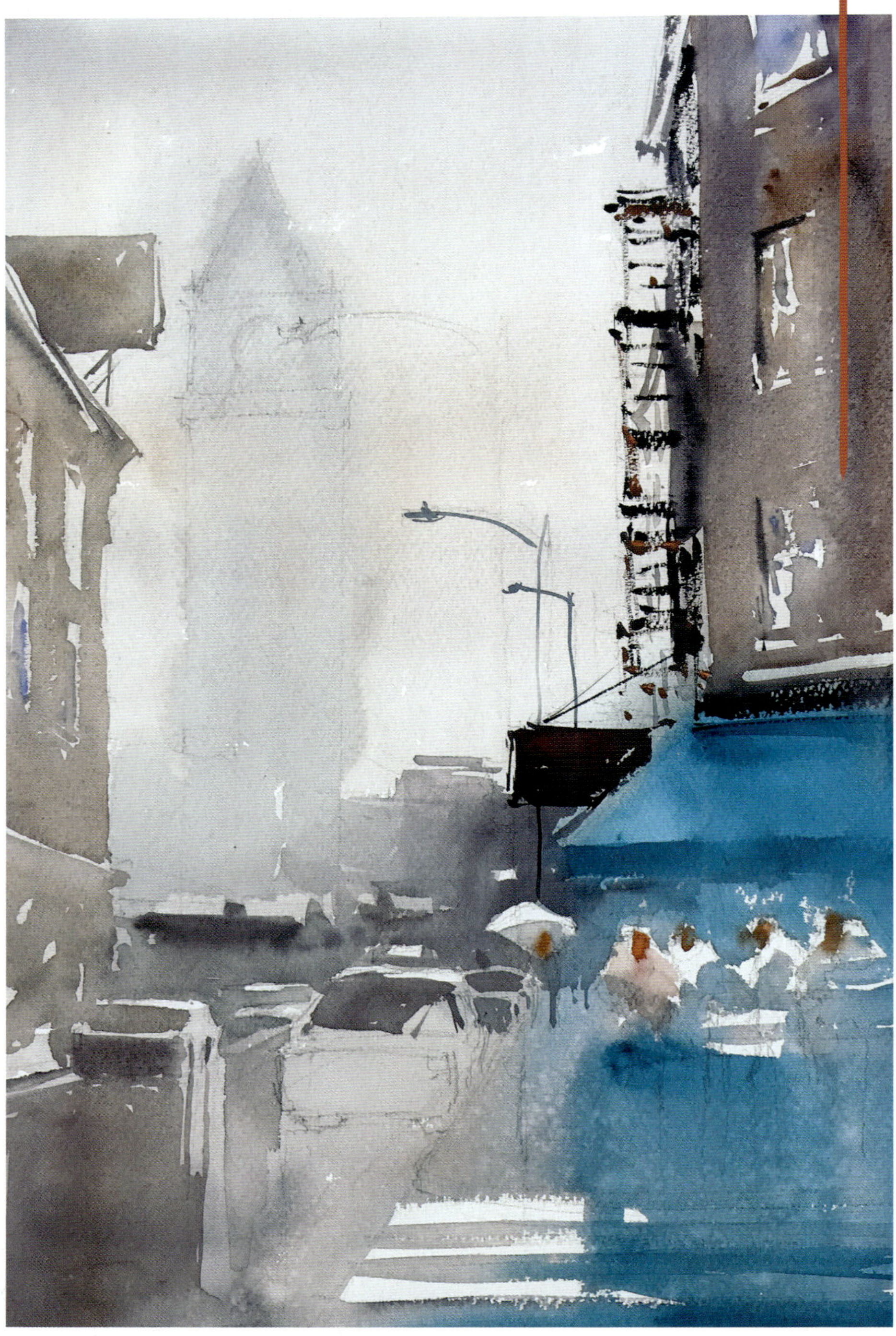

When painting on location you have to expect weather changes. When it's too hot, your washes dry too fast. Wind can rattle even the most experienced painter and cause you to pack up out of pure frustration. This time it was rain. My paper still hadn't completely dried from the first wash. So, knowing I had enough information to finish back in the studio, that's exactly what I did.

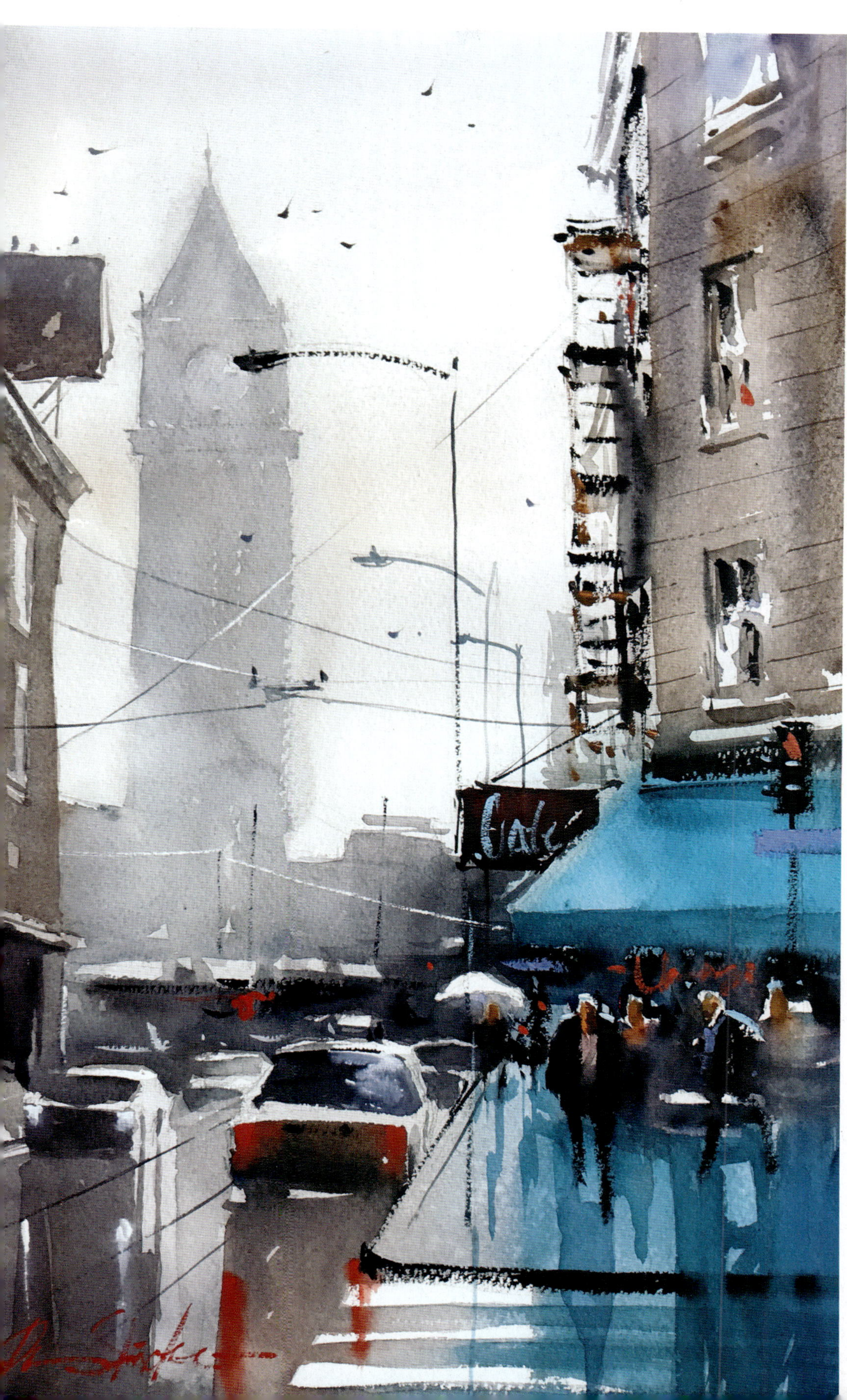

With 75 percent of the painting done and photo references taken before I started, it was easy to finish the painting back in the studio. I knew I had to work on my focal point. So I concentrated on adding figures and the rest of the details needed to finish the painting. Being forced away from your subject because of weather is not necessarily a bad thing. It allows you the freedom of not having to compete with the actual subject and can give you license to paint more freely.

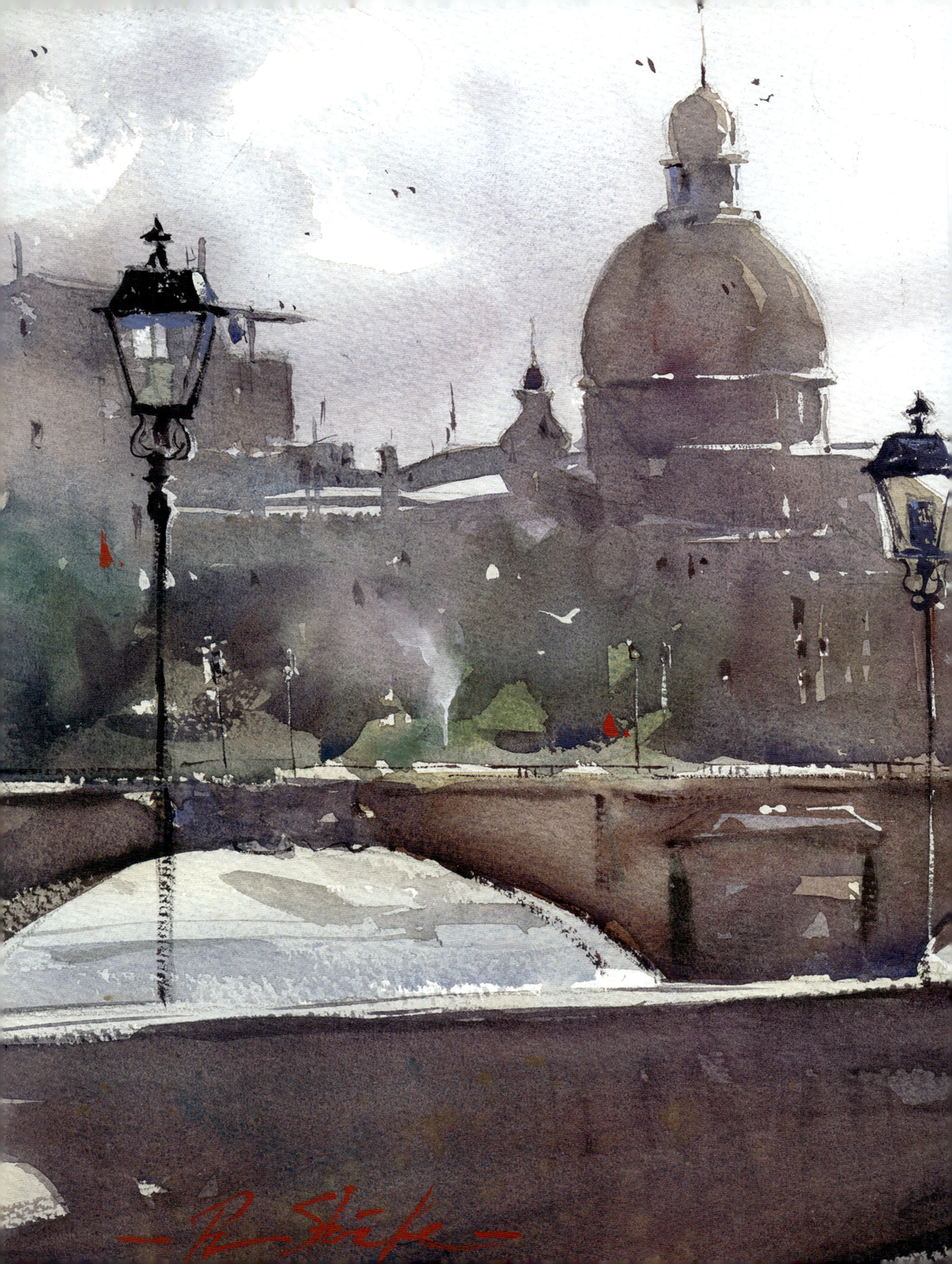

Composition & Tension

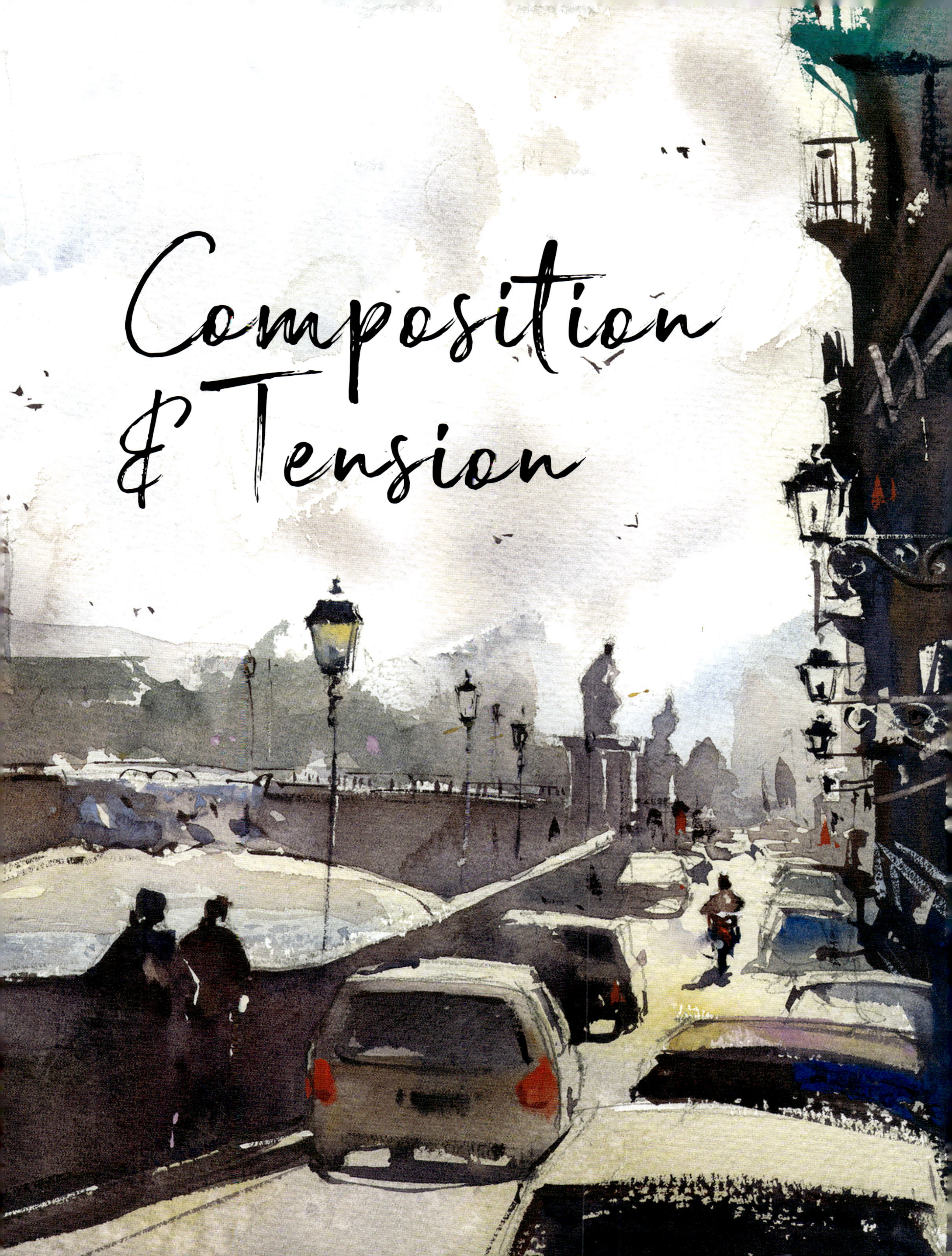

Placing Your Subject

While on location, it might be difficult to know where to place your subject on your paper. Knowing what you intend to paint is always a good idea. I have seen several paintings where the artist intended the viewer to focus on one particular area, but because of poor planning the viewer gets caught up or distracted by another area. Such indecision causes the painting to feel disorganized. Here are some rules to help you place your subject matter and avoid design issues.

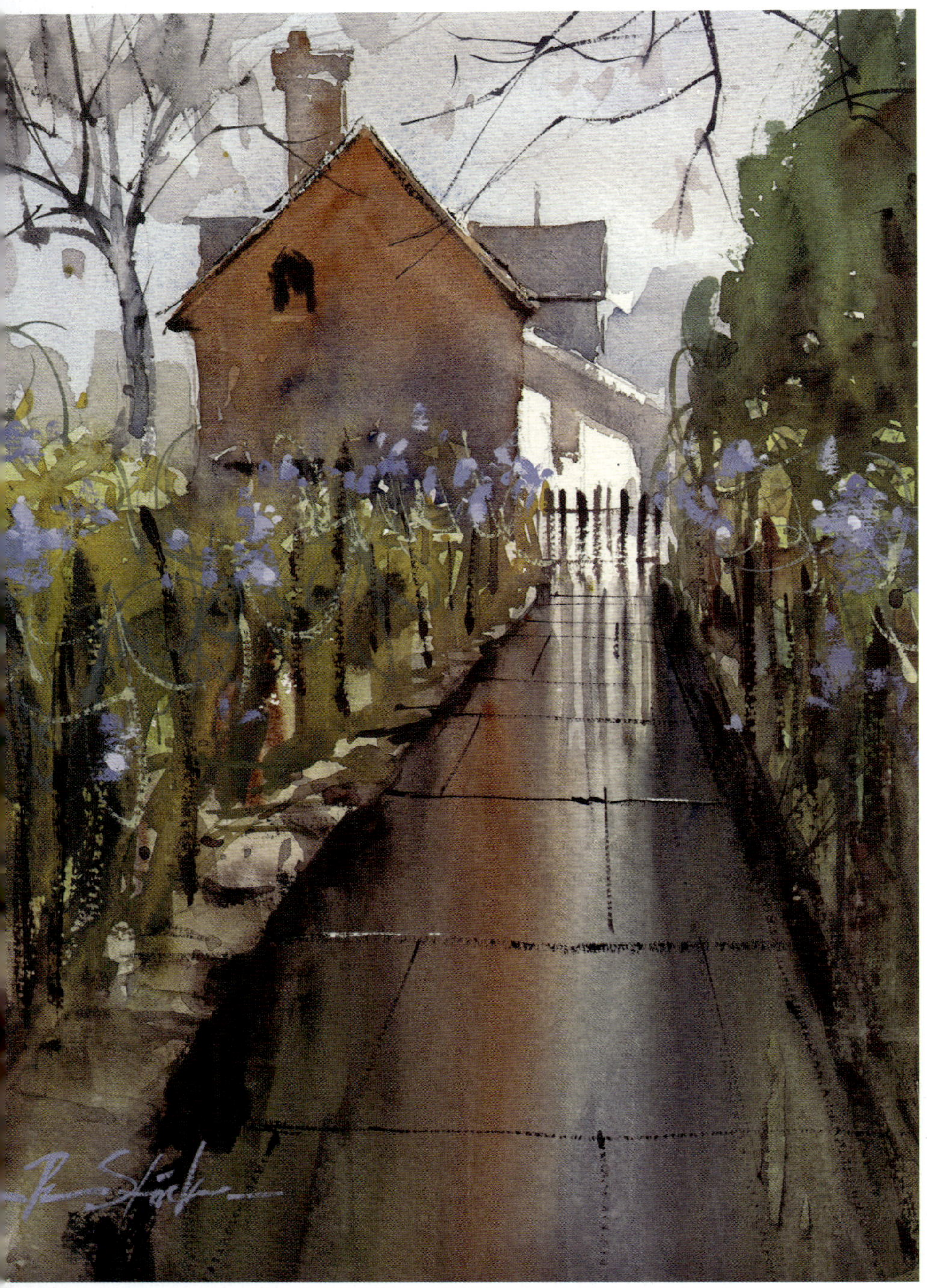

The English Garden. The Golden Rule (see page 53) works no matter the format, vertical or horizontal. Here my focal point is the top right intersection and my supporting element is the lavender flowers that I applied later with an opaque paint.

The Golden Rule

This basic rule of composition is normally applied during the sketching process, so that by the time you are ready to paint, you have already worked out the main design issues.

1. Begin by placing a half or quarter sheet of watercolor paper on your board so that you have a horizontal rectangle. Draw a horizontal line across the paper a third of the way down starting from the top.

2. Draw another line one third of the way up from the bottom.

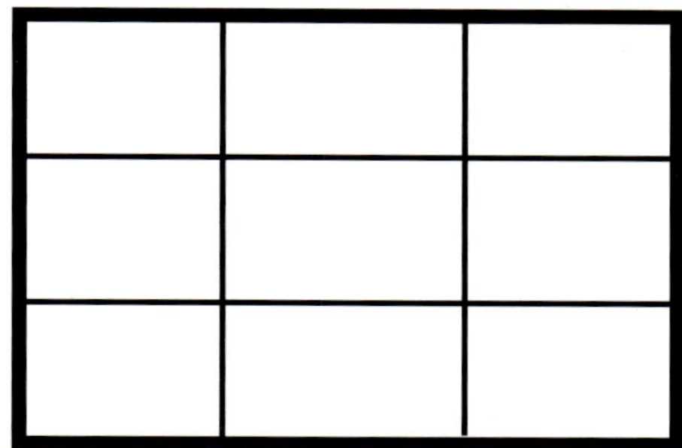

3. Now do the same vertically, so you are looking at a grid made up of four intersecting lines.

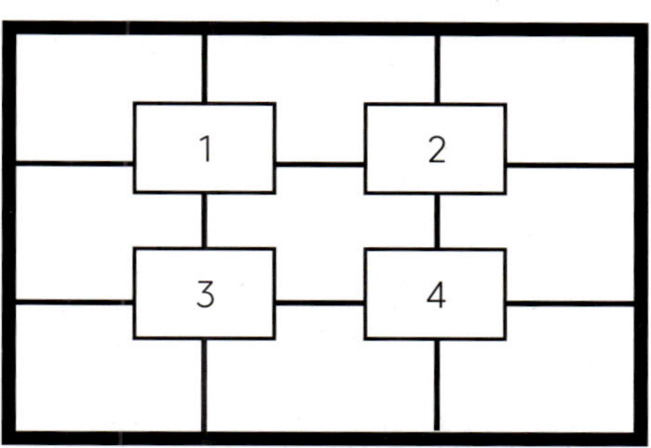

4. The next step is to place your subject in one of the intersections—1, 2, 3, or 4. This will work for most compositions. However, I encourage you to challenge this in your artistic pursuit, and don't be governed by unbreakable rules. There is no gravity in art.

Page 50, *Florence, Italy*

Tension in a Painting

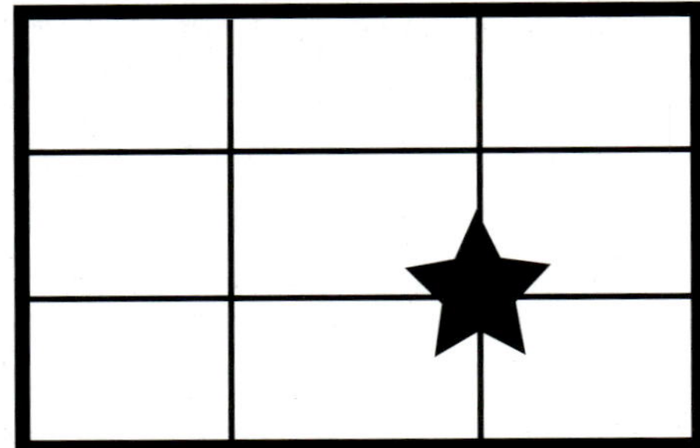

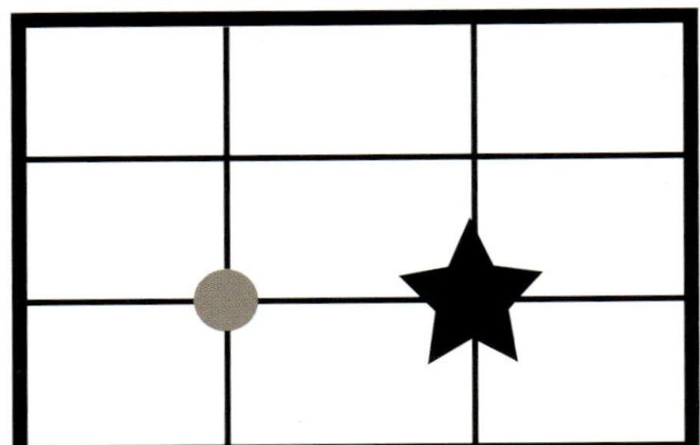

1. Here I have chosen a horizontal format with the bottom right intersection as my focal point. This choice is completely up to the artist and can dramatically change the mood of the painting.

2. After placing my main focal point, I then look for a balancing feature. This needs to be at one of the opposing intersections. This helps balance the composition and is often called "the bolder and the pebble." The pebble shouldn't be the same size or have the same value shift as the boulder. Remember that the pebble should support and balance, but never compete.

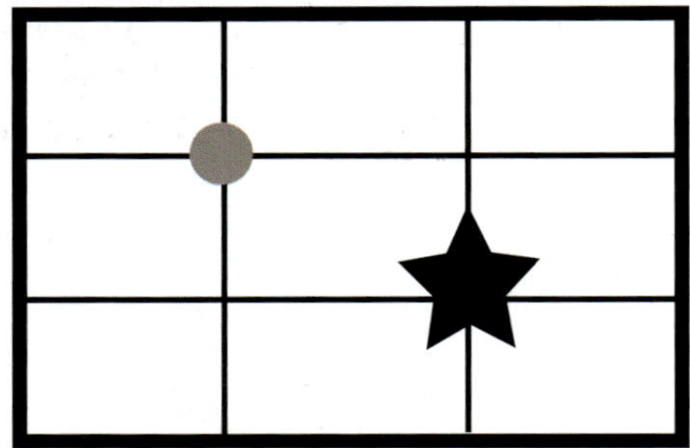

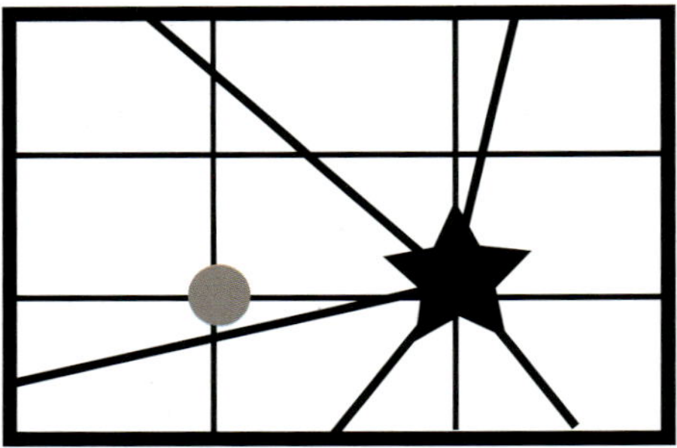

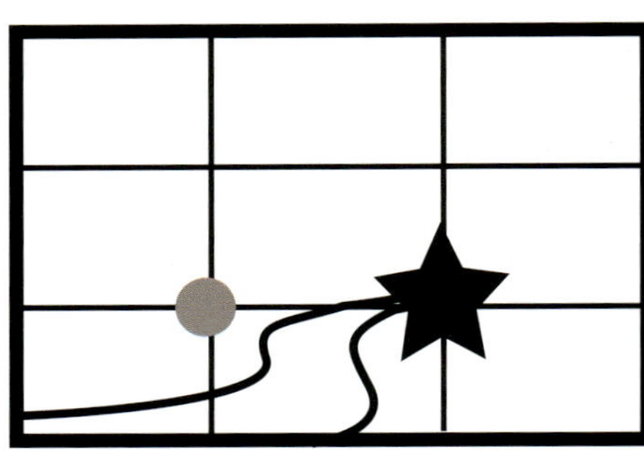

3. Here I have chosen the top left intersection for the supporting shape.

4. Using perspective lines to indicate buildings or roads provides a strong example of how you can direct the viewer's eyes to your focal point.

5. Curved lines can be used to indicate a road or river.

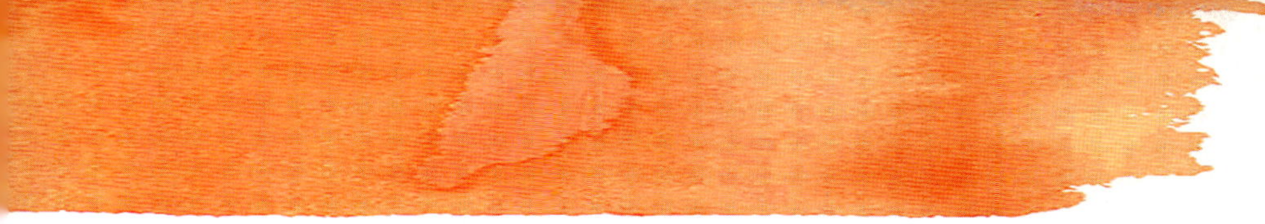

A Night Out in Prague

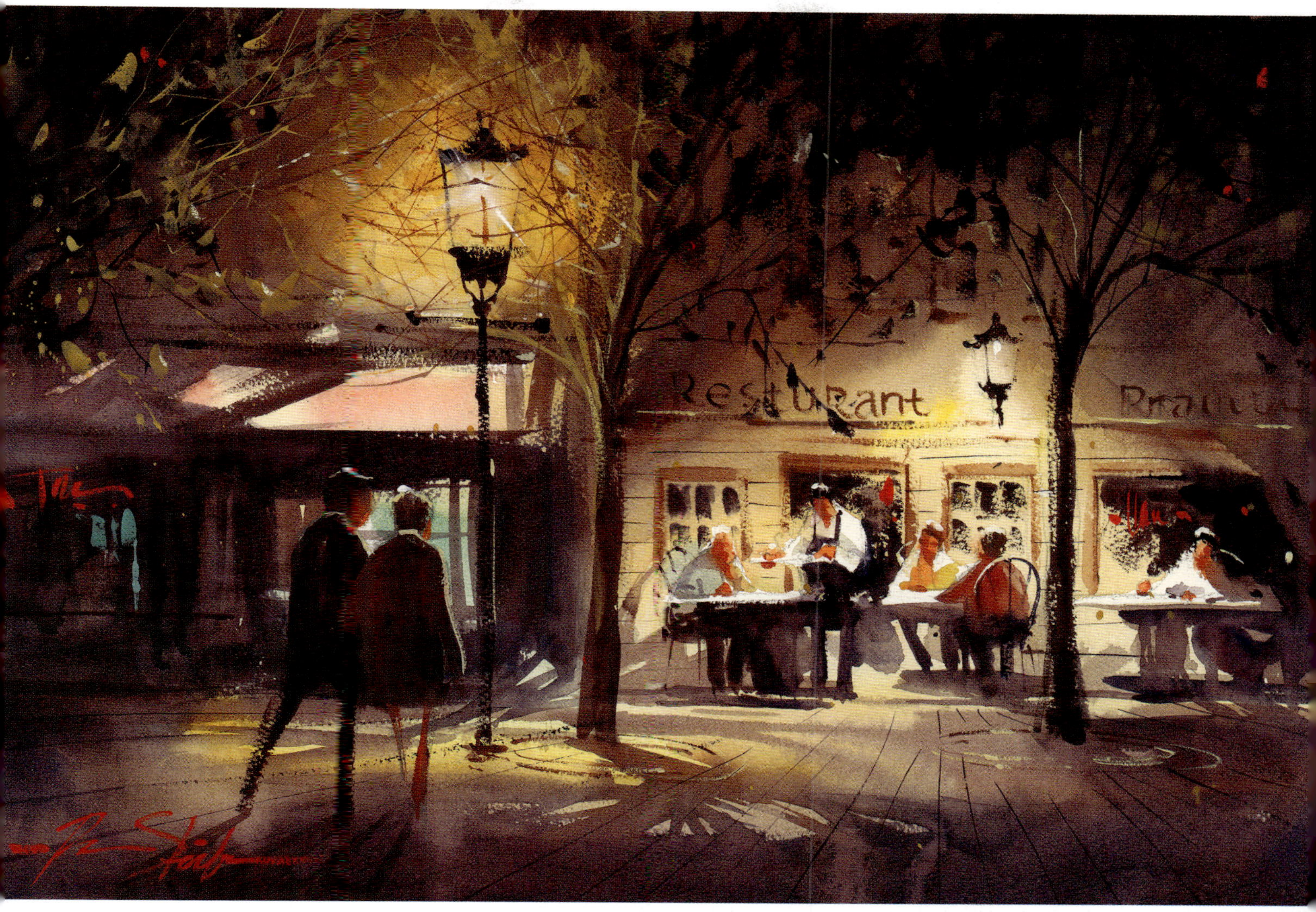

Keep the Corners Boring

Try this the next time you are setting up to paint on location. Take a quick look at your subject, and think about your focal point—it's probably what excited you to stop in the first place. Maybe it's the café umbrellas, or a sailboat, or a red barn. Place this subject close to one of the intersections on your paper. This should be your main concern, and it should rule the painting from beginning to end. The other objects in the setting still need to be painted, but with much less attention. As you move away from your focal point, the other objects should start to lose detail and importance. I believe we should interpret our subject matter in an impressionist manner; that is, at a glance.

By keeping your corners boring, you are avoiding unnecessary tension that might lead the viewer away from the focal point. I'm not saying to avoid putting an object in a corner; just try to make sure that it's connected, and that it drives the viewer's eye into the painting toward your focal point.

Simple Shapes

This section addresses an issue that I think is just as important as the shape itself, and that is how we see shapes in general and why we paint them differently to what we are really seeing. My focus in this section is to begin to challenge you to think about how and what we see as we go through life. Rarely do we sit and stare at everything we pass by. In fact, we are seeing much more then our mind registers, but the majority of what we see, unless it captures and holds our attention, is forgotten about a moment later. This is how I approach my paintings—as if we were only given a glance at our main subject and had to fill in the rest from memory.

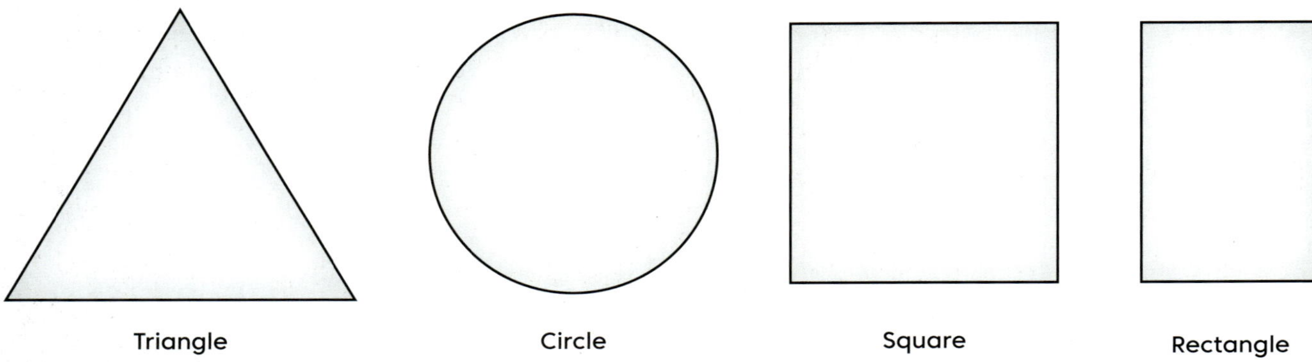

There are many ways an artist can control the viewer's gaze: line, color, shape, and most importantly, value. The greatest value shift should always happen near your target area (your darkest darks and lightest lights), but let's examine shapes for this next exercise.

The four shapes above are some of the earliest shapes of my memory. Most of us probably learned these shapes and visually imprinted them before we could walk or talk. By the time we reach adolescence, we recognize them subconsciously. For example, quickly look at the triangle. It is a shape we commonly see in our daily lives. The triangle can be seen almost everywhere; we see it in nature, mountaintops, trees, and water systems. In our cities it is ubiquitous: road signs, traffic cones, architectural design. It can even be seen in our clothing and the food we eat. It is this familiarity that can get us into trouble. So when we render these shapes, we need to consider the visual strength they have, i.e. their visual tension.

We all know that if we place a figure in a painting, it immediately draws the viewer's eye. This is because we recognize ourselves before we recognize any other shape. And this is exactly why we should learn how to paint figures as random shapes so they blend into their surroundings. We can use these ideas about connecting shapes as we create composition within a painting.

The figures in the paintings on the right are where I want the viewers to focus—particularly the figure crossing the street. This is your target area or "area of dominance." Regardless of how I paint the umbrellas, the viewer will always come back to these figures. However, if the umbrellas were rendered as perfect isosceles triangles, it would create negative tension above their heads, confusing the viewer about my intent in directing their eye around the painting.

J&M Cafe

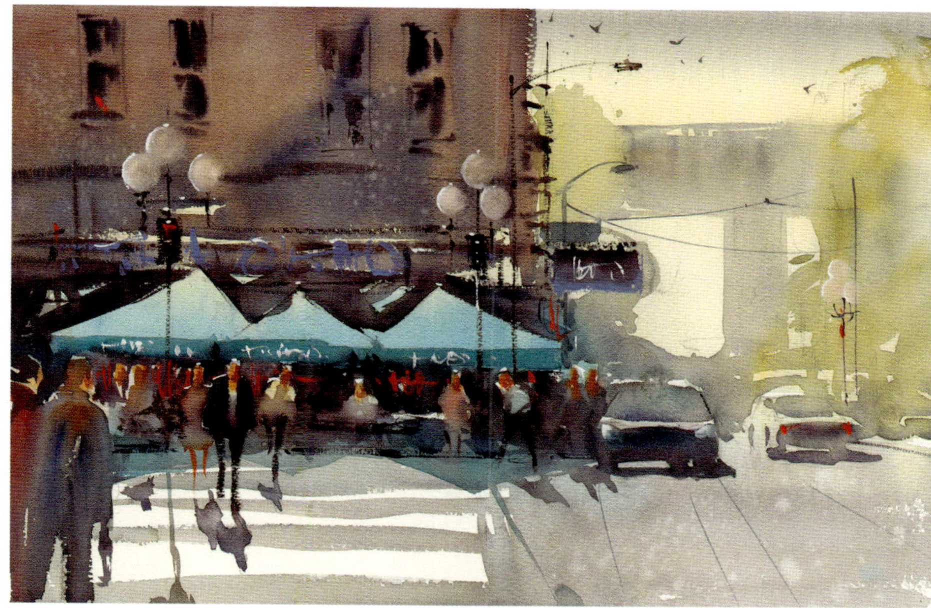

In this first image, the umbrellas are painted quickly with little precision so they become a secondary part of the composition and support for my focal point.

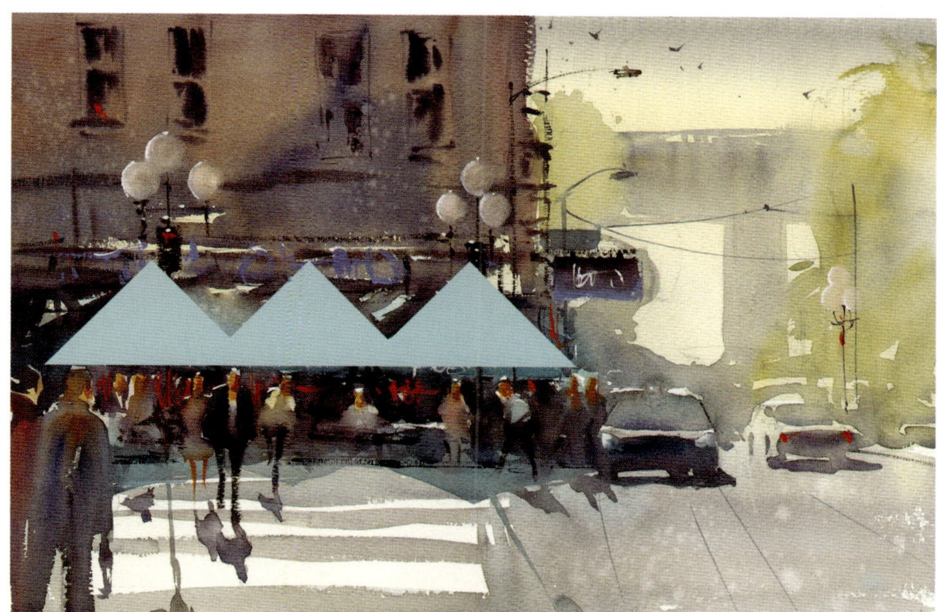

This second image has been digitally enhanced to show the umbrellas as perfect, regular, flat, equal shapes. If painted this way, they will cause an unintended tension and confuse the viewer about what they are and their purpose.

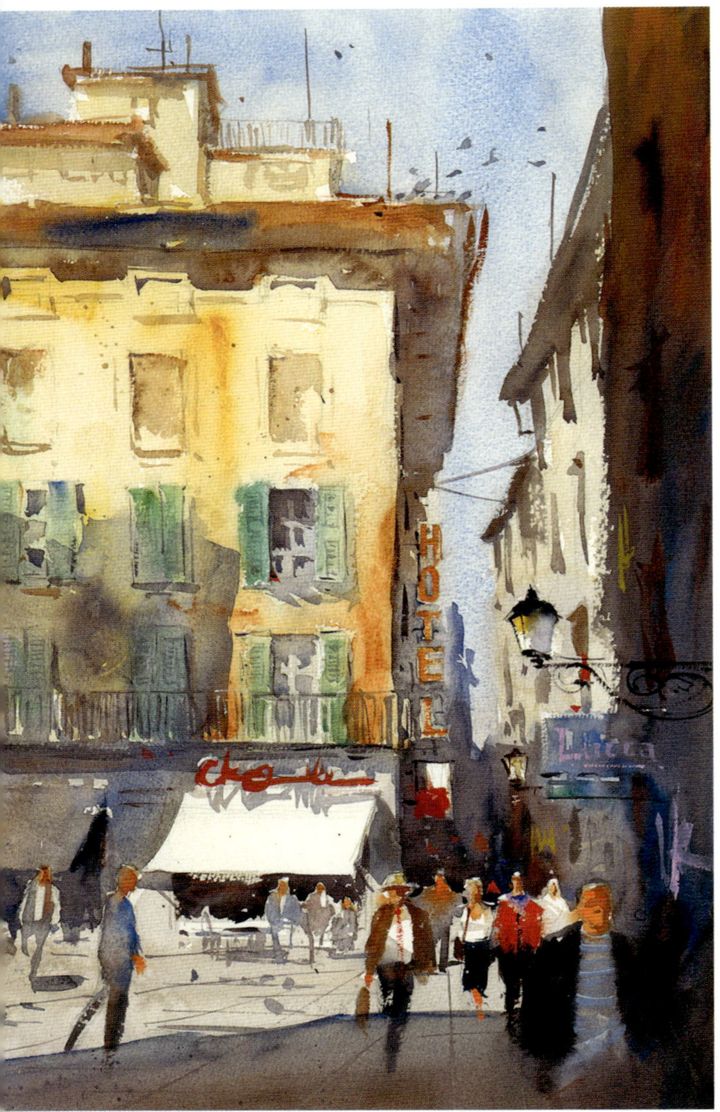

There is conflict between the perfect, dark-valued windows in the building and the figures in the bottom right-hand corner, which are my intended focal point. You can't paint these competing subjects with the same tension. One always needs to win.

Let's look at another example. The most common mistake I see is not with the circle, square, or even the triangle, but with rectangular shapes. Out of all of the shapes imprinted from childhood in our visual memory, we seem to want to paint rectangles as solid shapes with all four corners filled in completely. Don't do it. As these two images show, softening the rectangular windows makes all the difference. This can be one of the simplest ways to release tension and make a painting look less rigid.

Via Fillungo, Lucca

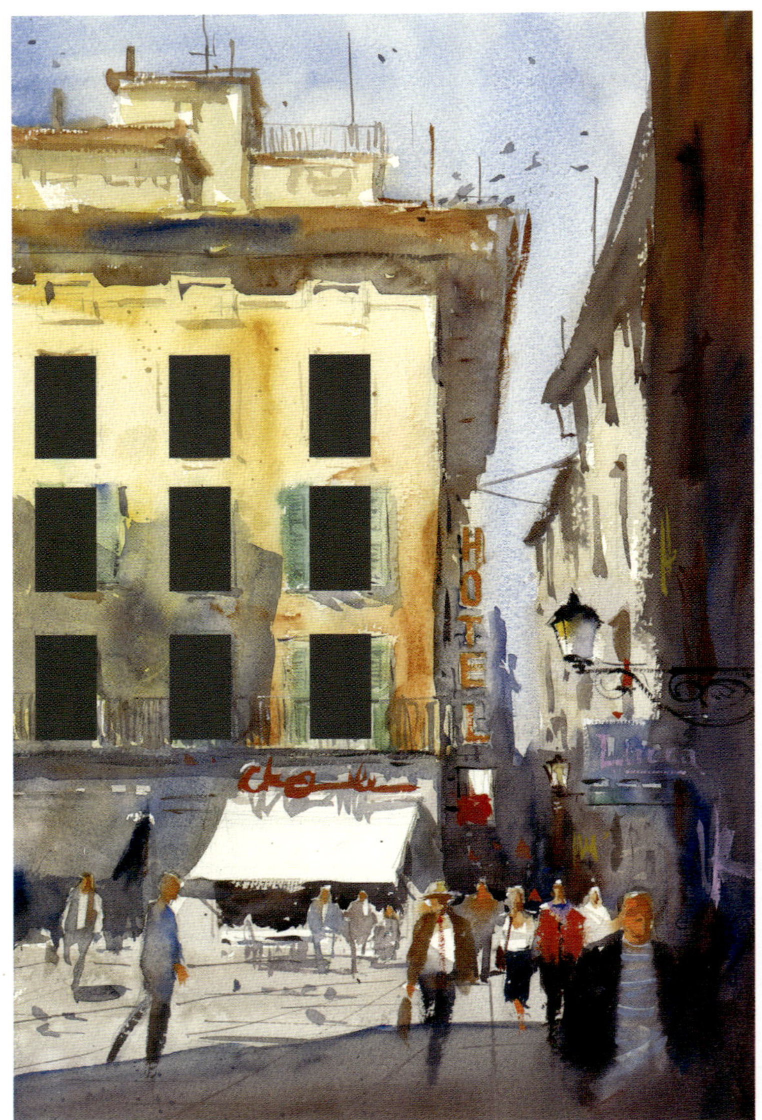

Lucca Sketchbook Painting

Here is a typical page from one of my sketchbooks (image at right). The bottom right sketch is a simple value study of what would eventually be the painting. In this graphite thumbnail I am trying to establish my basic shapes and values. In the top left image, I take the sketch a bit further by doing a color study. That is, color notes of the buildings, shadows, and some details of my focus; as you can see, I am applying what I've done in the value sketch here, just with paint. These lovely little watercolors can end up being great references for future paintings, or they can stand on their own as memories of the day. The brushstrokes and figure studies are done for details I may add to the later painting.

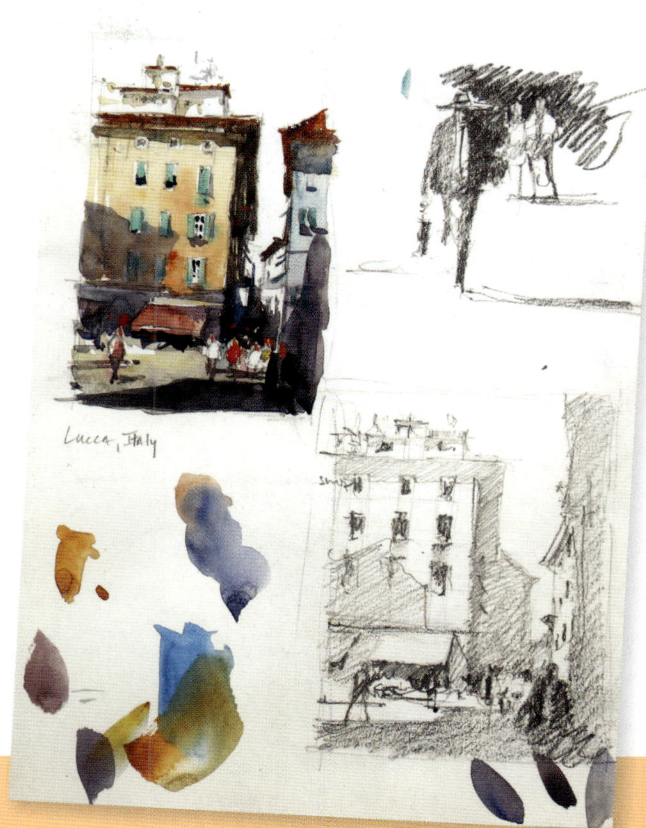

Tip

Here are four examples of the rectangle. It's not difficult to see the problem. Rather than painting a window solid from edge to edge in one value, commonly black, I tell students to paint windows as if they are driving by them in a car: quickly, not spending too much attention on shape or detail. If painted this way, the viewer won't get hung up on the negative tension of a solid shape. This allows the eye to travel over these shapes and settle on a more important area of the painting.

1. **Painted solid, from edge to edge in one value—negative tension, poorly executed.**
2. **Quickly painted using the texture of the paper—this allows the eye to travel over this shape to a more important area of the painting.**
3. **Quickly painted, indicating some detail and utilizing positive and negative shapes.**
4. **This is a combination of two and three.**

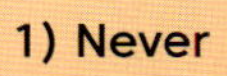

1) Never

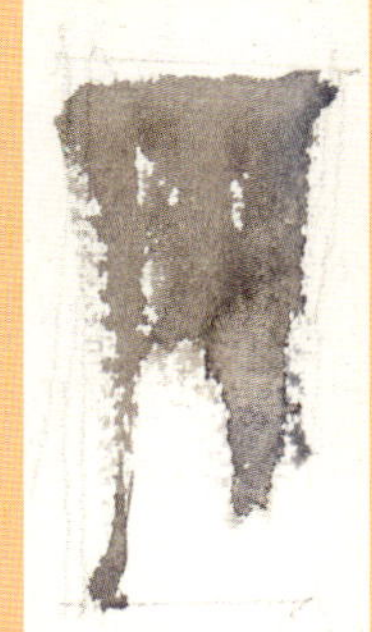

2) Acceptable

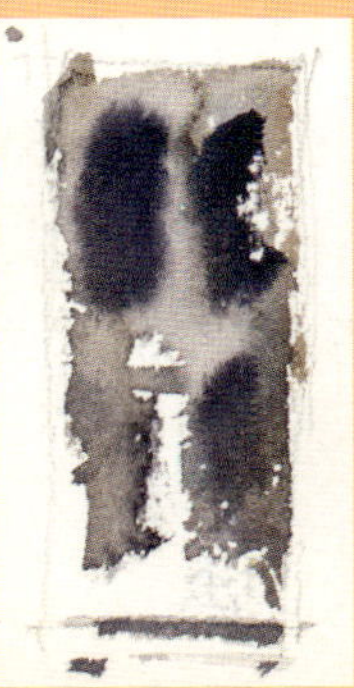

3) Acceptable

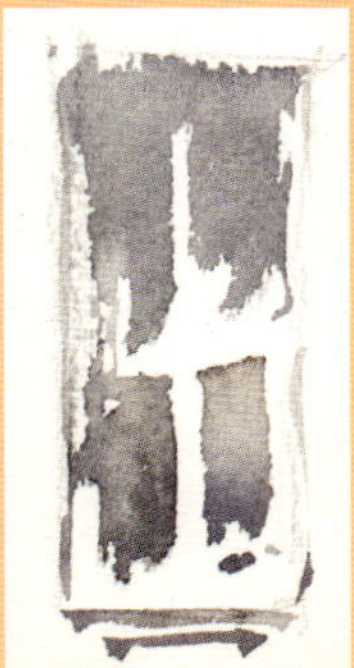

4) Acceptable

Tension

I believe that there is a certain amount of tension in almost every aspect of our lives. As artists, we naturally try and interpret this in our work. Throughout this book, I will describe the negative and positive tension we experience in color, value, and most importantly, design. To begin, let's look at the use of tension in as simple terms as we can—a single brushstroke.

Brushstroke (Flying White)

- **Is the brushstroke above positive or negative?**
- **Is it positive because it is darker than the rest of the paper?**
- **Is it negative because it is a small shape on a larger sheet of paper?**
- **Can it be both?**

Let me explain. One day while painting with a friend, I made an energetic dry brushstroke on a painting. My friend, Yuming Zhu, a master Sumi artist, declared it "flying white." I had never heard this term before and asked what he meant. He explained to me that he was taught to look at the lighter value as having equal weight to the darker value.

Most of us will only see the dark positive value as it breaks up into the white of the paper, creating a staccato or broken color; we won't pay attention to its lighter counterpart. It can be debated that without the lighter value, the darker value would sit flat and have very little interest at all.

This is the concept of tension. It is the balance we should try to achieve in our work. However, it's important to note that very often they will not be in equal proportions.

Behind Dagmar's

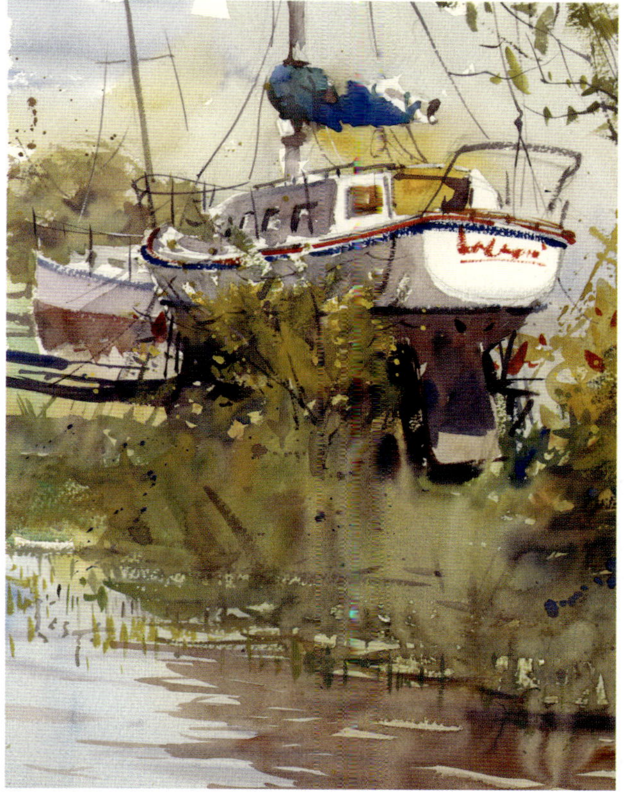

Notice the tension the boats create through value and shape. This would not be as effective if I had treated the foreground detail with the same attention, so a looser passage was applied.

Post Alley Shadows

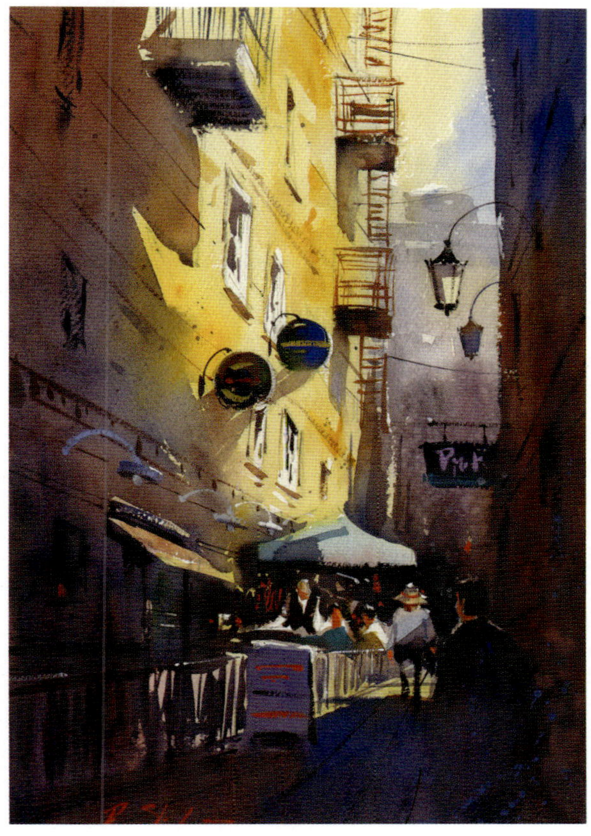

In *Post Alley Shadows,* see how the broken ribbon of light supports the much larger dark value of the shadow that connects the foreground and distant buildings into one shape.

I want to be clear. Don't think of negative and positive tension as good or bad. Think of them as equals, as in ***Brushstroke (Flying White)***. The blue is a positive brushstroke, but it is the white that adds the interest

As you compose your paintings on location or in the studio, start asking yourself, how am I going to balance this image?

- **Tension in color:** the positive and negative tension comes from simply choosing the right or wrong color combinations.
- **Tension in value:** this comes from the incorrect amount or placement of lights and darks in your composition.
- **Tension in design:** this refers to the arrangement of shapes, value, and line within your painting.

Breaking the Horizon

Here are some quick tips on how to change tension in your paintings by simply changing the horizon. But as I mentioned on page 16, there is a paradox with the horizon line. The issue lies when you move from your drawing to your painting. At the drawing stage, the horizon line is the most important line you make. It establishes a line on which your vanishing points rest and the parallel lines of your object converge, so that distance and form are created. Without it, you can't have organized form or consistency of line within your objects. In your drawing, the horizon line is strong and absolute. However, when making the leap from drawing to painting, you must diminish the visual power of the horizon line—in other words, reduce its tension. You do this by breaking it.

Breaking the horizon can be achieved by connecting it to shapes or by losing it altogether. Even though the horizon line was the first line I drew in all of these sketches, I have done my best to try to eliminate it altogether, so that when I begin painting there is no hesitation to paint through or connect a distant shape to one in the foreground.

CHOICE 1.
HIGH HORIZON
This example illustrates a simple way of how to achieve action and movement in your image. Notice how the viewer is pulled into the image simply by showing more of the foreground.

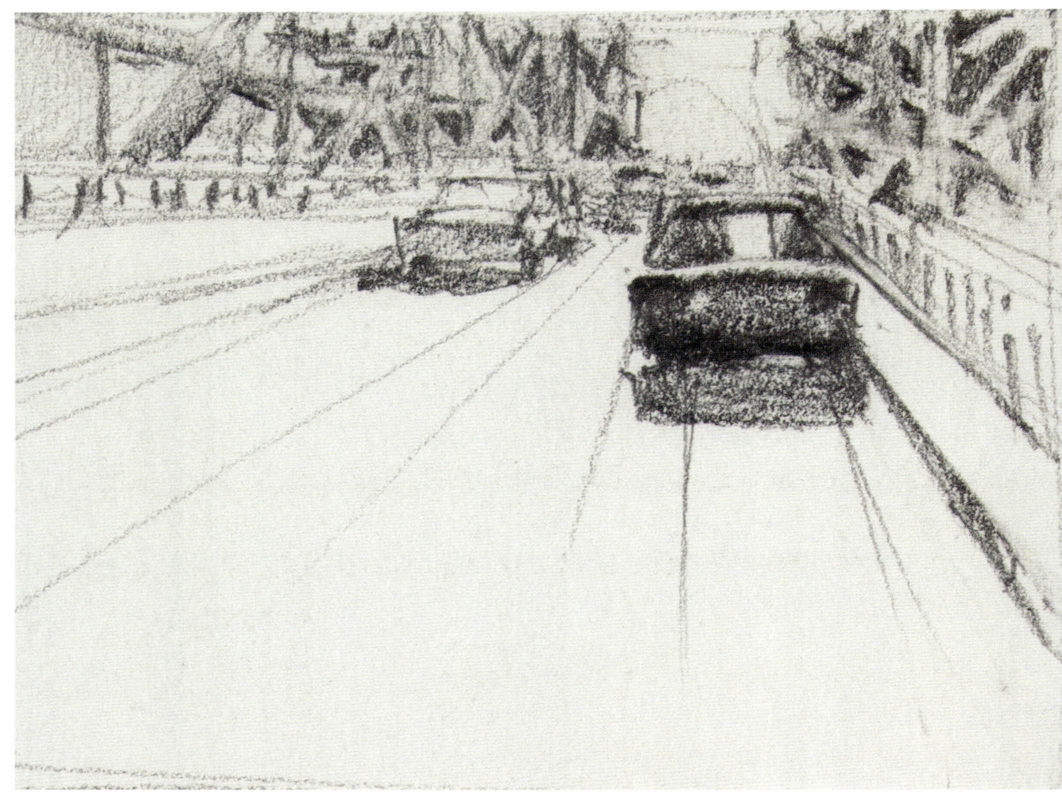

CHOICE 2.
MID HORIZON

This is the more common choice for most artists because it is normally the viewer's vantage point. It is a more balanced design and is commonly what you, the viewer, is seeing in a real-life situation.

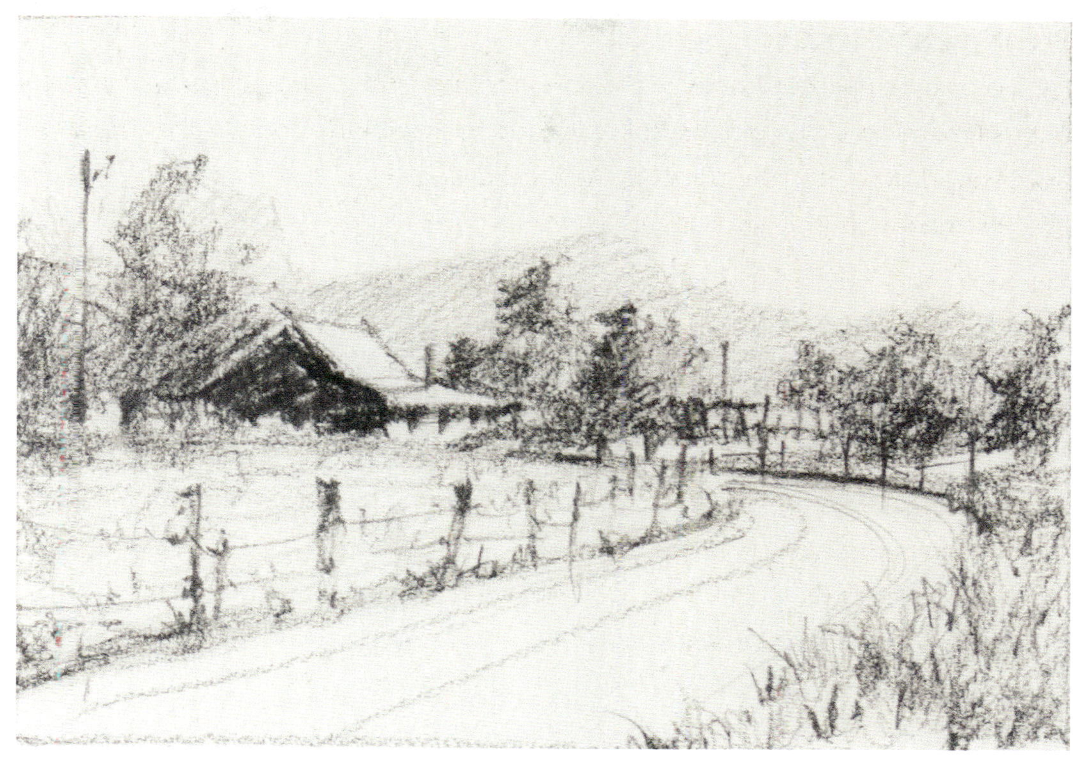

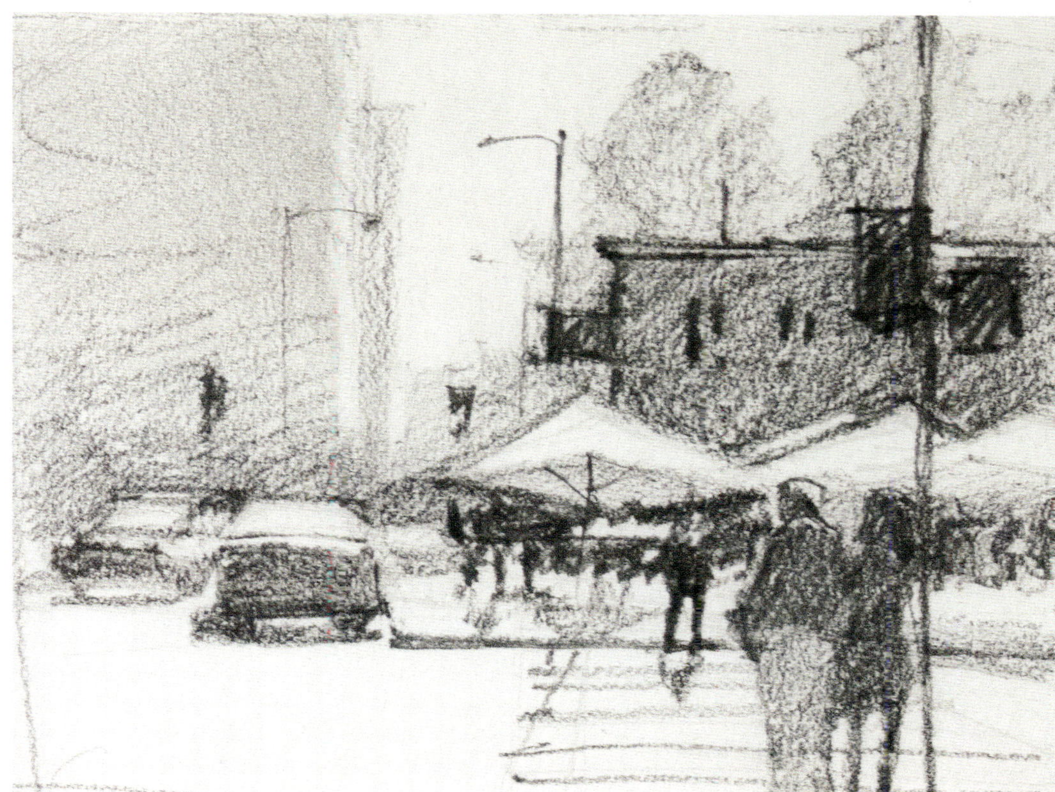

CHOICE 3.
LOW HORIZON

A lower horizon line can help you create drama within your paintings. Use this opportunity to create distance, but don't forget to connect the painting.

Page 64, *Game Day Safeco Field*

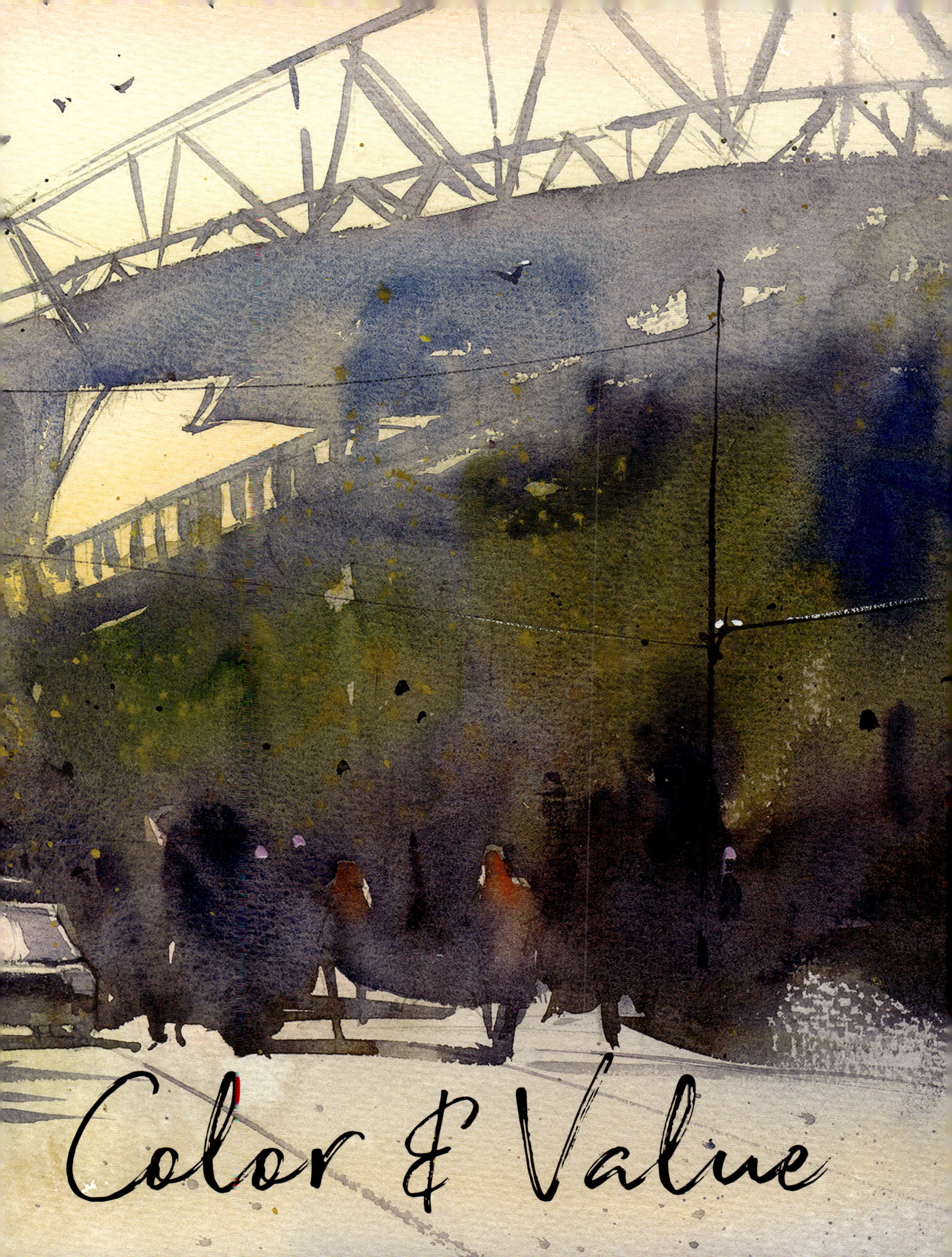

Color & Value

The Color Wheel

The practice of painting a color wheel is worth the time and effort for any artist. I have painted dozens over the years and have learned something new with every one. It is important to note that with so many brands of watercolor on the market, one could do a color chart for every brand and achieve a wide range of secondary and tertiary colors. It is important to understand how color can affect the mood, focus, and tension of a painting, and how the power of good color harmony can make the difference between a good and bad painting. We know that the primary colors dictate the color wheel; that work has been done for us. We also know that mixing red and blue make violet, red and yellow make orange, and that yellow and blue make green.

The Analogous Palette

An analogous color wheel or palette is when you select one primary color, like red, and use the adjacent colors around it to create an overriding color theme for the painting. The analogous palette is perfect when you want to convey mood to the viewer. I suggest painting individual wheels using just one set of colors around each primary color. Make one wheel with all of your reds, another with all of your blues, and the last with your various yellows. What you'll end up with are wheels of color temperature. This is a great way for you to figure out your warm and cool reds, blues, and yellows.

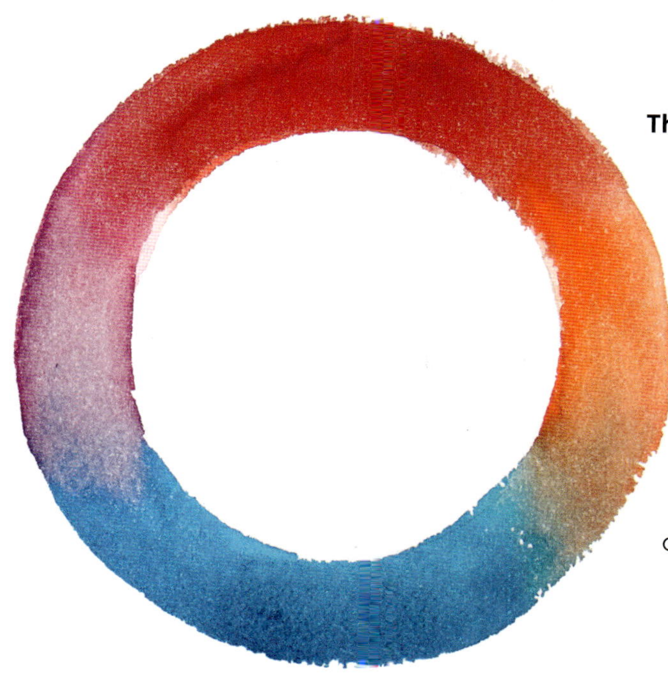

The Split Complementary Palette

I like to use this palette on location because it simplifies the process, and I usually come home with a more interesting painting. A split complementary deals with a similar concept as the analogous with one basic addition. If you begin with a red-orange color scheme, you would then add one of the complements like blue-green to help balance the painting. By doing this you are creating interest and color harmony that will help connect your painting.

The Harmonious Palette

The power of good color harmony can make the difference between a good and bad painting. When it comes to color, the most common questions I hear from students are: "What color is that?", "What color should I use?", and the famous, "What is your favorite color?" For the record, I'm sure I asked my mentors similar questions when I first started out. Frequently the answer I was given was not really about color but about value. Like me, I believe that most artists confuse color with value. Value can have a greater affect on color than you think.

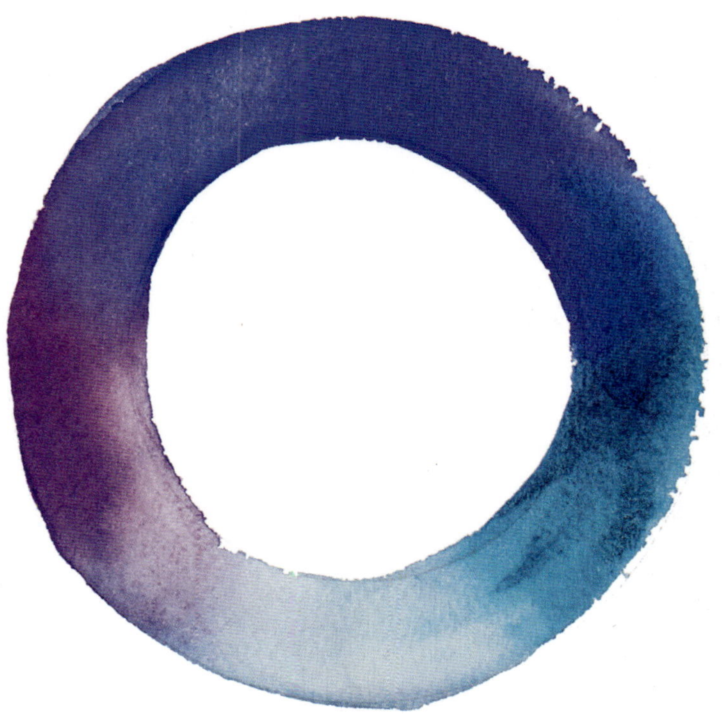

Think in terms of values instead of color.

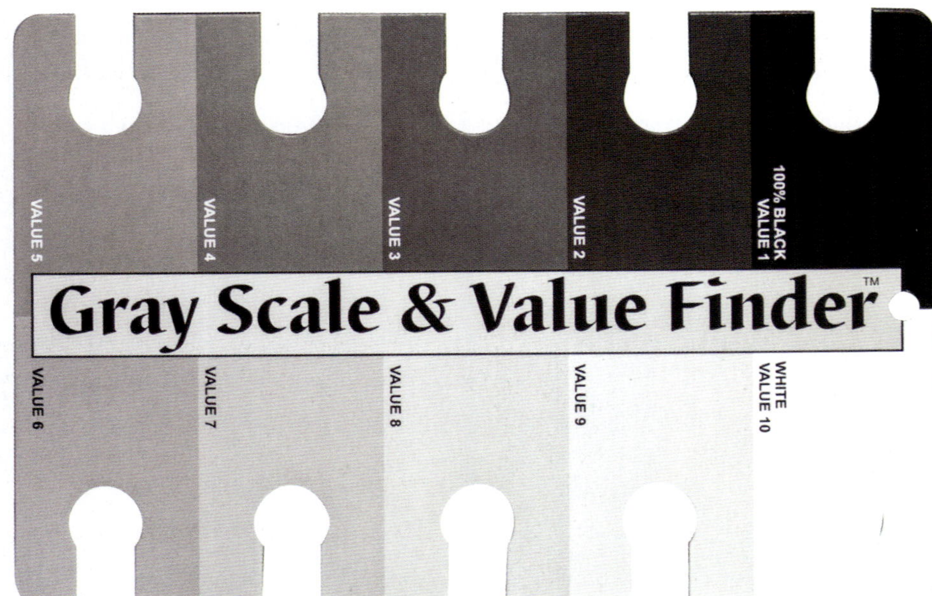

It's easy to see how we can recreate value in the studio. Now let's see where it can be applied in the real world.

It is easier to look at a red bus and decide which red to paint than it is to look at the same red bus and decide what value it possesses. As soon as I started to understand how value could affect my work, I began seeing my subject in a different way. No longer was I concerned with what red to use, but rather what value—or more appropriately values—to use so that I could create form, or shape, and distance, in what I painted. The next time you're pondering what color an object is, make sure you understand the values of it and its surroundings.

But for now, let's discuss the power of good color harmony in a painting, how a limited palette can make a big impact, and why painting with grays can make colors look more intense.

Figure 1

Figure 2

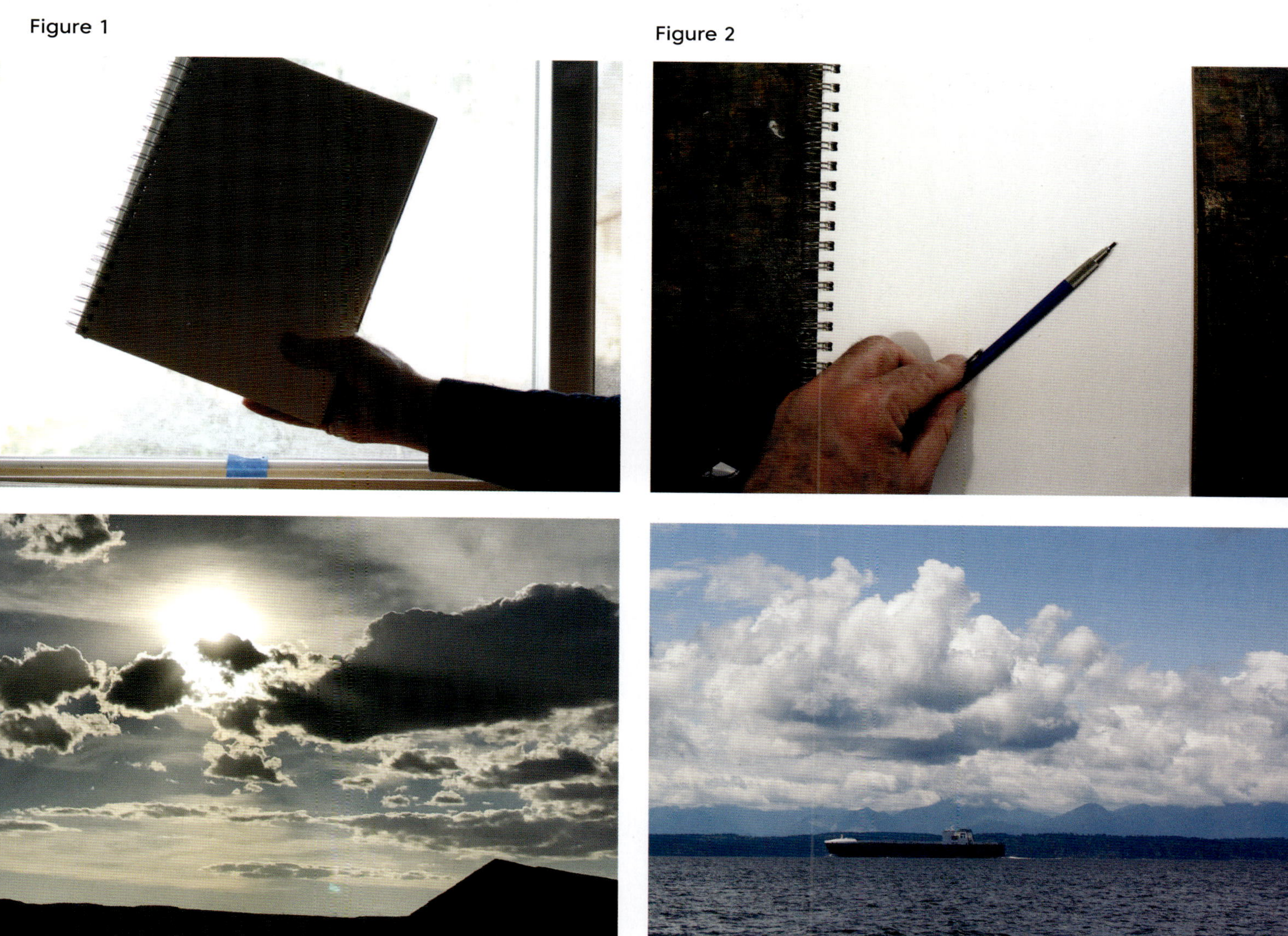

Figure 3

Figure 4

In figures 1 and 3, the values fall into the 1 or 2 range of the scale (see value scale on page 68), whereas in figures 2 and 4, both the sketchbook and cloud fall into the 9 or 10 range. After teaching for a number of years, I often see this common mistake made. Perhaps subconsciously we don't believe what we are seeing, and so we tend to paint a preconceived idea of our subjects, rather than what is truly there. In this case, a white cloud or white sketchbook painted with a dark value.

Color Chart

Cadmium yellow light
Yellow ochre
Cadmium orange
Cadmium red light
Alizarin crimson
Maroon perylene
Cobalt blue
Cerulean blue
Turquoise
Viridian

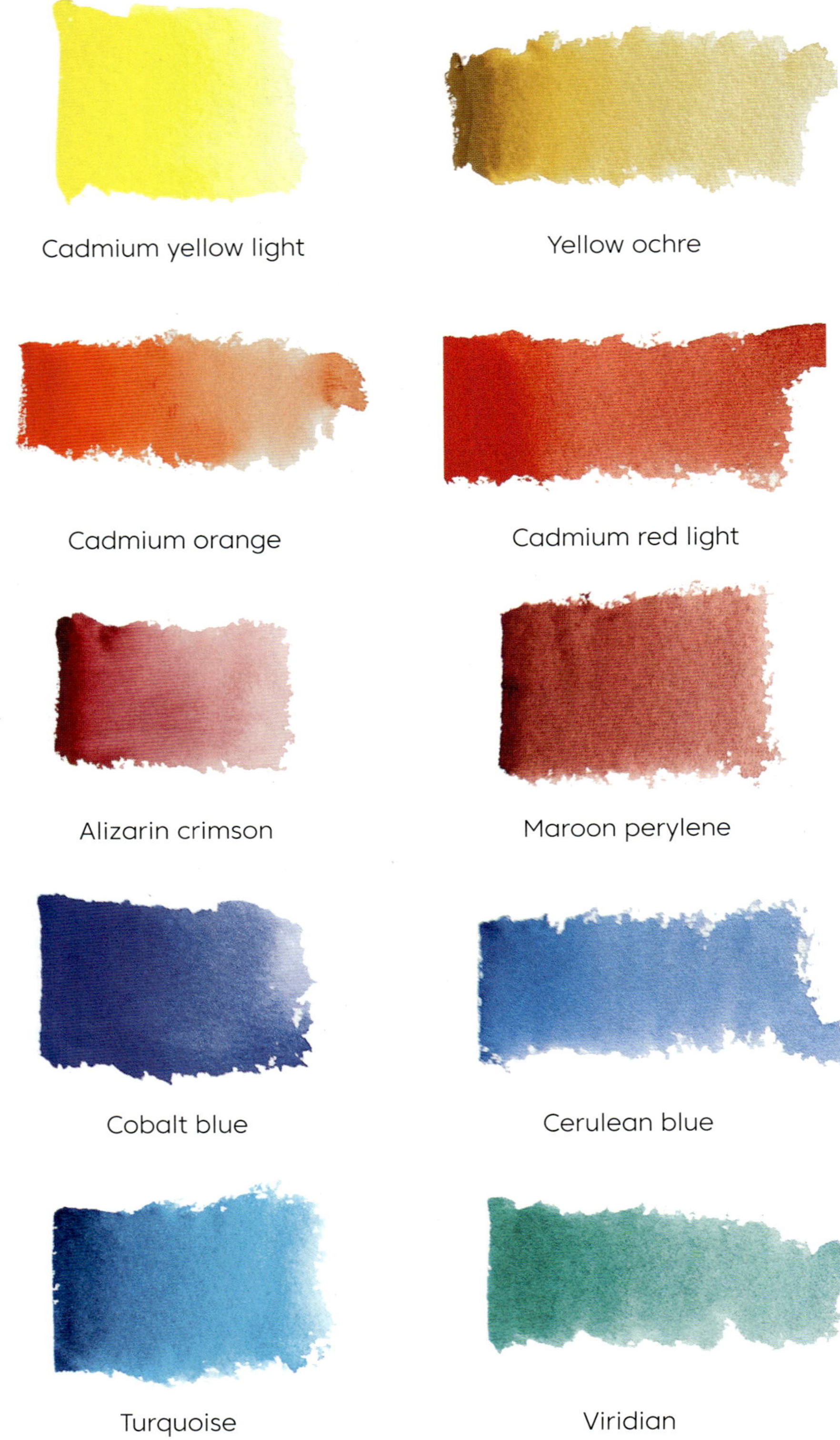

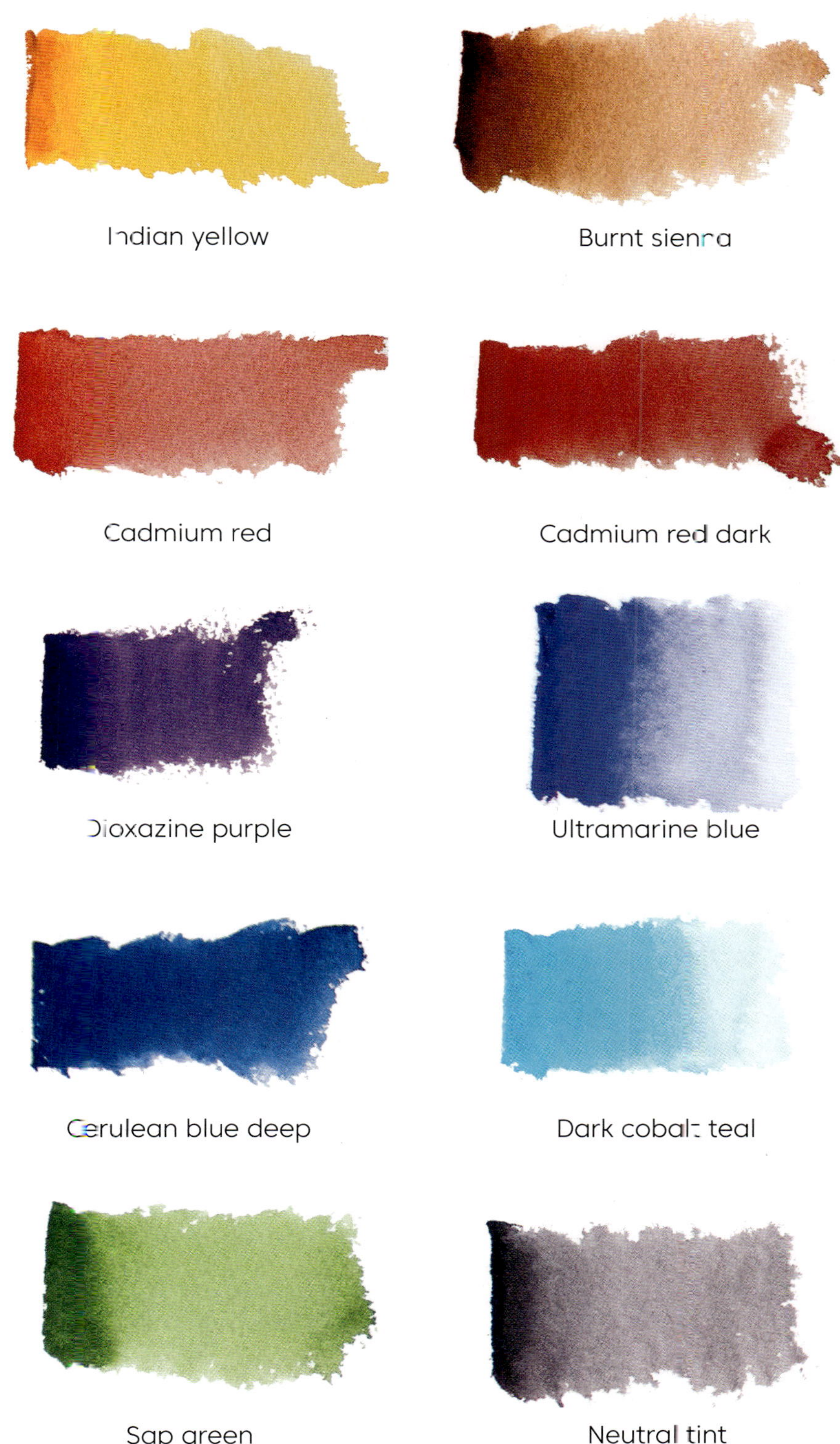
Indian yellow
Burnt sienna
Cadmium red
Cadmium red dark
Dioxazine purple
Ultramarine blue
Cerulean blue deep
Dark cobalt teal
Sap green
Neutral tint

Color Washes

Here are three examples of two sedimentary opaque colors, cadmium red light and cobalt teal, mixing on the paper.

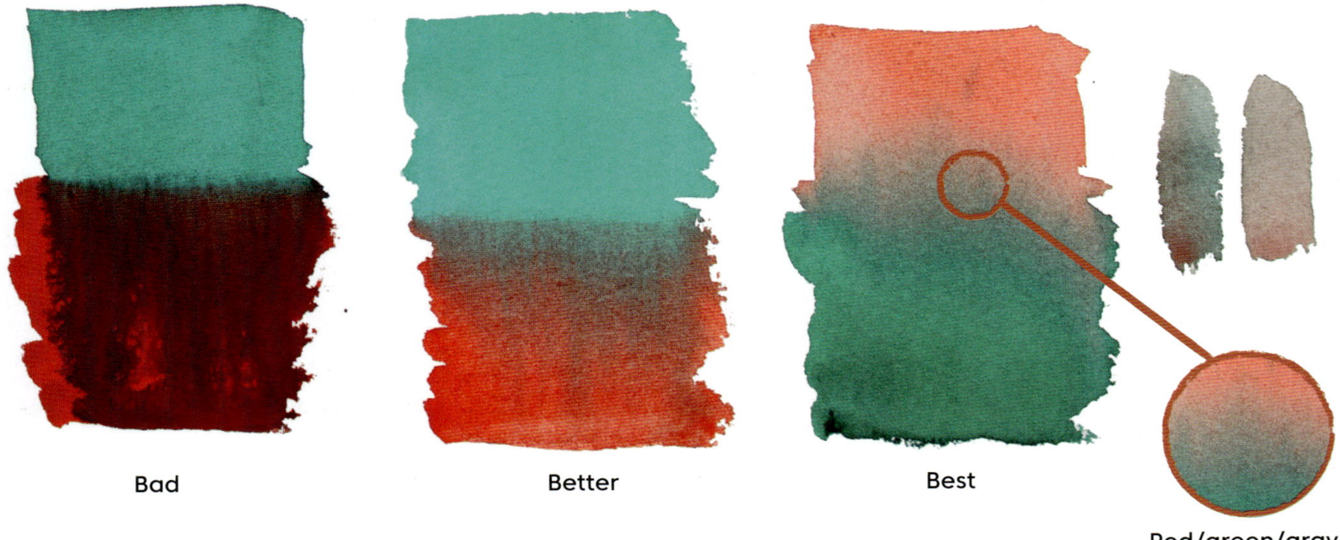

Bad: The left swatch shows the two colors mixed at different consistencies, and where one color (the red) was allowed to set up before adding the teal. The result is a muddy, undesirable transition.

Better: The center image shows a better gradation, but you can still see the demarcation line of the red. This is due to the red setting up or being allowed to dry to a point where the red and green could not mix and merge properly.

Best: The image on the right was painted with the two colors at the correct consistency but also at the correct drying stage or time, proving that if the two colors remain wet, they can be blended properly.

The two brushstrokes to the right of the washes are the two colors mixed on the palette: one with more red in the mixture, one with more turquoise. This shows the difference between mixing colors on your palette versus mixing on the paper.

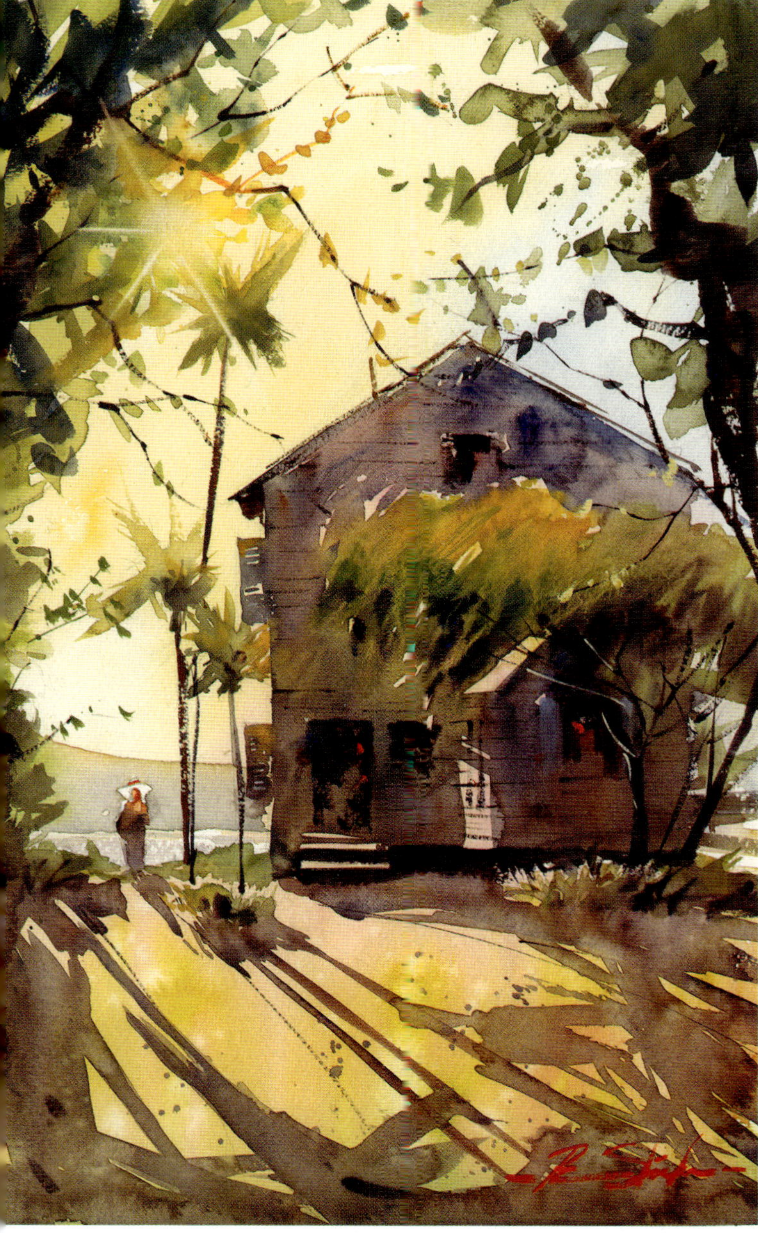

Kona Sunrise

Mixing Your Greens

I prefer to mix my greens on the paper rather than the palette. The combinations from allowing two colors to merge on the paper are endless and can often be more exciting than the colors you use straight from the tube. This reaction is one that is unique to the watercolor medium.

Yes, it's true, if you mix blue and yellow on your palette in equal ratios, the result is usually green. However, if you allow the same two colors to mix on the paper, you can create a green/gray that may work better for what you are trying to achieve.

Another common combination I use is ultramarine and yellow. On the near right, I added ultramarine blue—a sedimentary, transparent color—over a wet wash of Indian yellow: a staining, transparent color. Then, on the far right, I mixed them the other way around, with the Indian yellow added to the ultramarine. The separate brushstrokes above are the same colors as they appear after mixing on my palette.

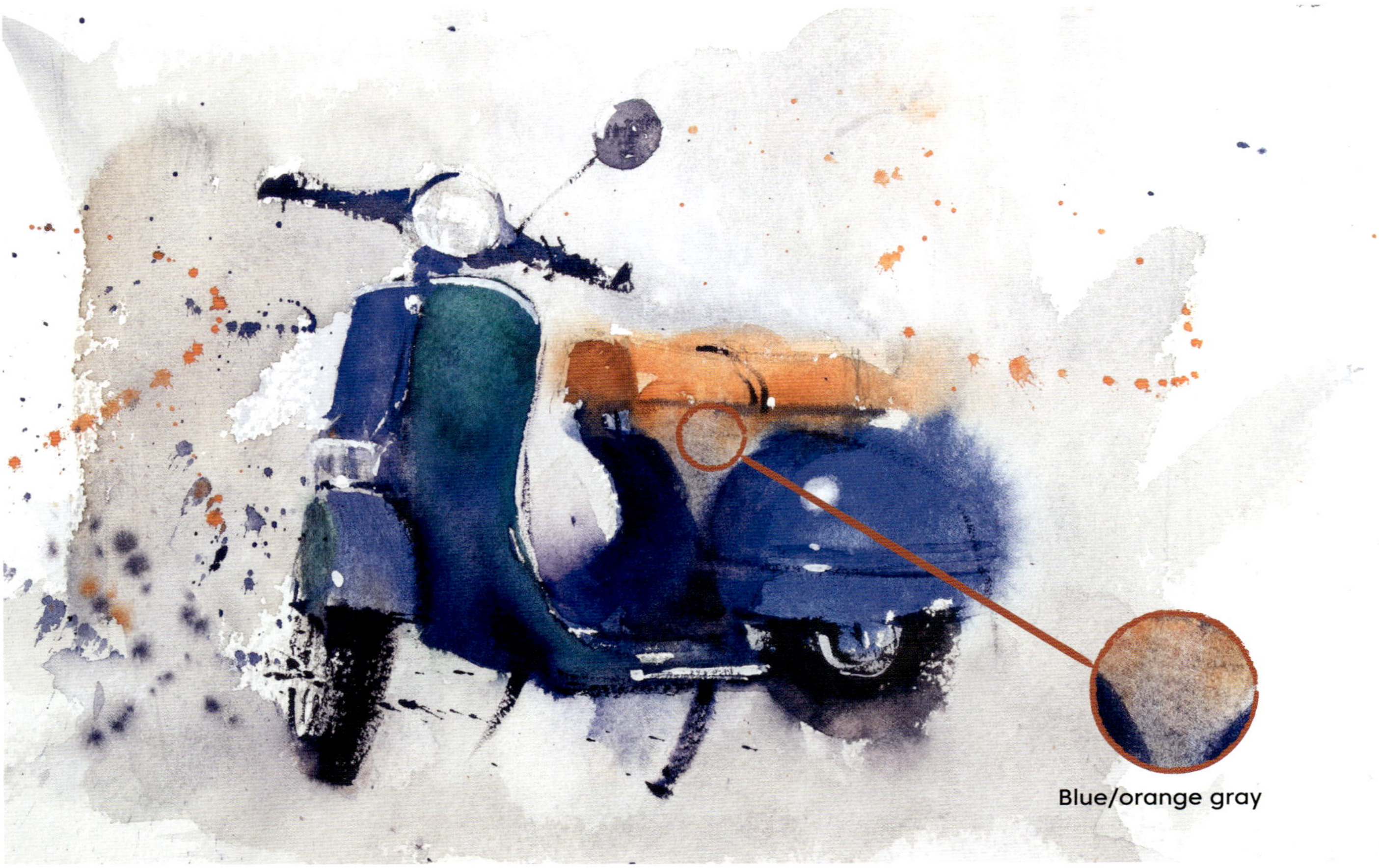

Blue/orange gray

The Blue Vespa

Practice this type of experiment wherever and whenever you can. Knowing that you have limited time can help you loosen up and result in a great image for your sketchbook. The lighter gray background wash was mixed on the palette, using the same colors that I used for the scooter.

It's easy to see why I used these two colors together because they contrast so beautifully. Cadmium orange is an opaque staining color, while cobalt blue is a semitransparent color, and both granulate well. I consider these colors to be two of the most beautiful in my palette. Not only are they almost perfect complements, but when combined they create a particularly unique visual spark.

Shown here is a more obvious example of how by lifting my brush I allow more water and color to flow down the right side of the wash. One way to avoid this is by lifting the brush after you've moved past the tape line.

I judge success by the intensity of color and watermarks. Where I feel this didn't really work was when I didn't get to the orange fast enough, and I didn't judge the weight or intensity of the turquoise correctly. I'm constantly trying new combinations, not only with color, but with timing and consistency of paint. These studio-made color swatches are great exercises that you can add to your artist sketchbook, so when you approach a painting you don't hesitate to try new ideas. This way you can focus on painting with purpose and energy.

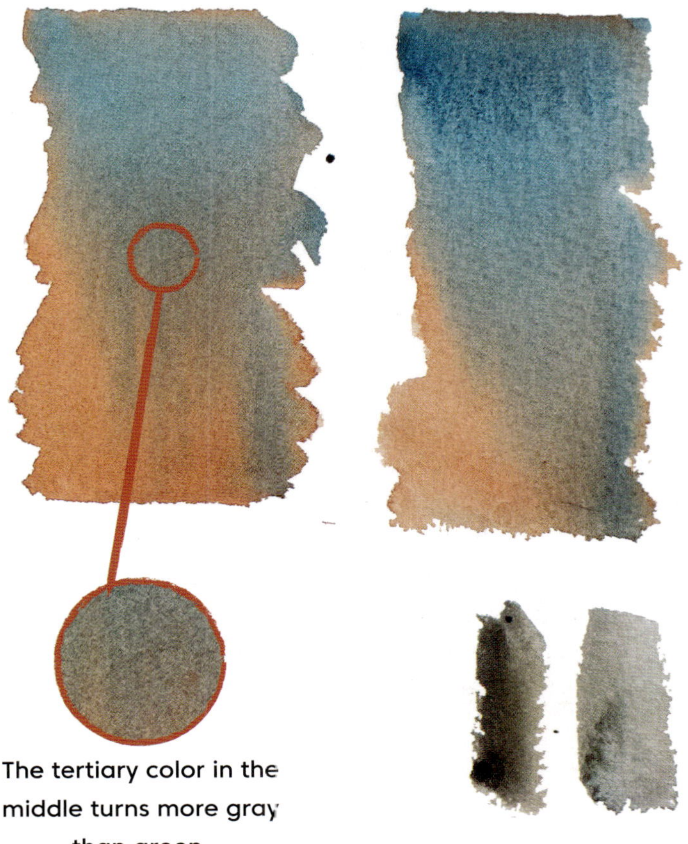

The tertiary color in the middle turns more gray than green.

Mixing Your Darks

Instead of using commercial premixed blacks, here are some ideas for color combinations that I mix to achieve my darkest darks.

Notice the two blacks below (ivory black and lamp black). They can be used for your darkest darks, but when dry they can leave a flat appearance; when disturbed into a wash, the result is a dull, unexciting gray.

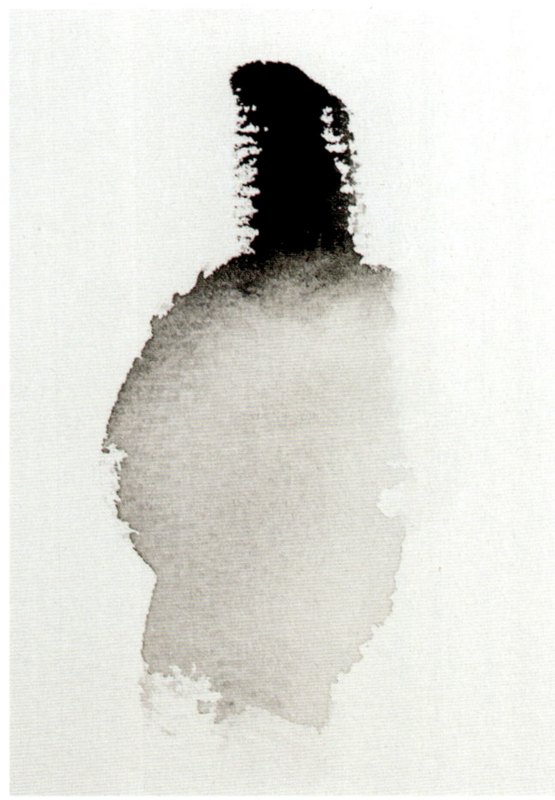

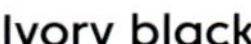

Ivory black

Lamp black

The combinations on the opposite page still achieve your darkest darks, but they are created by mixing two colors together. The result is a much more interesting wash, and the dark area will have a trace of light that will make your darks really sparkle. To make the most of this technique, play with the percentages of your color mixtures—usually a cool and a warm color. Add more of the cool color, and you will produce a perfect dark for a winter or dreary day scene. Add more of the warm color, and you will get that particular warm dark of a hot day.

Ultramarine and maroon perylene

Turquoise and alizarin crimson

Dioxazine purple

Purple burnt sienna

Color vs. Gray

The importance of painting with grays cannot be overstated. Grays are as important as any primary or secondary hue on the color wheel. We all know that by mixing red and yellow we get orange; however, many struggle to understand how to mix warm or cool grays, which, in fact, are more commonly seen than primary and secondary colors.

Some artists run into problems when they try to achieve a gray tone by building up layers of color. This results in dull, muddy areas. When referring to grays, I am not speaking of a color you can purchase in a tube, but rather the color that is the outcome of mixing two or more colors. I'm also not referring to several colors being stirred around on your palette that invariably end up a drab monotone hue. Nor am I talking about building up layers of washes on your paper. If mixing color on your paper is important, then grays on your paper are equally important. The combinations are endless and they can give your painting the mood and interest you're looking for.

Rain Delay
If it weren't for the red awning and the reflection on the ground, this painting would be a study in grays; it shows why painting with grays is so important. Grays act as a supporting color/value to the brighter areas of color. They connect our shapes and help with perspective. Remember that cool grays recede the horizon and warm grays advance it.

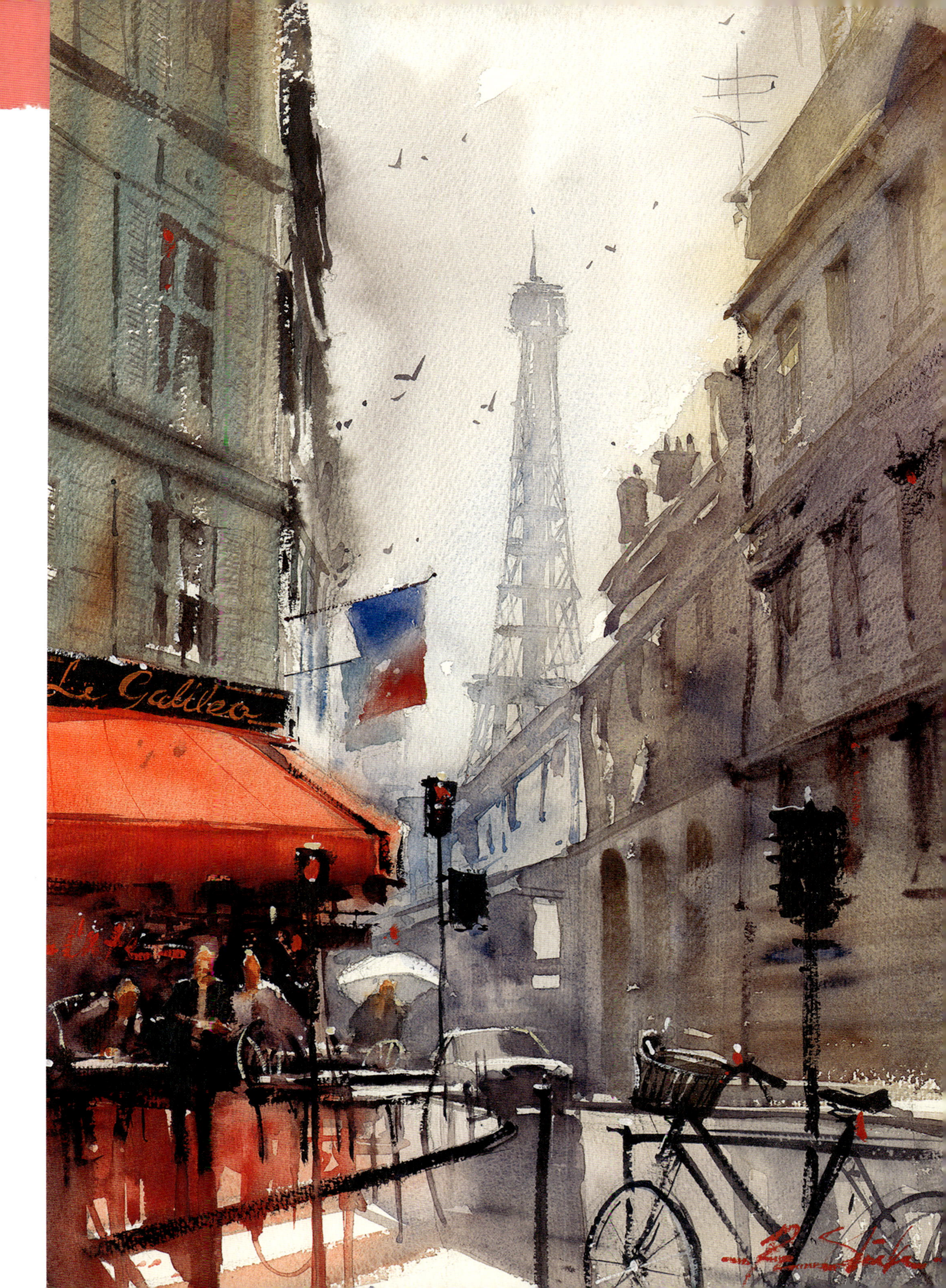
Le Galileo

Here is a simple example of the range of grays that can be accomplished by mixing two colors. On the warm side, I used burnt sienna and on the cool side, ultramarine blue. The warm, cool violet/gray that these two colors create where they merge (known as the middle third), bring interest to what could otherwise be a dull and rather boring area of the painting because it supports the colors rather than competes against them.

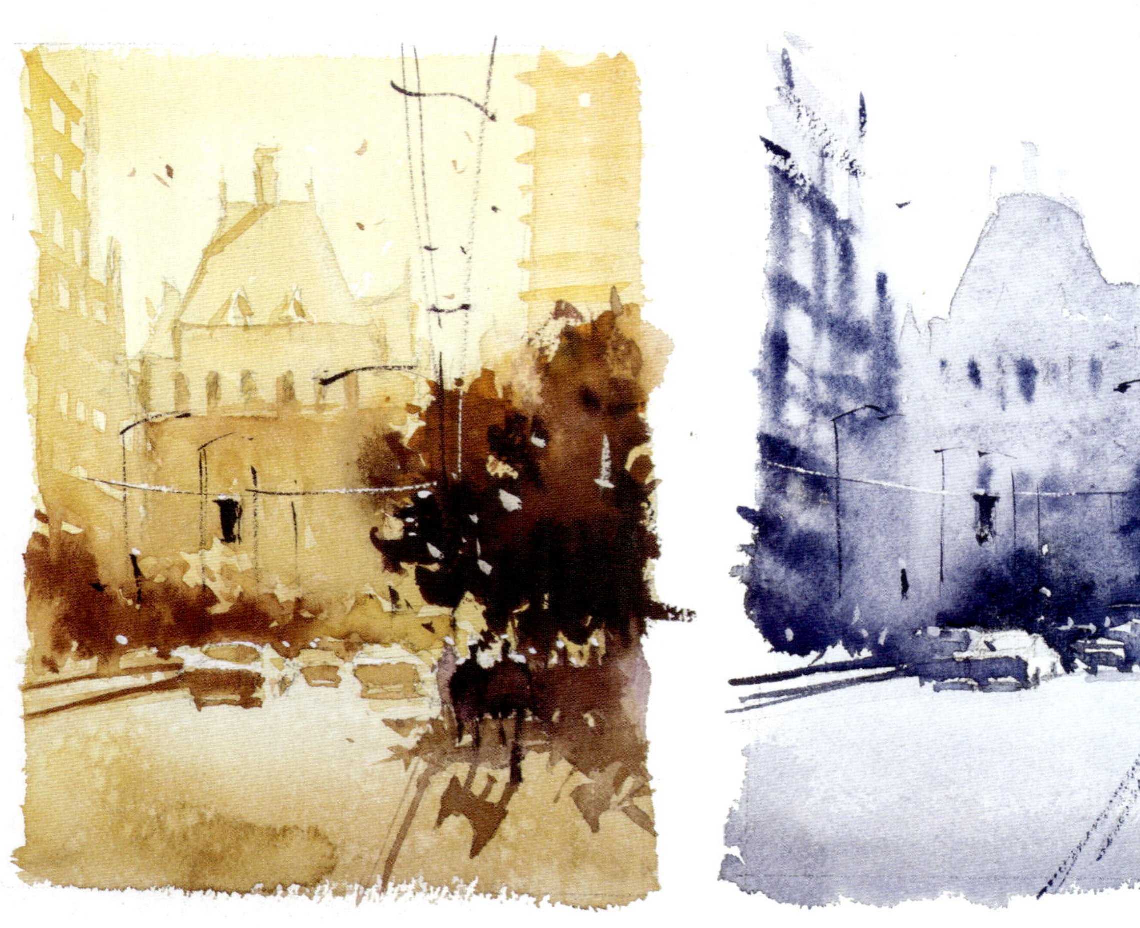

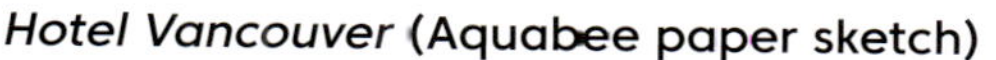

Hotel Vancouver (Aquabee paper sketch)

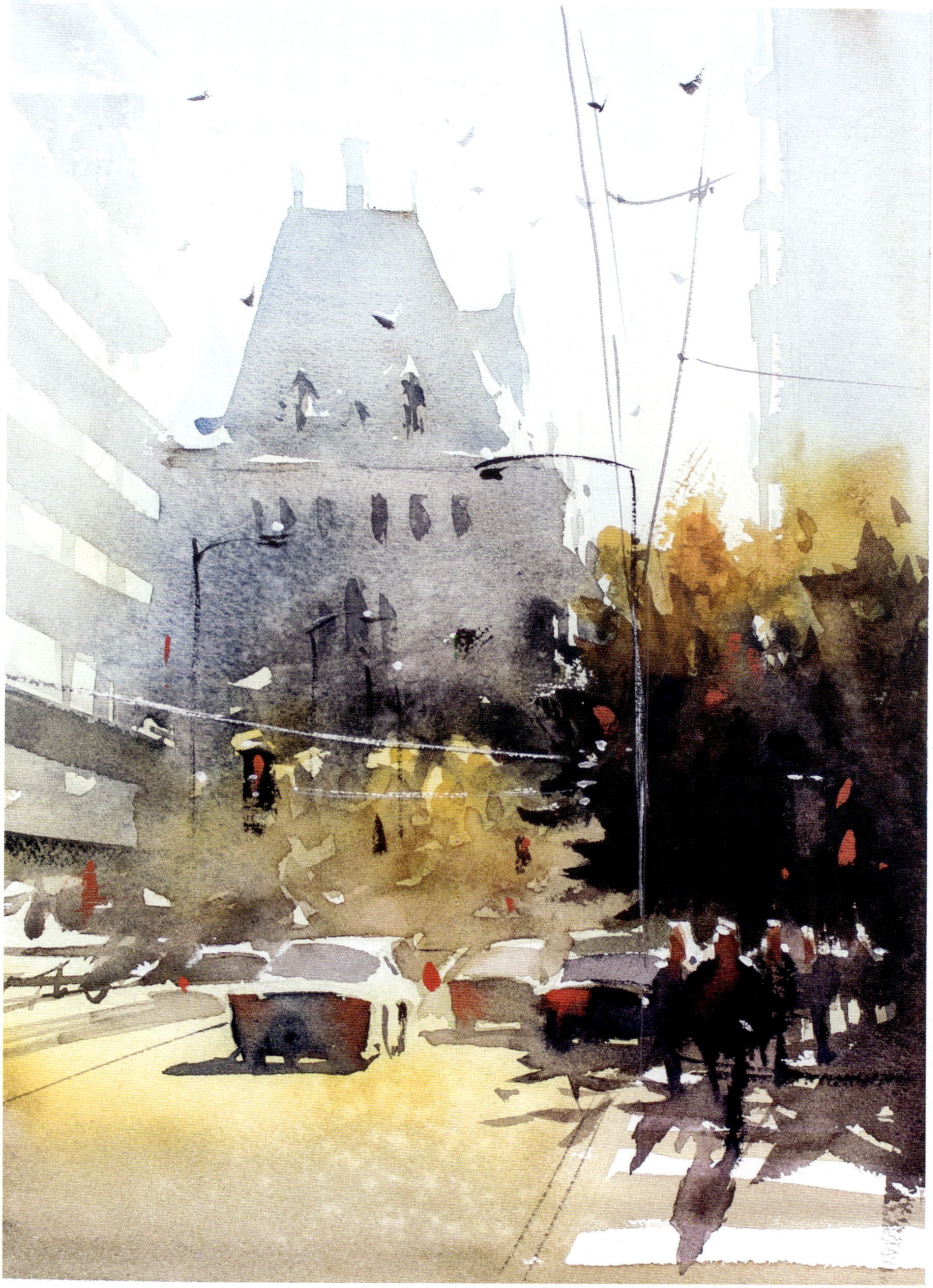

Color Swatches

These are some of the common color combinations I use. They show how you can mix complementary colors without graying them—although there are some failures. By mixing on the paper, the two colors hold their integrity and create a tertiary color. But if the two colors were mixed on the palette, the result would be gray.

Here is a mix of cadmium yellow light, which is a sedimentary opaque color, and dioxazine purple, a staining-transparent color. The smaller color swatches are the two colors mixed on the palette. From left to right, I started with a greater concentration of the yellow, gradually mixing in more and more of the purple. Diluted into a light wash here, dioxazine purple is one of the darkest colors in my palette and can quickly turn this wash black or into a #1 value. (See scale image on page 68.)

The large swatch (above) is an example of the two colors mixed on the paper at the same consistency and value. If the colors are allowed to mix on the paper, the result is a tertiary color that can be used to create mood, light, and interest.

Here is one of my favorite combinations: a mix of burnt sienna, a sedimentary-semitransparent earth color, and turquoise, a staining transparent color. There seems to be endless variety when these two colors are mixed together on the paper. They provide one of my favorite combinations for old buildings, wet-street scenes, and figures.

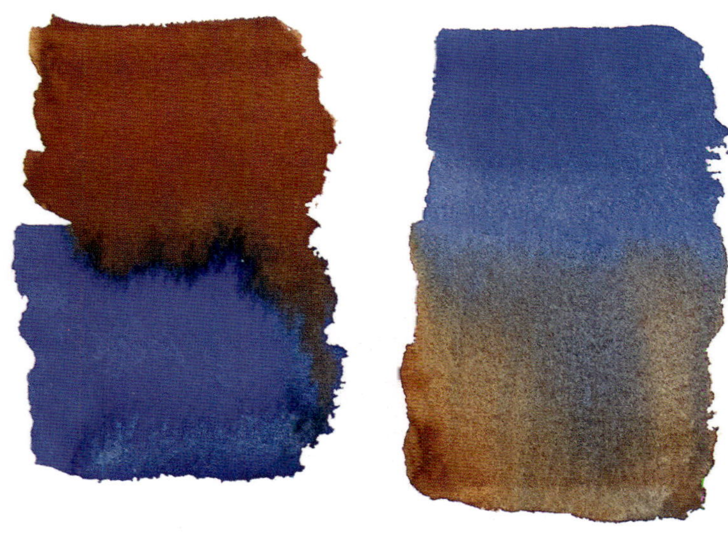

This shows burnt sienna and ultramarine blue, sedimentary transparents, mixed together on the paper. The left side shows an example of the two colors mixed at incorrect consistencies, which can give unpleasant blooms and watermarks. On the right, the same two colors are mixed with a more consistent ratio, resulting in a more pleasing wash with a lovely gray-violet aspect. Note that some watercolor brands will turn green instead of gray.

For this swatch, I used two sedimentary opaque colors: cadmium red light and cobalt teal. These can be difficult to mix together because of the strength and weight of their pigments. The result where they merge is a dark, muddy gray.

Nice Marina Step-by-Step

Once in a while you come across a subject that you just can't wait to paint. I saw the finished painting of the harbor in Nice, France, in my mind's eye the moment I arrived. It can be tempting to just jump in and start without doing any planning, but my advice is to take a few minutes to do a thumbnail sketch so that what you are seeing in your head ends up on the paper.

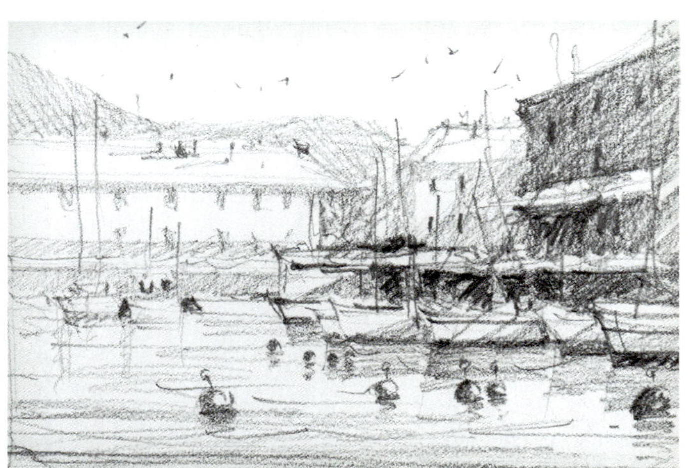

The first stage of this painting started with two main washes: the large gray wash that takes up two-thirds of the painting and the turquoise wash in the bottom right-hand corner.

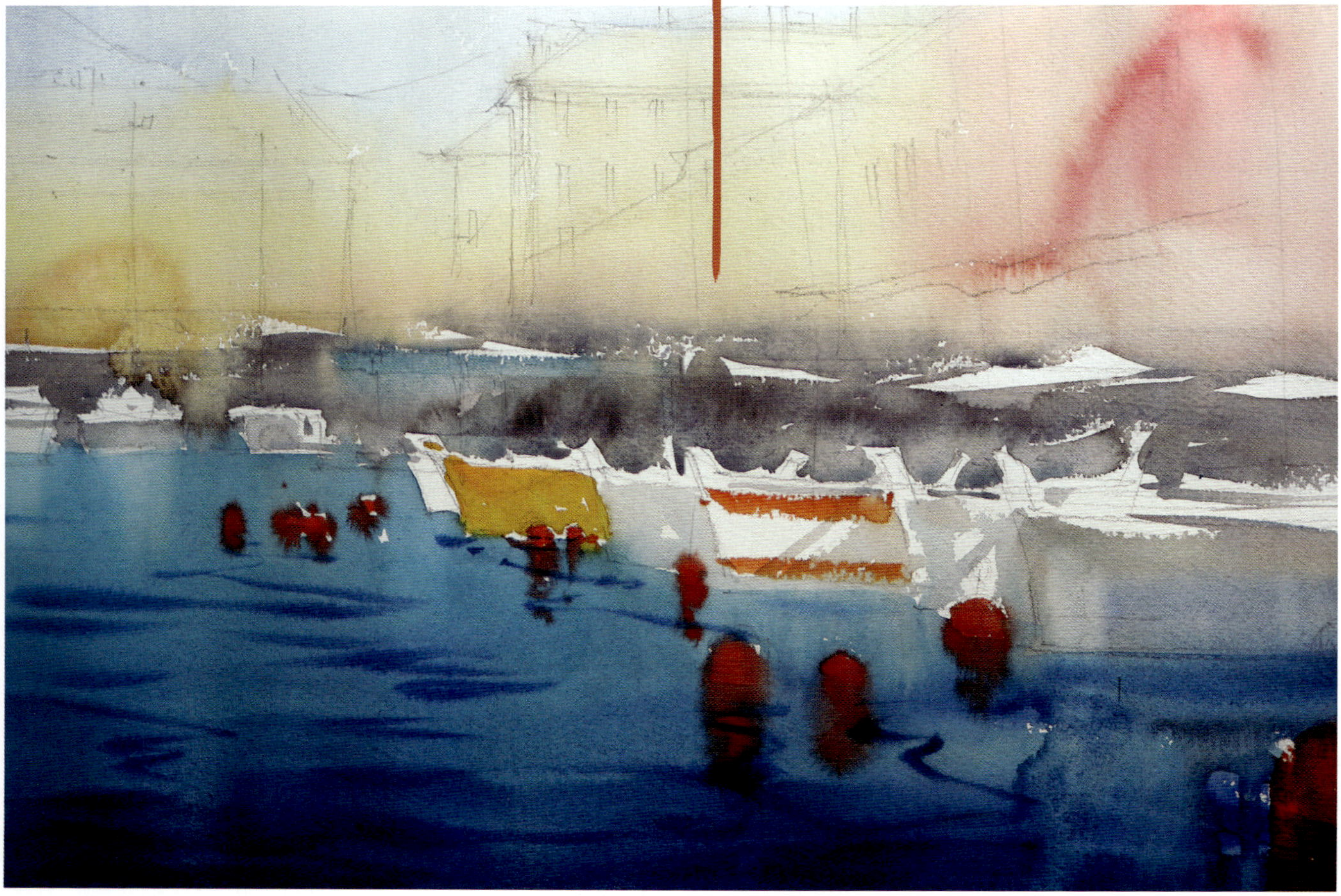

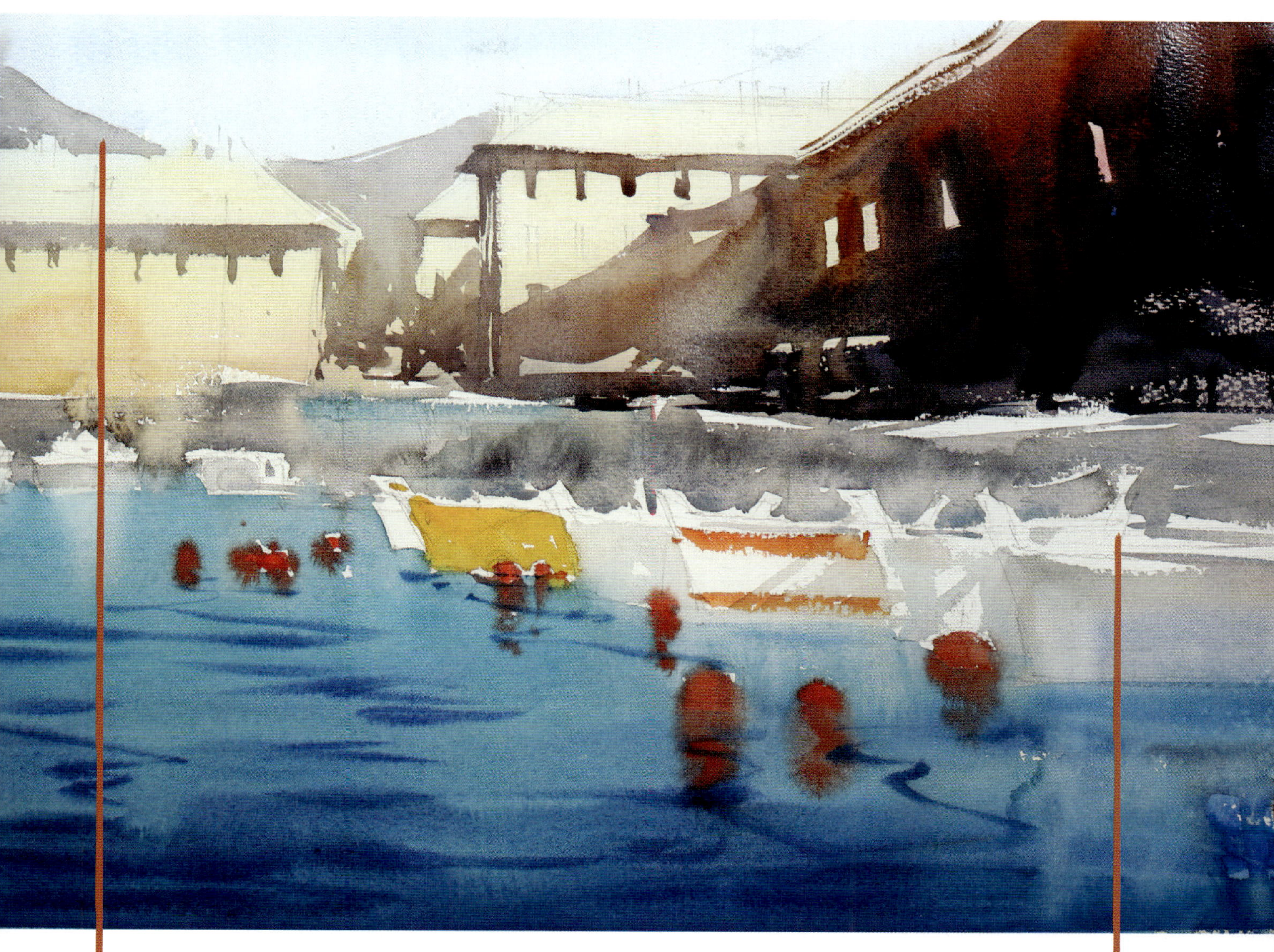

After everything was dry, I started at the distant hills and worked my way into the buildings.

Before this wash was dry, I applied a strong dark that connected the background and foreground shadows.

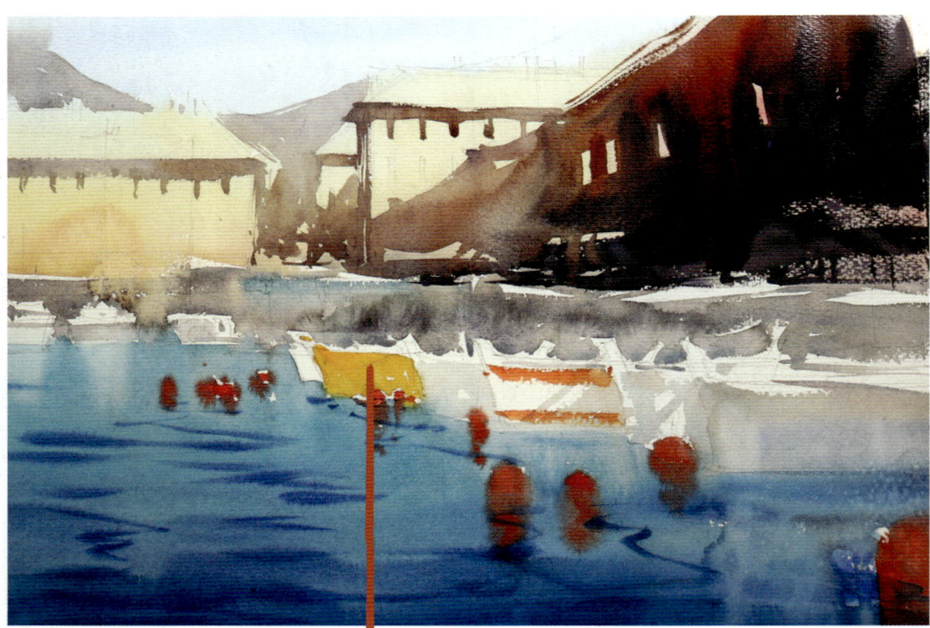

Next I started adding some finesse (windows, boat details, and connecting shapes) to help merge the mid and foreground.

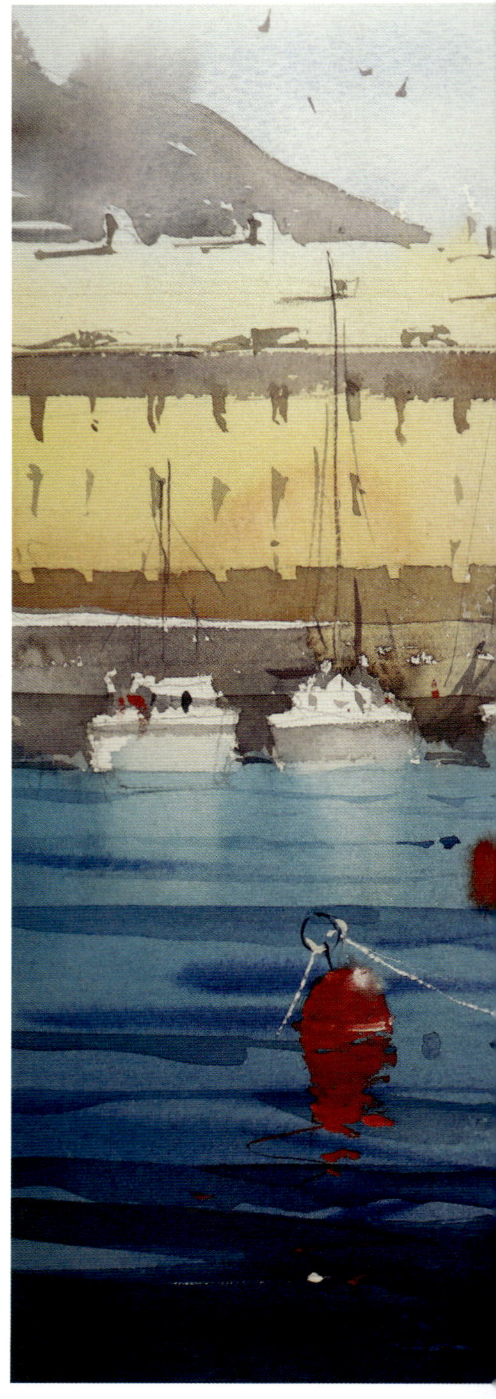

Page 88, *Big Island Boat Rentals*

Finally, the finishing touches. I reinforced the boat and buoys, added boat masts, rigging, and other details, as well as movement in the water and wave shapes.

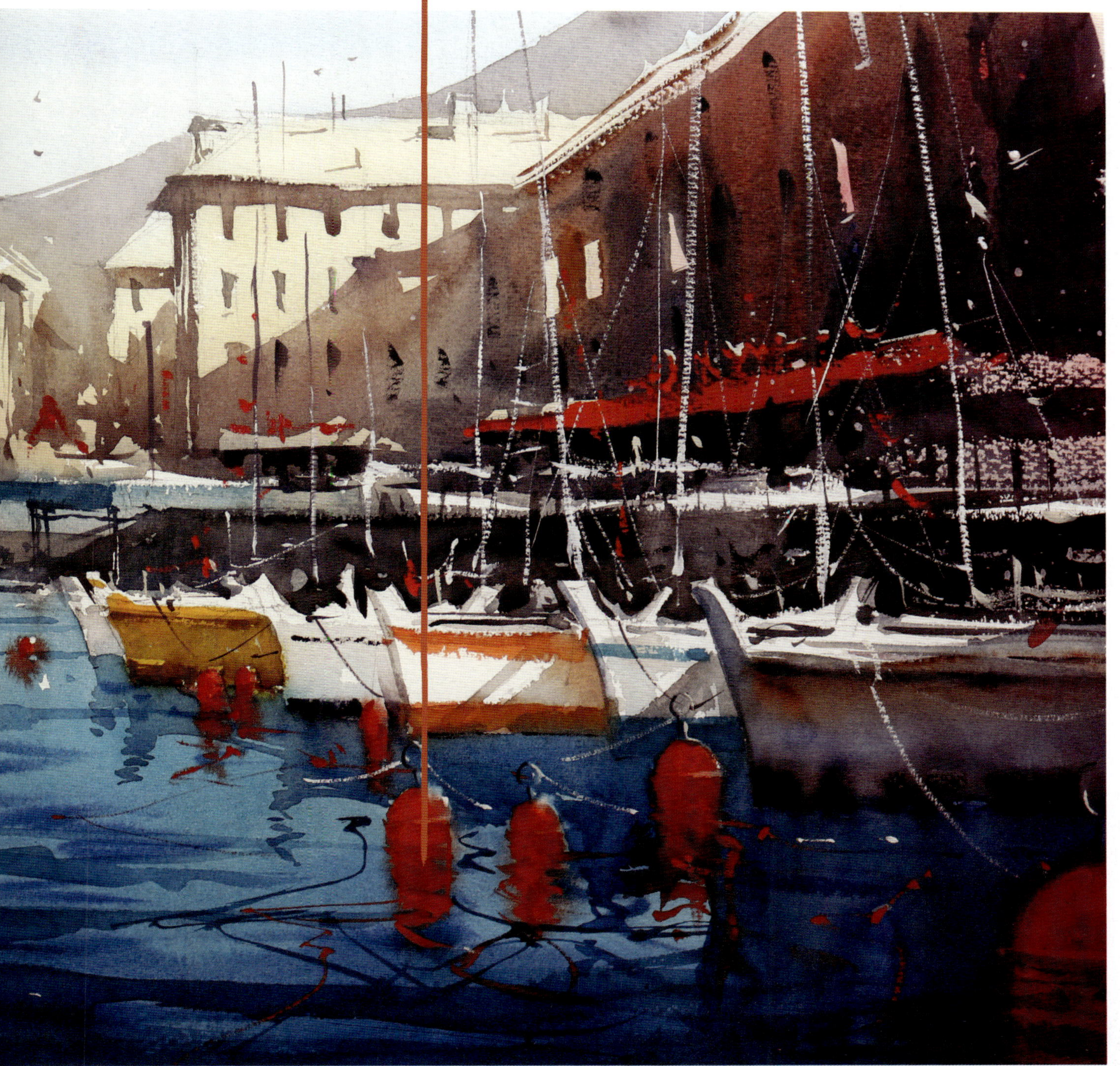

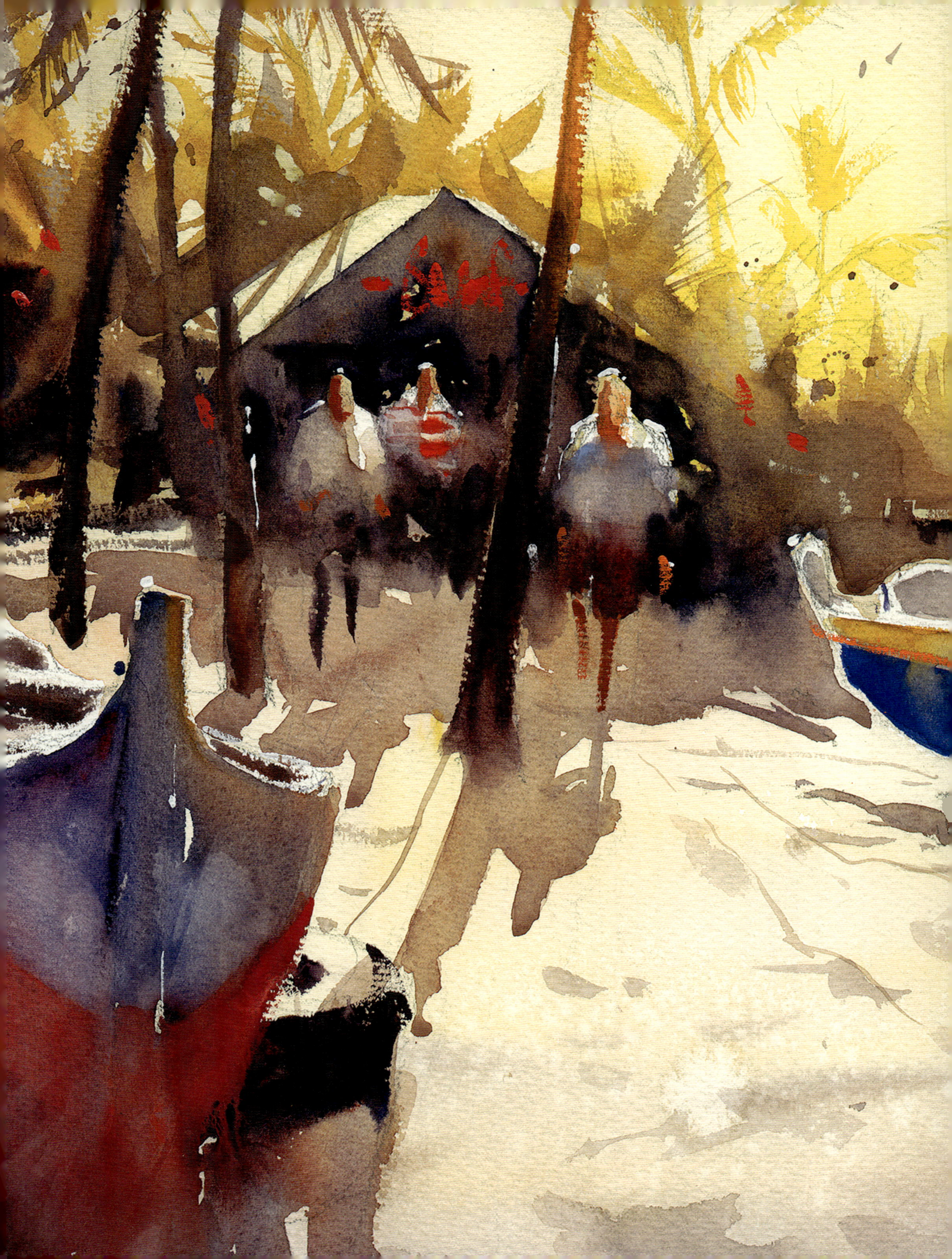

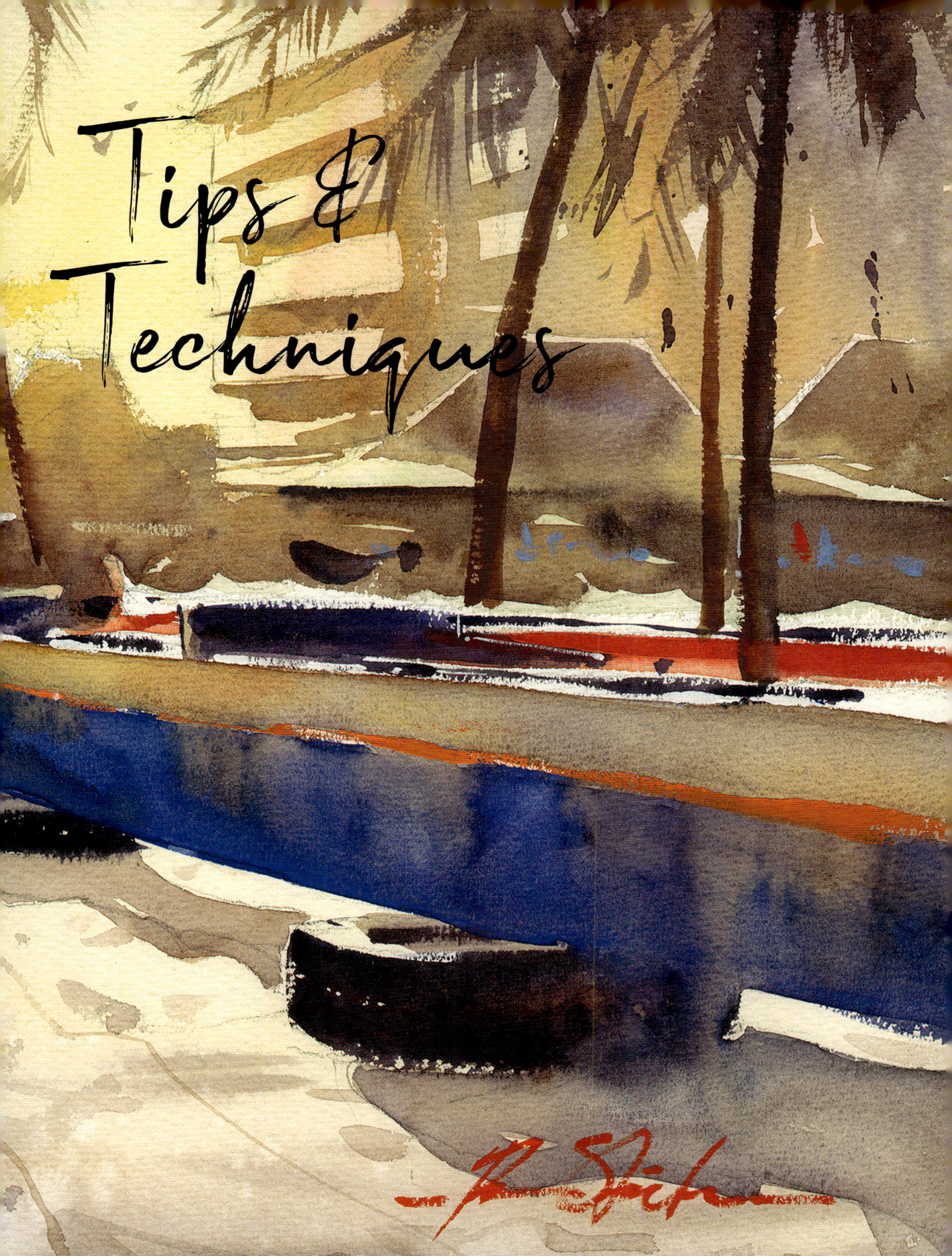
Tips &
Techniques

Developing Techniques

In this chapter, I thought it would be instructive to look at a few techniques I have developed over the years that might help you achieve more successful paintings. Techniques, however, can have "traps" of their own. If not continually developed, your work can become stagnant and uninspired. The good news is that no two people can make the same brushstrokes. Just like our tastes in music or food, we are all individuals, and if given time, that individuality will come to the surface. My focus in this section is to show you new techniques to build and improve; consider this a challenge for you to develop these techniques into your own style.

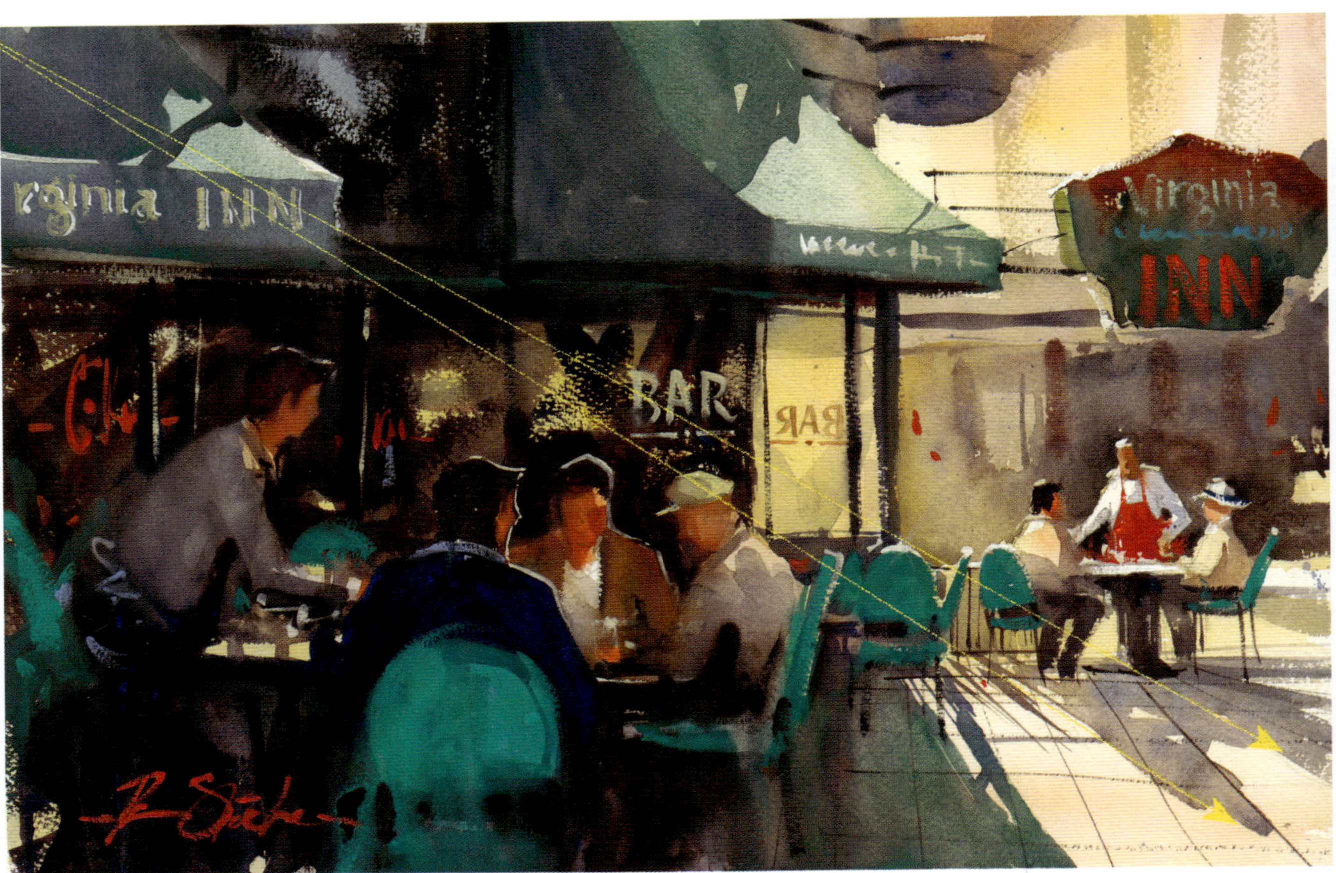

My goal was to connect this painting using one large shadow starting at the top left and ending at the bottom right. I applied one continuous wash to avoid watermarks and blossoms (blotches).

Shadows

Shadows are constantly on the move. Light sources frequently change positions—the sun as an example—and affect our shadows in many ways. As light sources change position and intensity, dramatic things can happen to shadows. A shadow that starts out cool and dark in value can become quite warm and full of color in a short period of time.

Caution: Two common mistakes I see when people paint shadows are the shadows are not connected, and they are painted as mirror images of the objects casting them. Very rarely do we see this occur in real life, and it only confuses the viewer. Remember, the surface on which the cast shadow appears can affect the shadow's appearance as much as the object casting the shadow.

Tip Don't forget, the ground affects how the shadow appears just as much as the object casting it—in this case the chair.

Tip Here I've isolated some figures and their shadows to show how they should be connected.

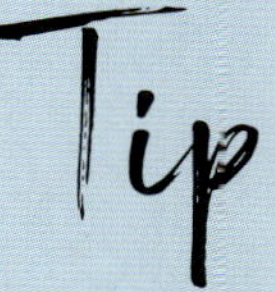

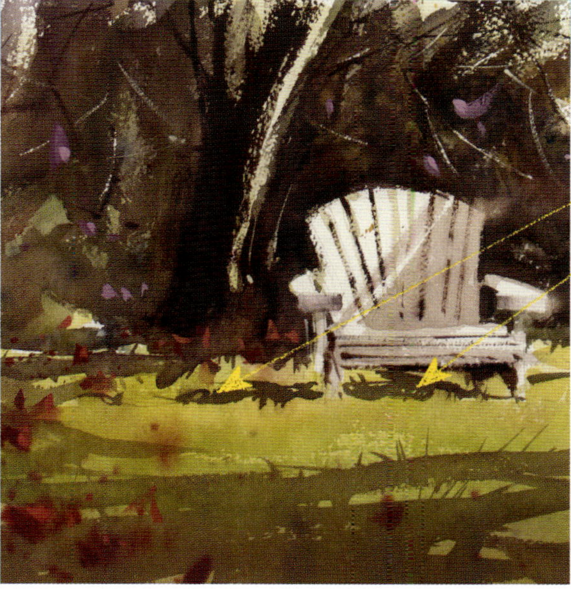

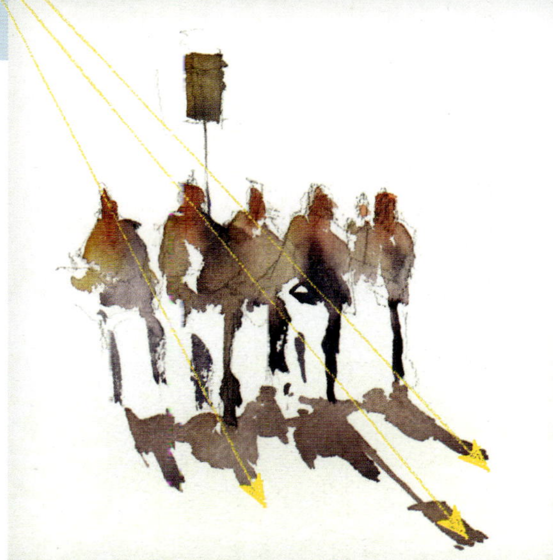

Reflections

Unlike shadows, reflections only move when the surface that is reflecting the image moves. In other words, if the surface moves so does the reflection. If the surface is still, as with a wet street, then the reflection stays put. However, if the surface is a moving body of water, for instance, the results are quite different.

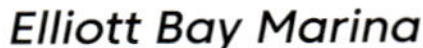

Elliott Bay Marina

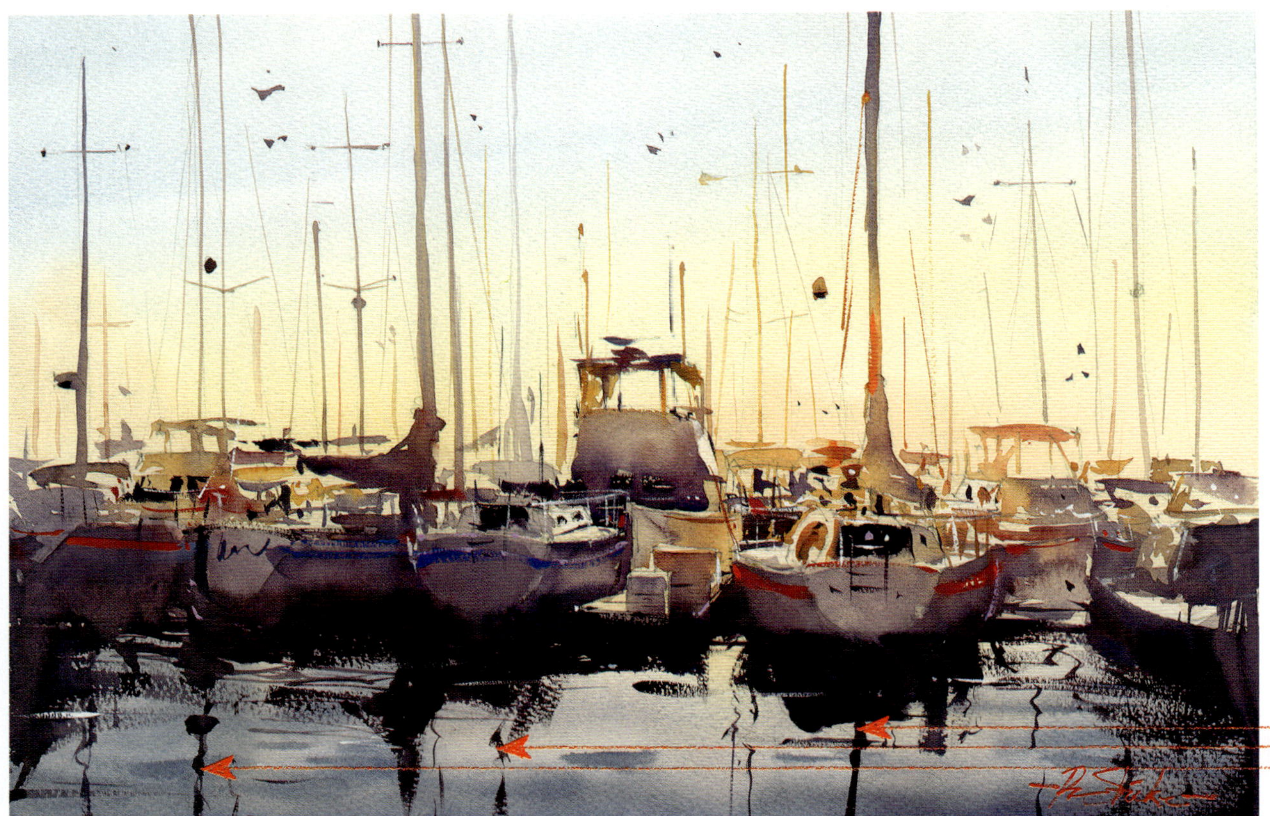

When the reflections of multiple objects meet, such as boats resting in a harbor, the result is an abstraction of these objects. For painters, this can create great opportunities and allow us to paint with more freedom. The results are brushstrokes that have been applied with energy and abandon, giving the vibrancy of life to the composition.

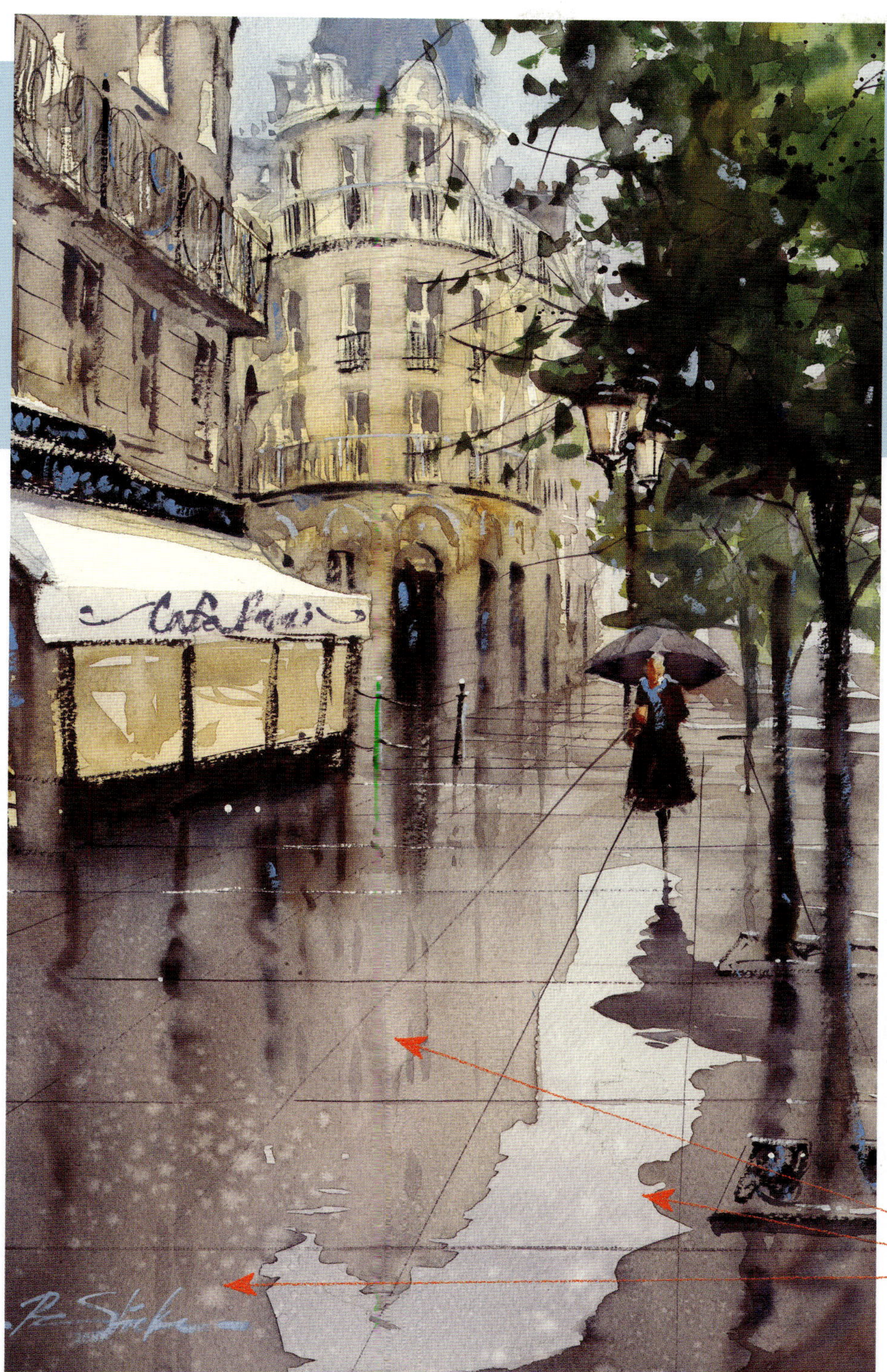

Solo in Paris

Tip

If objects overlap, connect their reflections. Try not to overthink reflections. The simpler the better.

Caution: Be careful about connecting your reflections, and don't confuse them with shadows. Reflections only fall in one direction, downward.

Perspective

Sitting instead of standing while you paint can drastically change your perspective. Sitting can skew the perspective of vertical lines, and it also hinders your movement, which usually results in a tighter finished product.

Caution: Be aware of the consequences of sitting while you draw or paint.

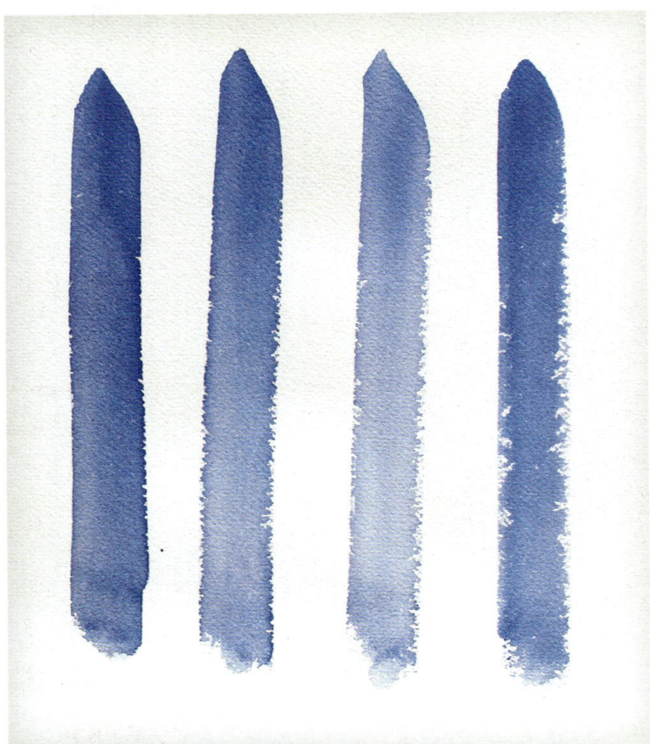

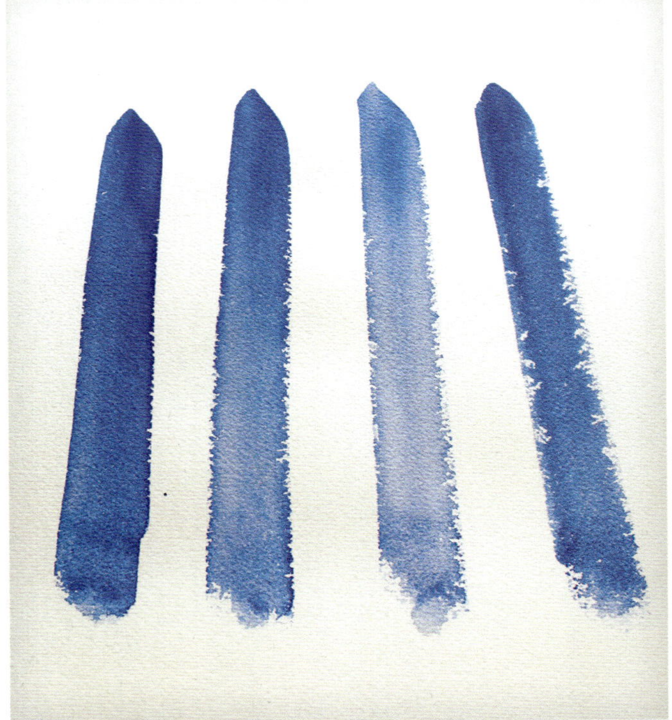

Tip

If you can't stand for a full painting, then I suggest standing while you draw. This way your vertical lines and perspectives start out on a strong foundation. Once you have the skeleton drawn out, you can sit to complete the painting. I personally prefer standing while painting. This gives me the ability to step away from the painting and observe it from a proper distance, while also giving me the ability to keep my drawing loose.

Breaking Tension

One of the best ways of creating or breaking tension in your work is the way you approach horizontal and vertical lines.

Tip

In the photo at below left, notice how the edge of the market sign creates a tangent next to the edge of the building. It lacks depth and will confuse the viewer if a shadow is cast onto the building. The photo at right shows a change in position, which makes a huge difference to the perspective. Before you start drawing on location, double-check these small details and make adjustments as necessary. These relatively minor points can make a big difference in your finished work.

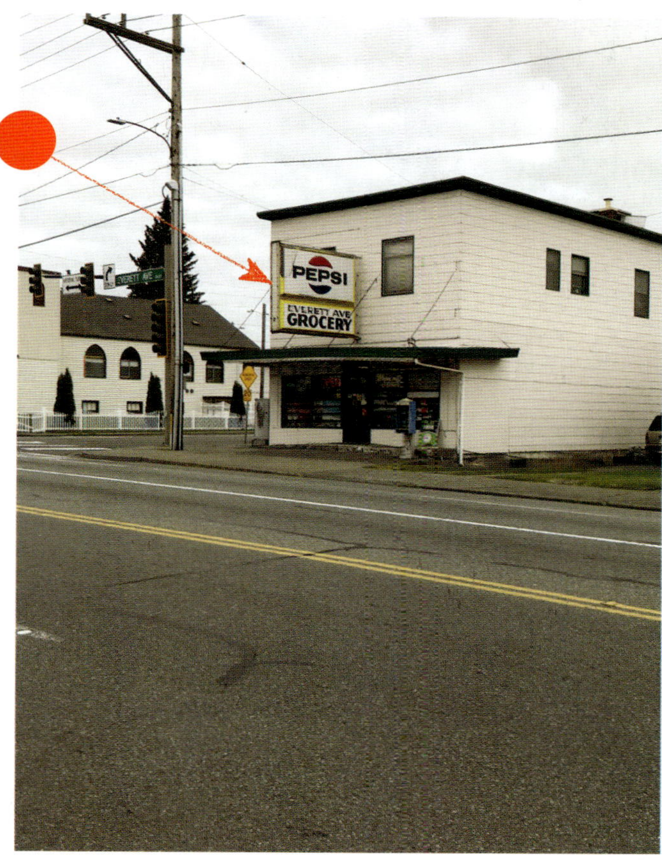

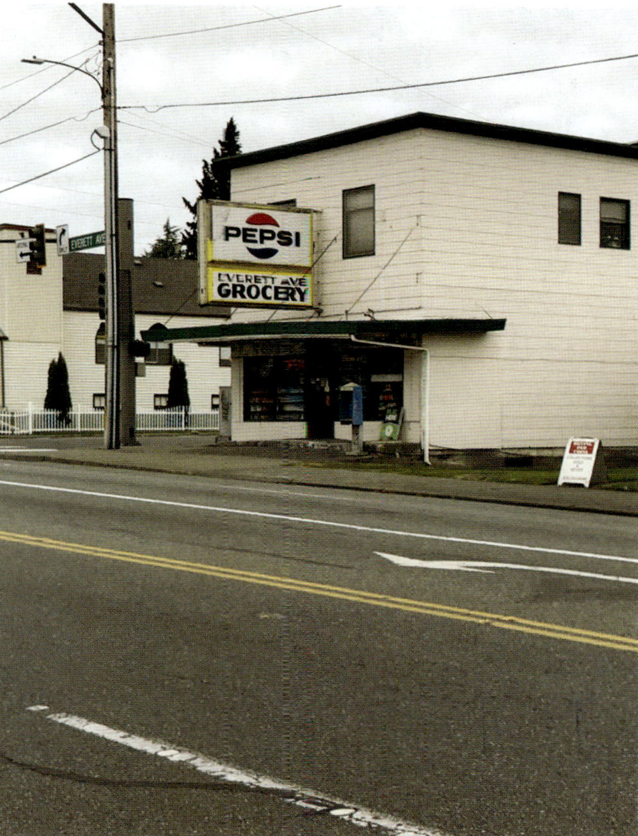

Caution: The trap here comes down to how you treat edges and lines in your paintings. Some of these issues can be solved in the drawing process, but once you start painting, your drawing can get lost underneath your washes. This means you have to make these decisions as you paint.

Detail

When it comes to detail, "If you can't hit it with a baseball, then don't paint it." I use this analogy because it is an easy way to remember that by painting details that are too far away or insignificant, you only slow your brush down and distract the viewer from what you are trying to say in your painting as a whole.

Narbonne Street (Aquabee paper, sketch)

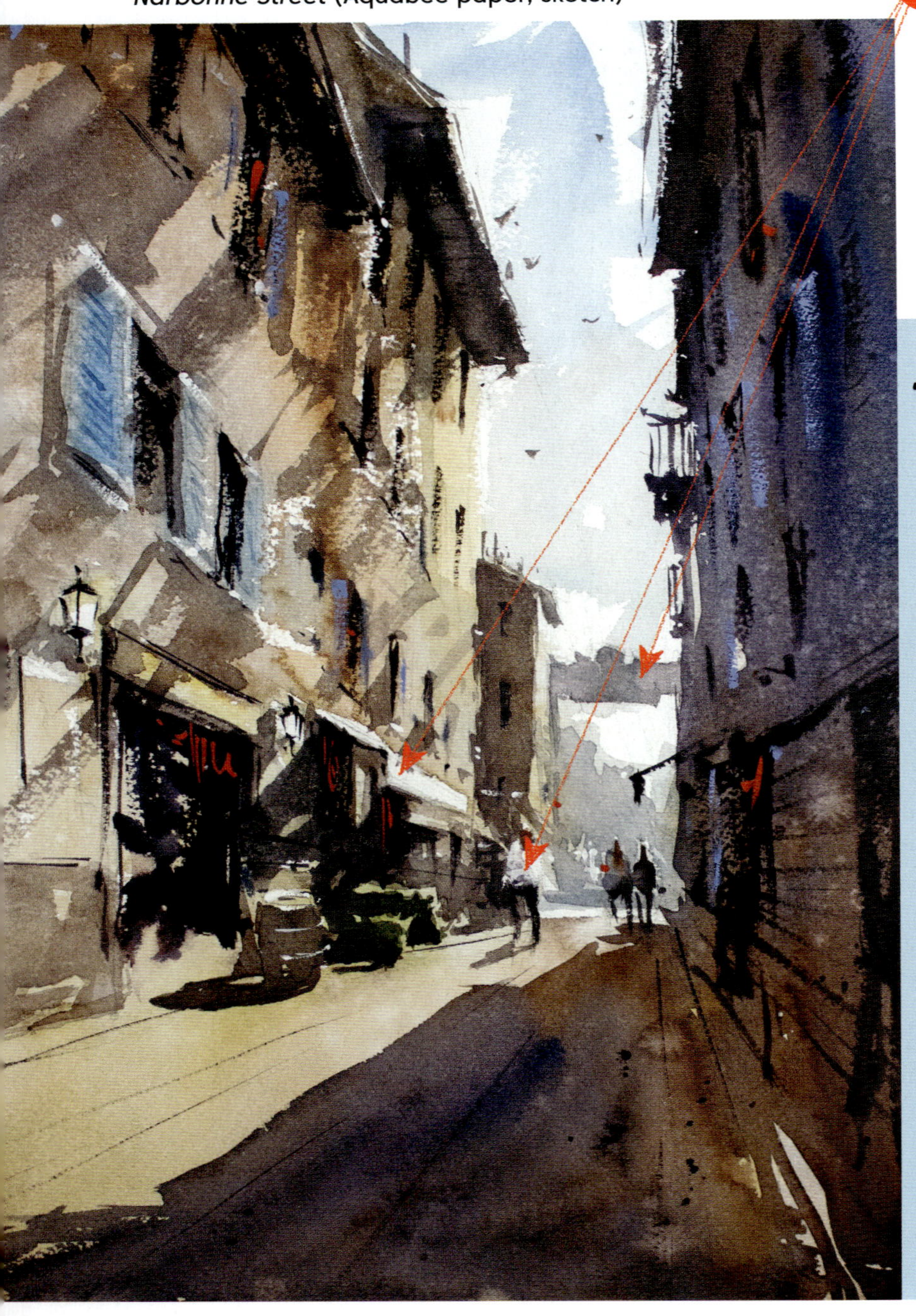

Tip

One of the key ways to avoid bad or negative tension is to avoid painting details. Ask yourself if the details will necessarily help your painting. It is possible to convince the viewer that they are looking at an entire city block by applying just a few well-thought-out shapes.

The quiet areas—or "abstract areas," as I refer to them—are often the very elements that support the painting. The focus shouldn't be on painting every vehicle in the parking lot or every shoe on every figure's foot, but on the important elements that convey a message to the viewer. These areas can also allow for the most exciting color transitions by providing accidental rewards and opportunities for your medium to take on a life of its own.

If you can't hit it with a baseball, then don't paint it.

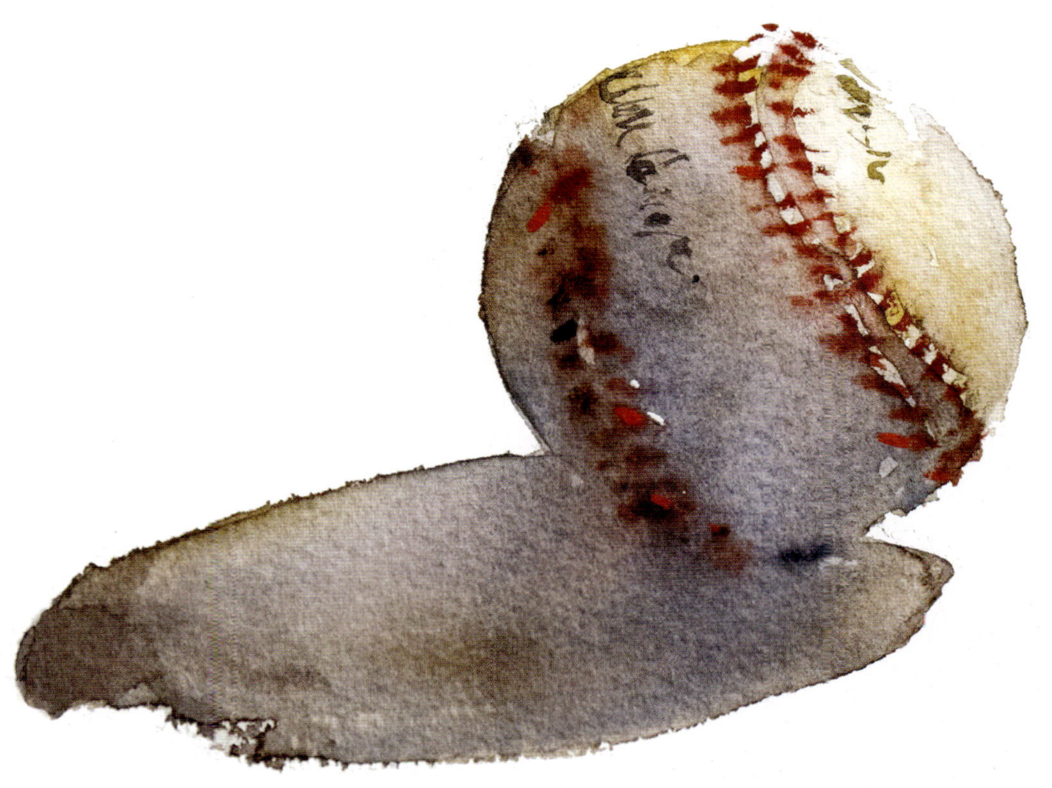

My Final Tip

Finally, the best tip I can give any painter is the same advice I received myself many years ago. **Paint often, and paint a lot.** Push yourself to try new techniques, and then develop them into techniques you can call your own. Your failures will always outnumber your victories, but keep listening to that voice inside that keeps calling you back to your palette.

Page 98, *Virginia Inn*

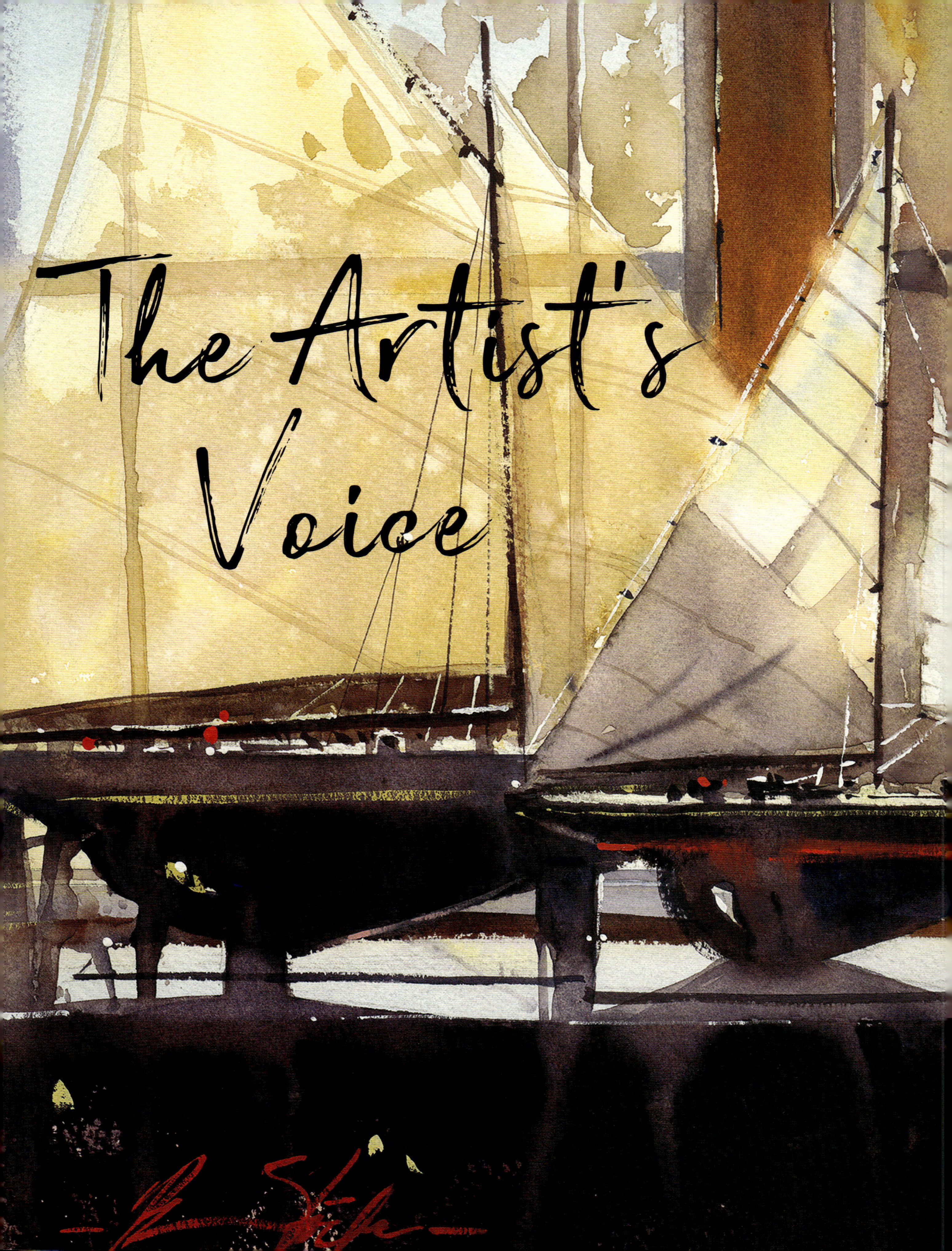
The Artist's
Voice

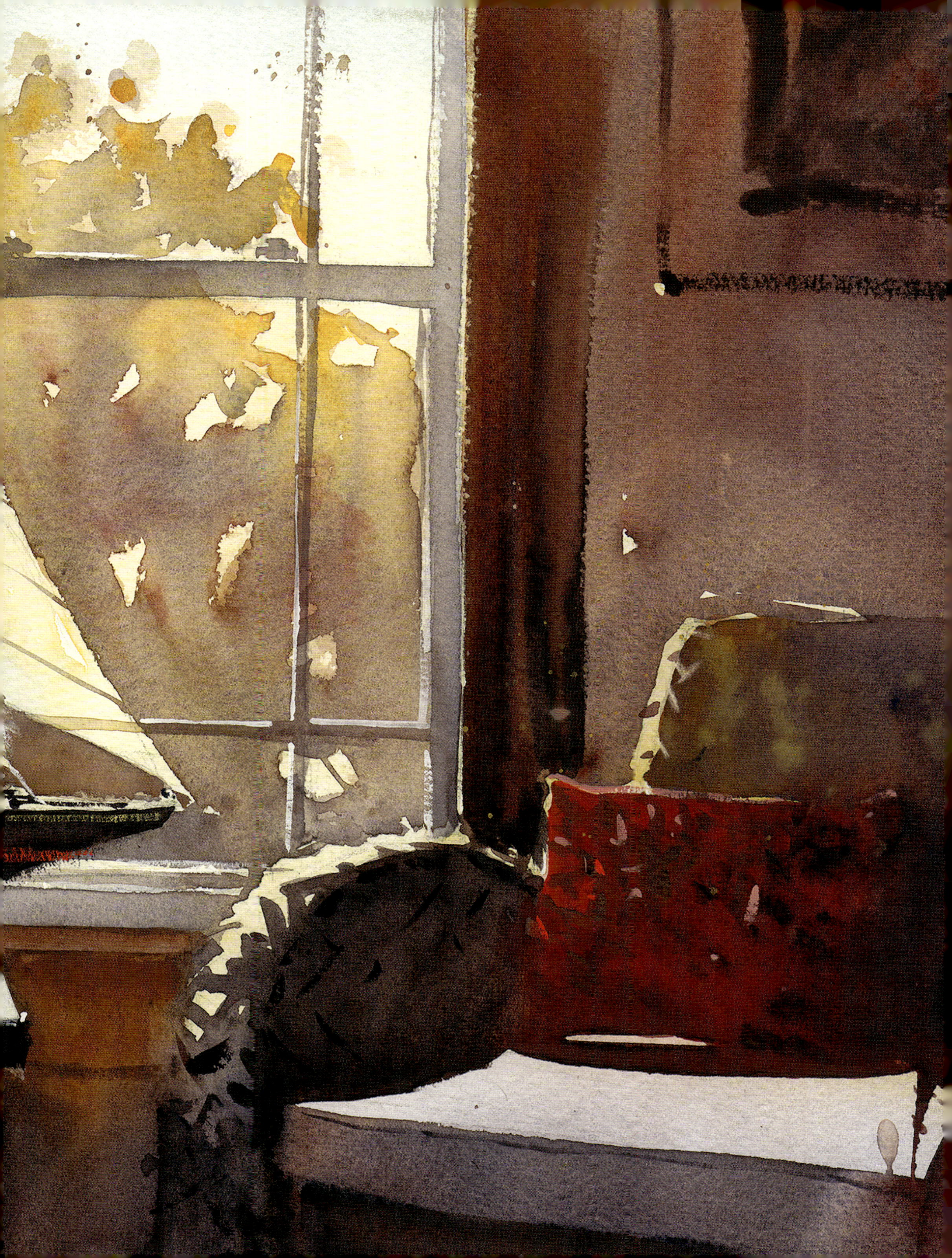

Define Your Voice

I believe what separates us most as artists is quite possibly the one thing we have most in common. That is, the time we spend painting. Those hours, days, and years we spend honing our artistic skills start to develop, over time, a unique calling card and style that separates us from one another.

Take someone who is just beginning to paint. They are timid about most everything: drawing, color choices, brushwork—even which equipment to purchase can be daunting. Believe me, I know this from experience. I used to question everything, and my work showed it. Years later, I still have those questions; I still fall into the traps I've warned you about in this book. The difference now is that I have compiled a memory of how and when to apply certain washes to the paper. Maybe my drawing is closer to what my idea of a shape should look like, and my equipment has been carefully selected from a room full of equipment I've purchased and no longer use. But more importantly, I know what I want to say in my work. I'd like you to start considering this in yours. It is as important as the techniques you will learn over time.

Painting *en plein air* can help you when it comes to finding this voice. Stick with it and make it part of your routine, and it will benefit all of your work in a positive way. By working *en plein air,* your brushstrokes become reactionary rather than calculated.

Look at the three paintings of the Public Market Center that follow. They are essentially from the same location but have completely different moods.

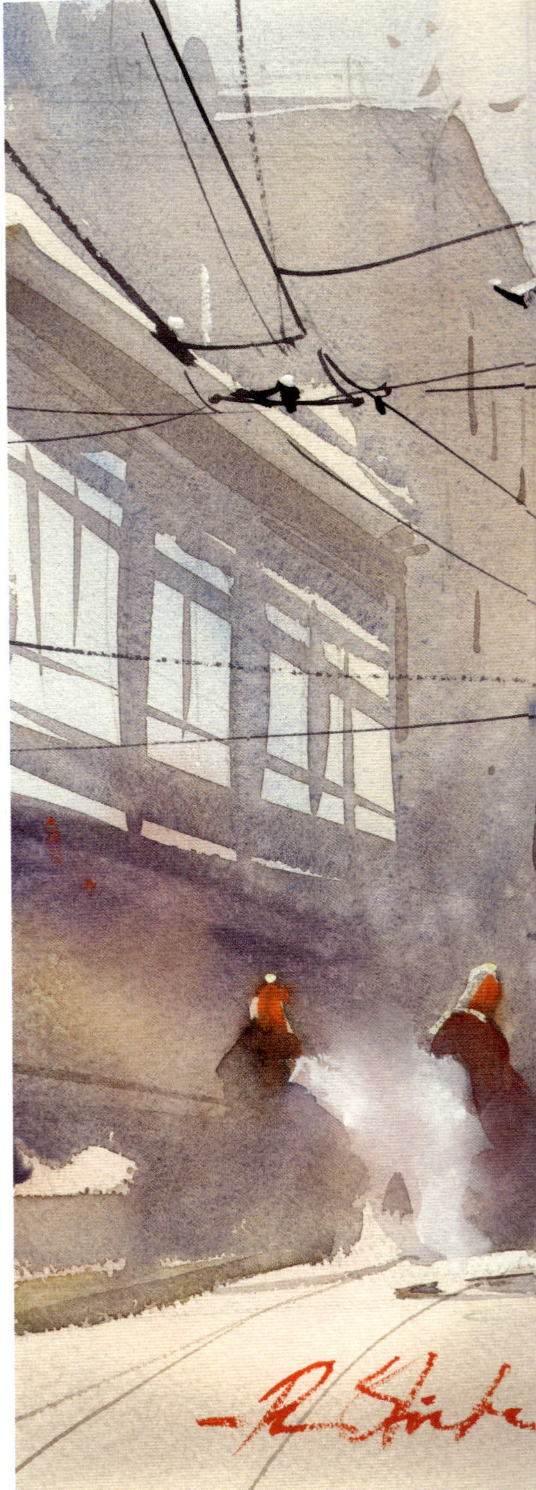

Morning Market

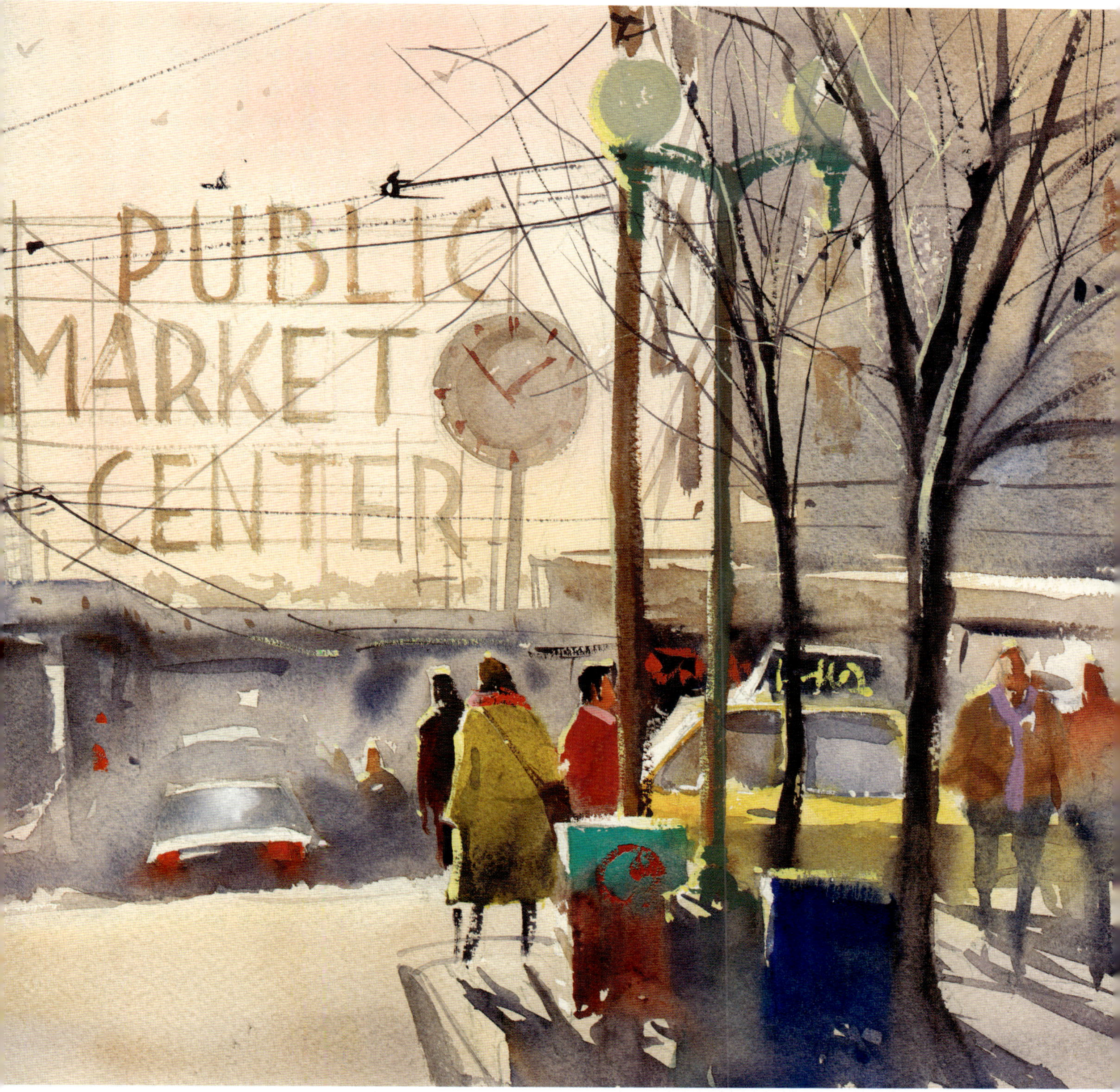

Here I have abandoned almost all of the detail that this busy location offers and have instead guided the viewer to one single figure (the woman in the yellow coat). I couldn't have done this without the large milky wash that connects almost two-thirds of the painting.

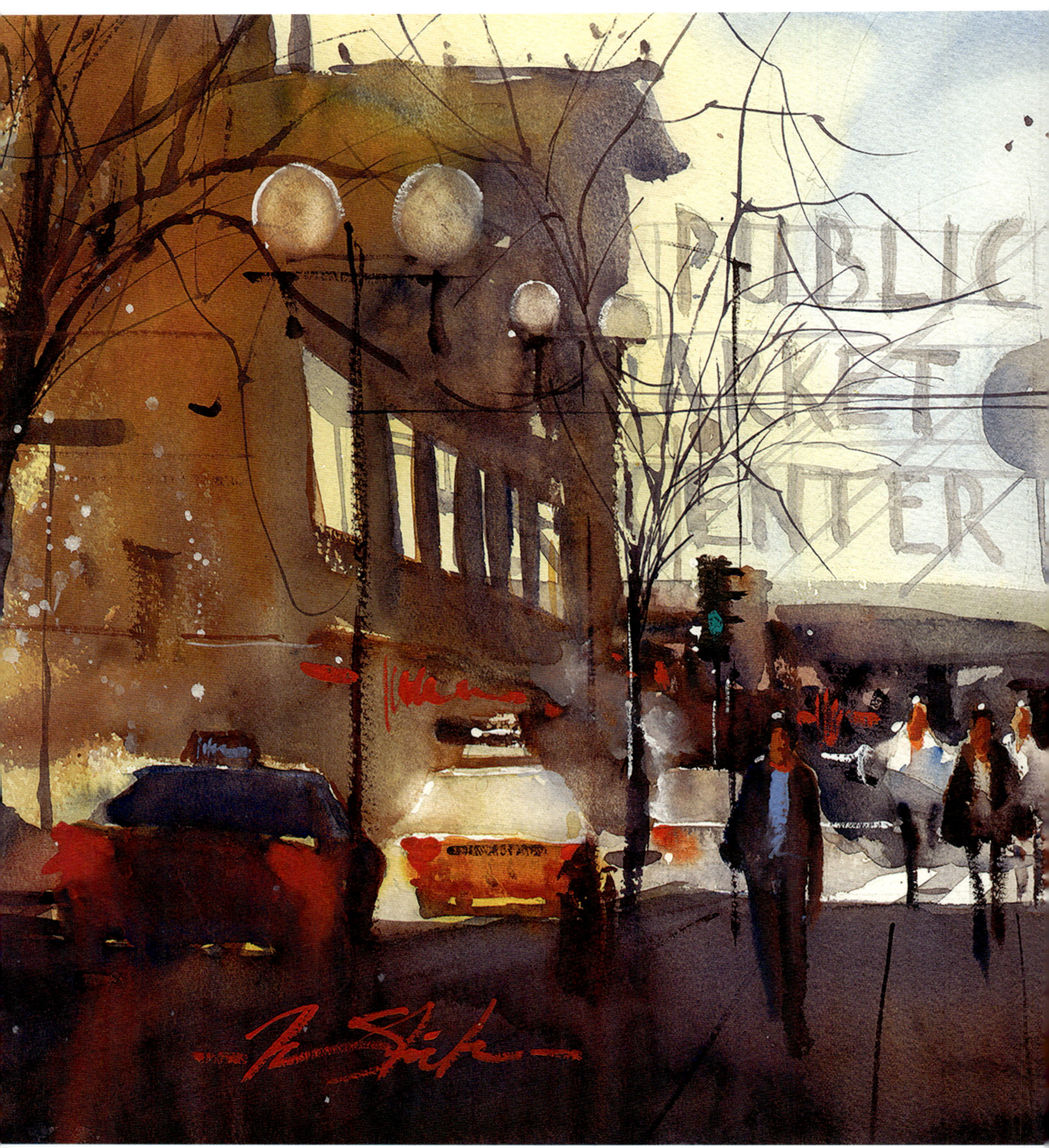
PUBLIC
ARKET
ENTER

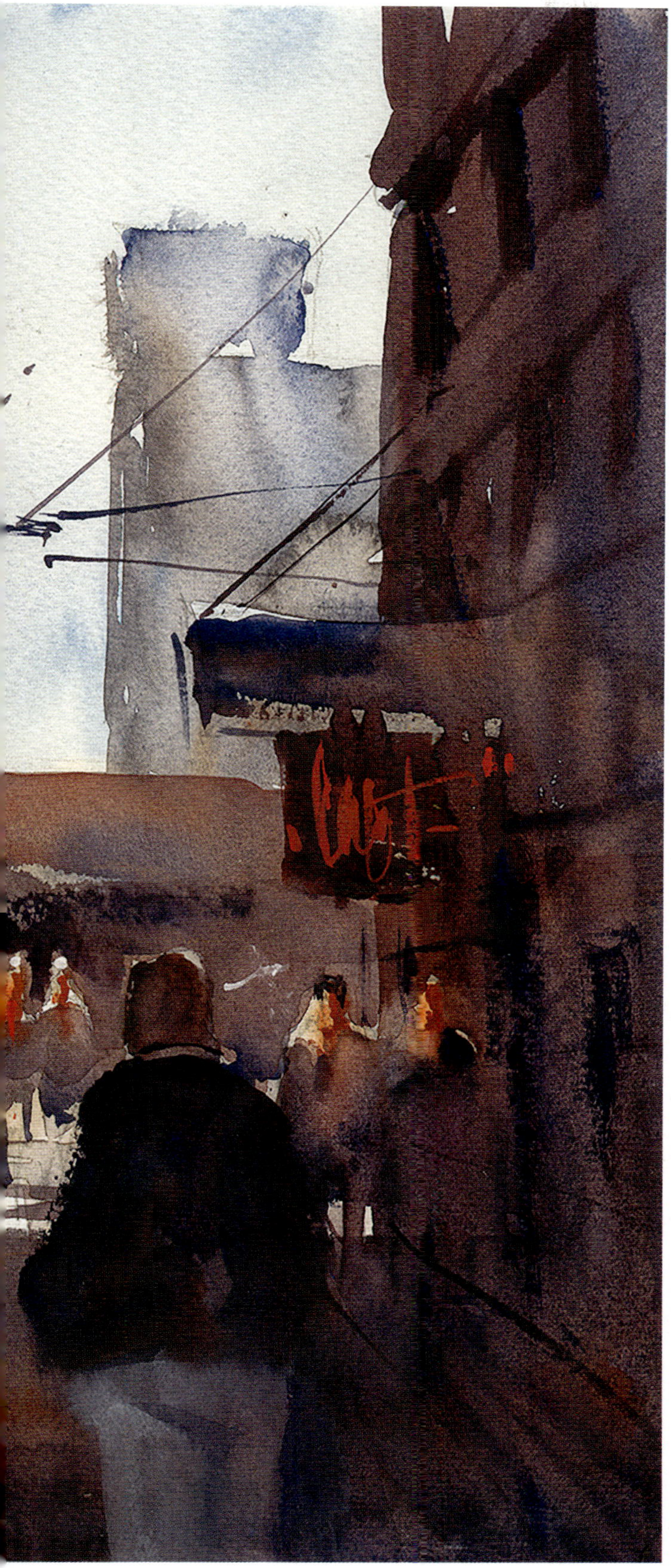

If you squint at this image, it really comes down to three basic shapes. The sky, the buildings, and the shape that tells the story: the ribbon of light that captures the taxi and the figures.

Mid-morning Market

This time the composition is all about the light. The figures, shadows, and architectural perspective are telling the viewer the same thing—look at the light!

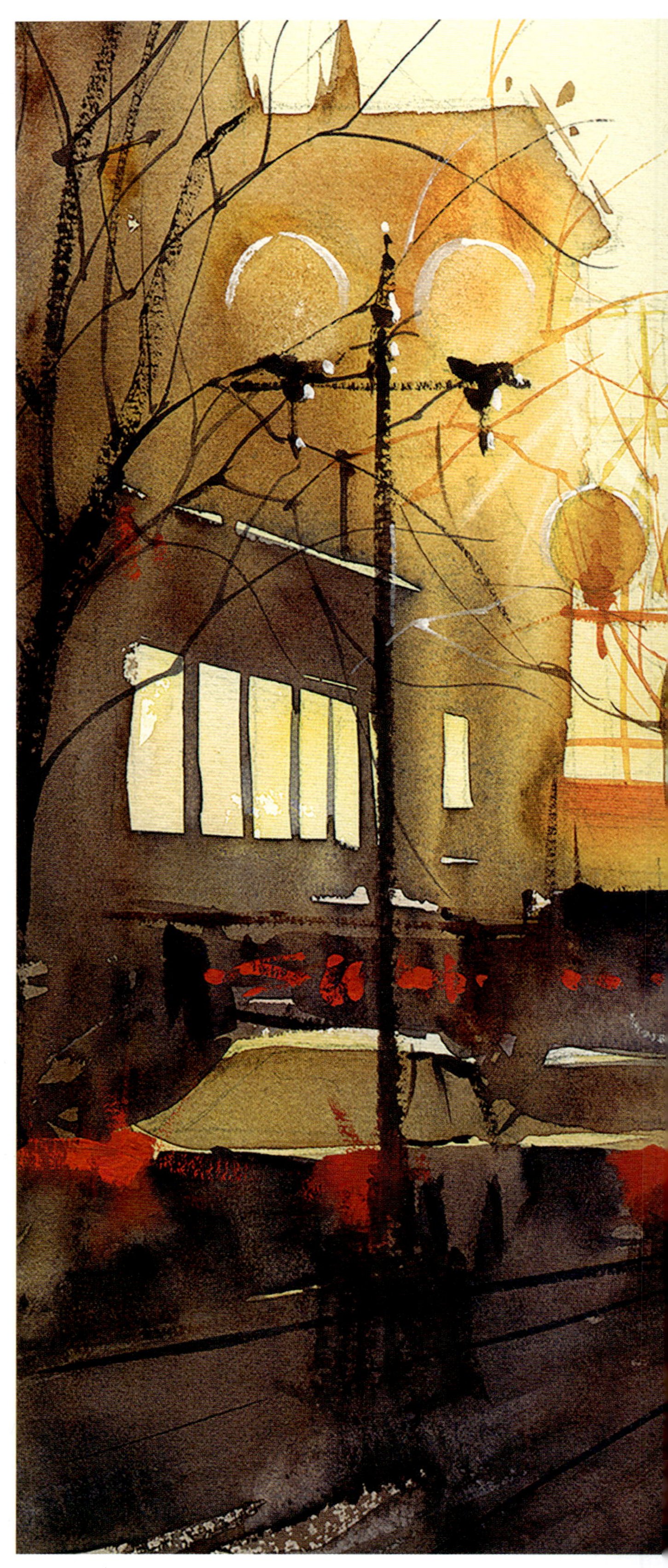

Afternoon Light Market

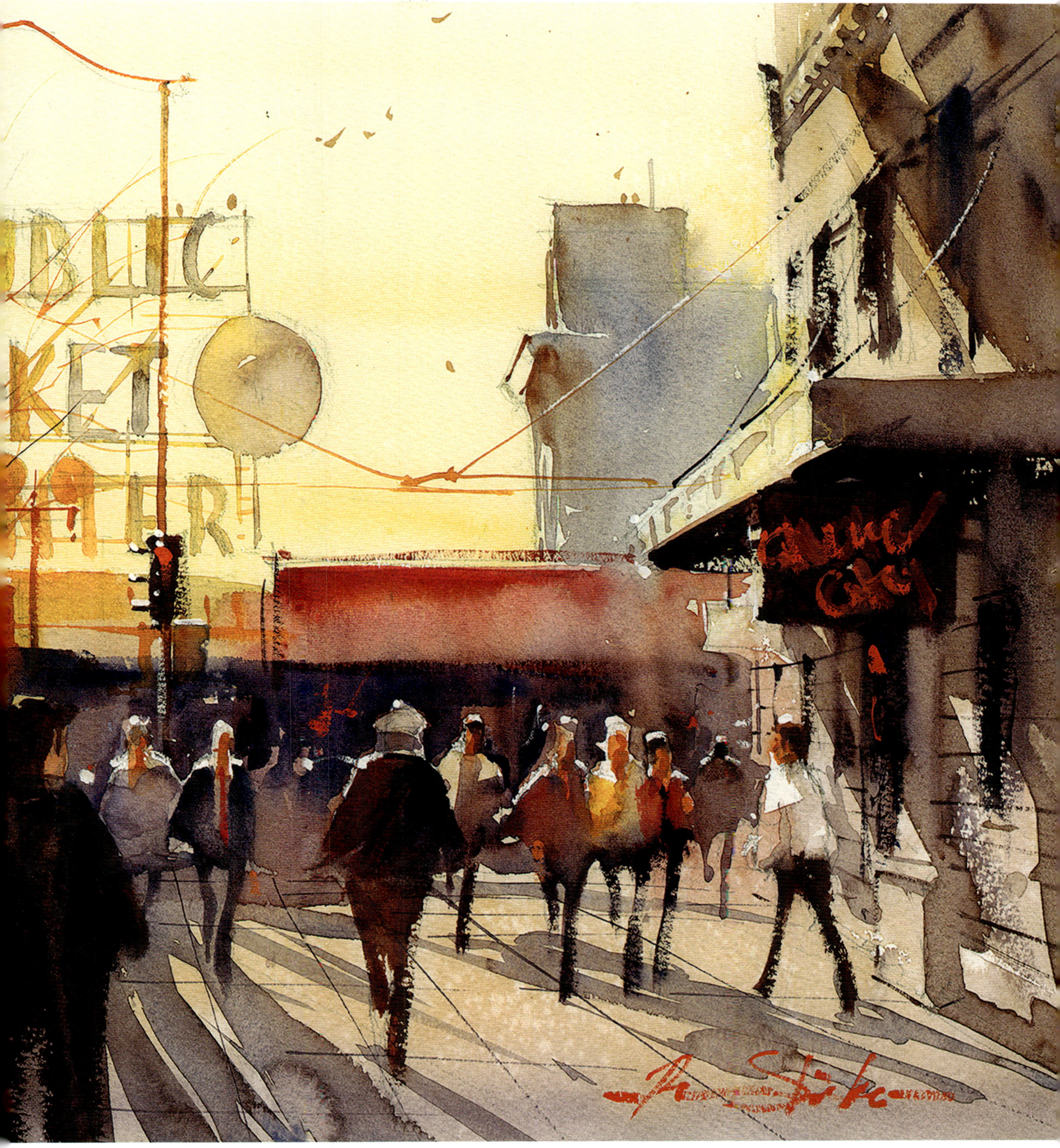

Intersection in Prague Step-by-Step

This step-by-step illustration shows how to bring your artistic voice out in your work. The actual painting was done on an overcast day with soft shadows and muted colors. I felt that a more exciting palette was needed for this intersection in Prague. Changing your color palette and stylizing your shapes are just a couple of ways you can begin to find your artistic voice.

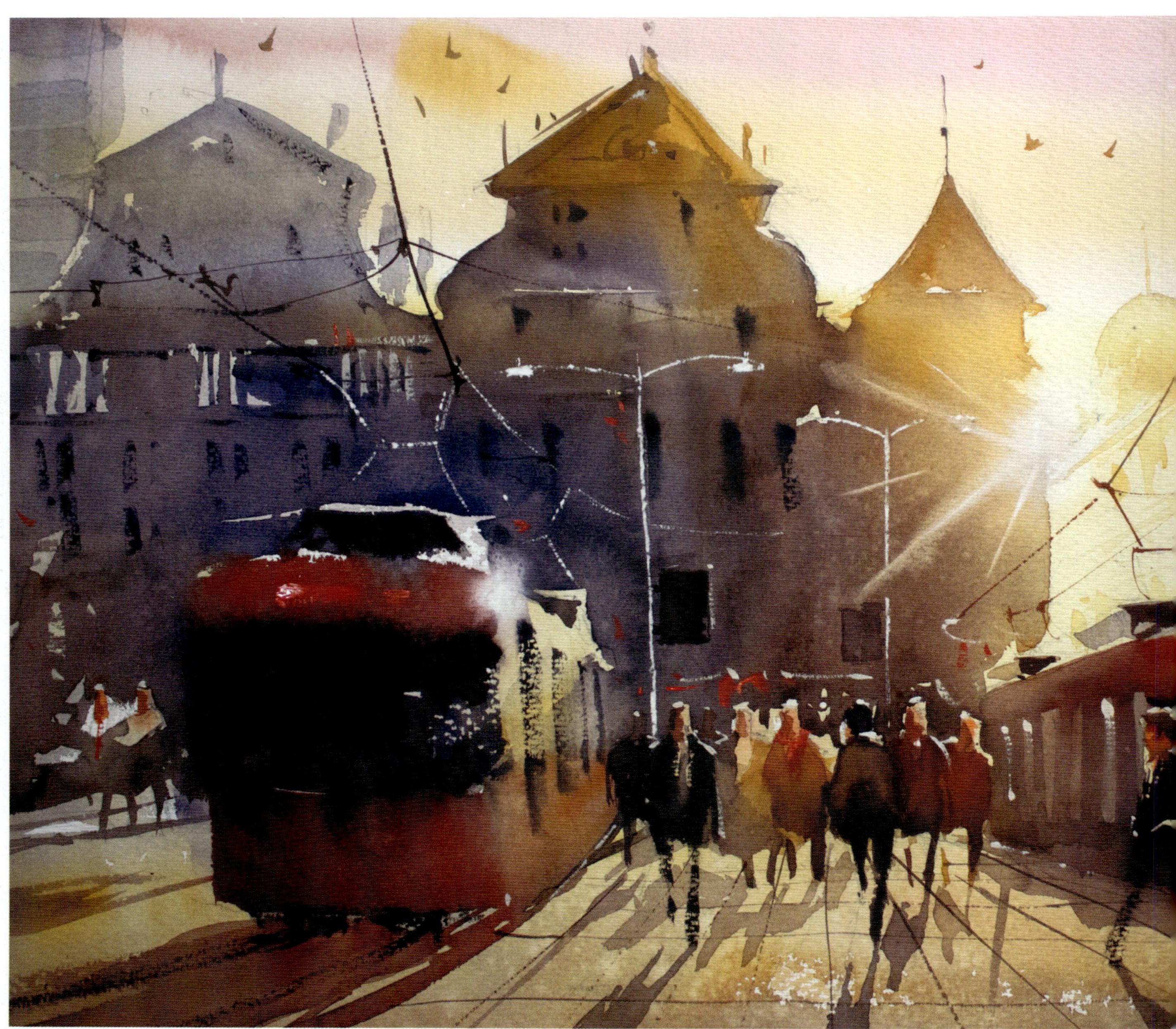

I first applied a loose wash of Indian yellow and alizarin crimson right across the sky, the buildings on the right side, and in the foreground of the painting.

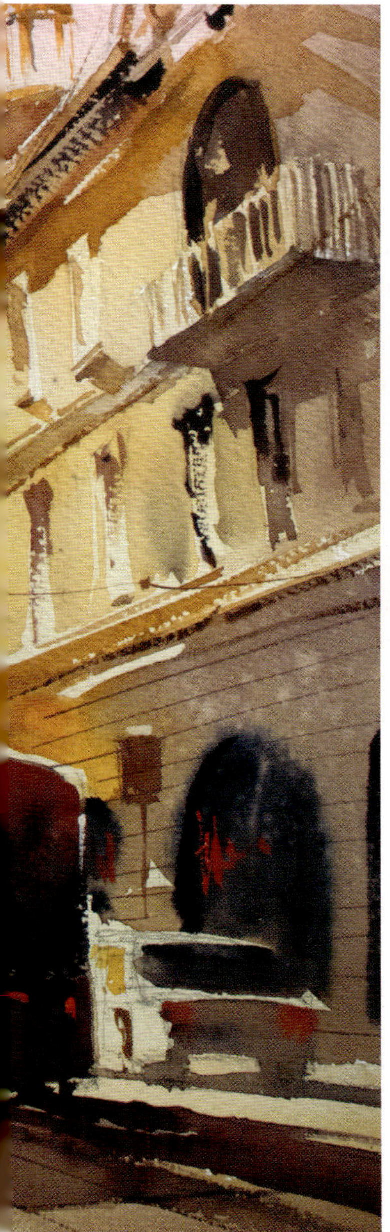

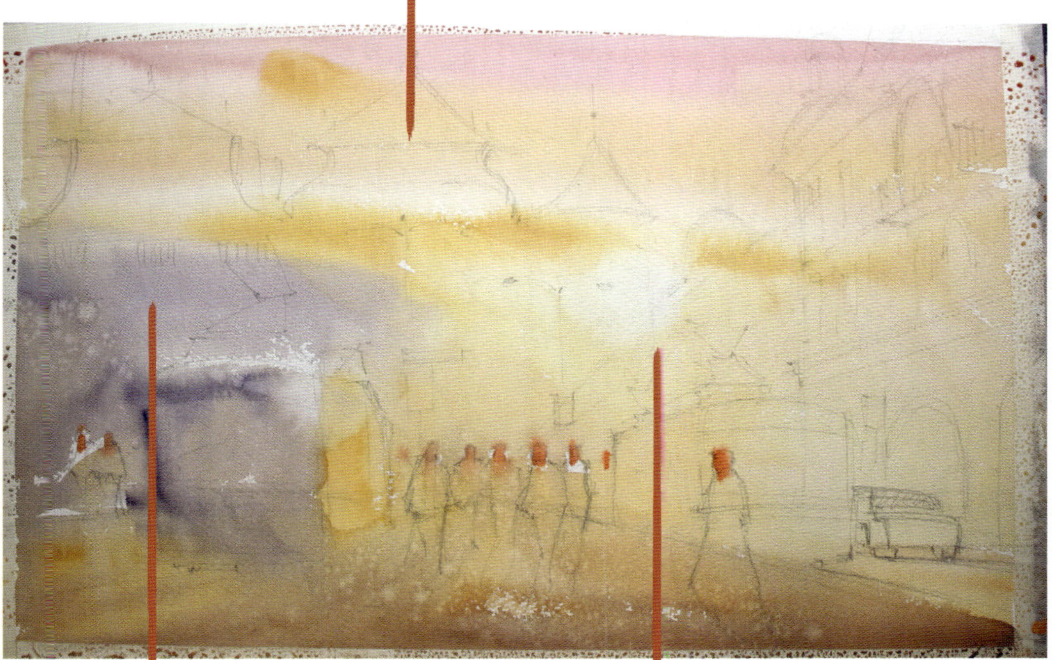

While still wet, I finished with a wash of purple on the buildings and main train on the left-hand side of the painting.

Before the wash was dry, and with a thirsty brush, I pulled some of the color out of the sky, right on the edge of the building. This is my main focus. It's what will dictate the mood of the painting and what will determine my shadows.

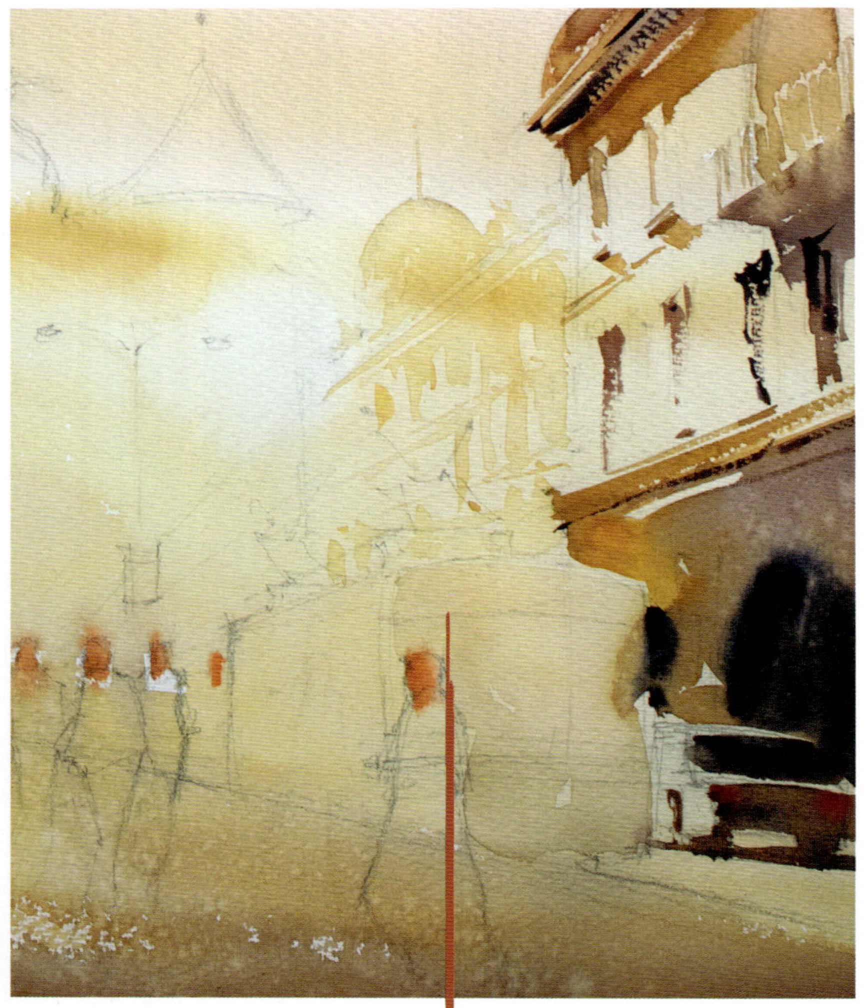

I had to establish some atmosphere in the background. With a few quick brushstrokes I indicated windows and some architectural detail on the distant buildings. I increased the value of my wash and did the same on the building on the right.

Next came the most difficult part of the painting, which was to connect the large building shapes to the trains and figures in the mid and foreground. I started with a wash of Indian yellow on the top and right side of the buildings, then quickly transitioned to a wash of burnt sienna and purple. It's important to note that the color was not mixed on the palette but on the paper—one poured into another. This makes for a much more interesting gradation of color and helps create the feeling of light.

Lastly, just before the wash was dry, I used a paper towel to pull the color from the building using a diagonal motion to create the effect of light streaming from behind the building.

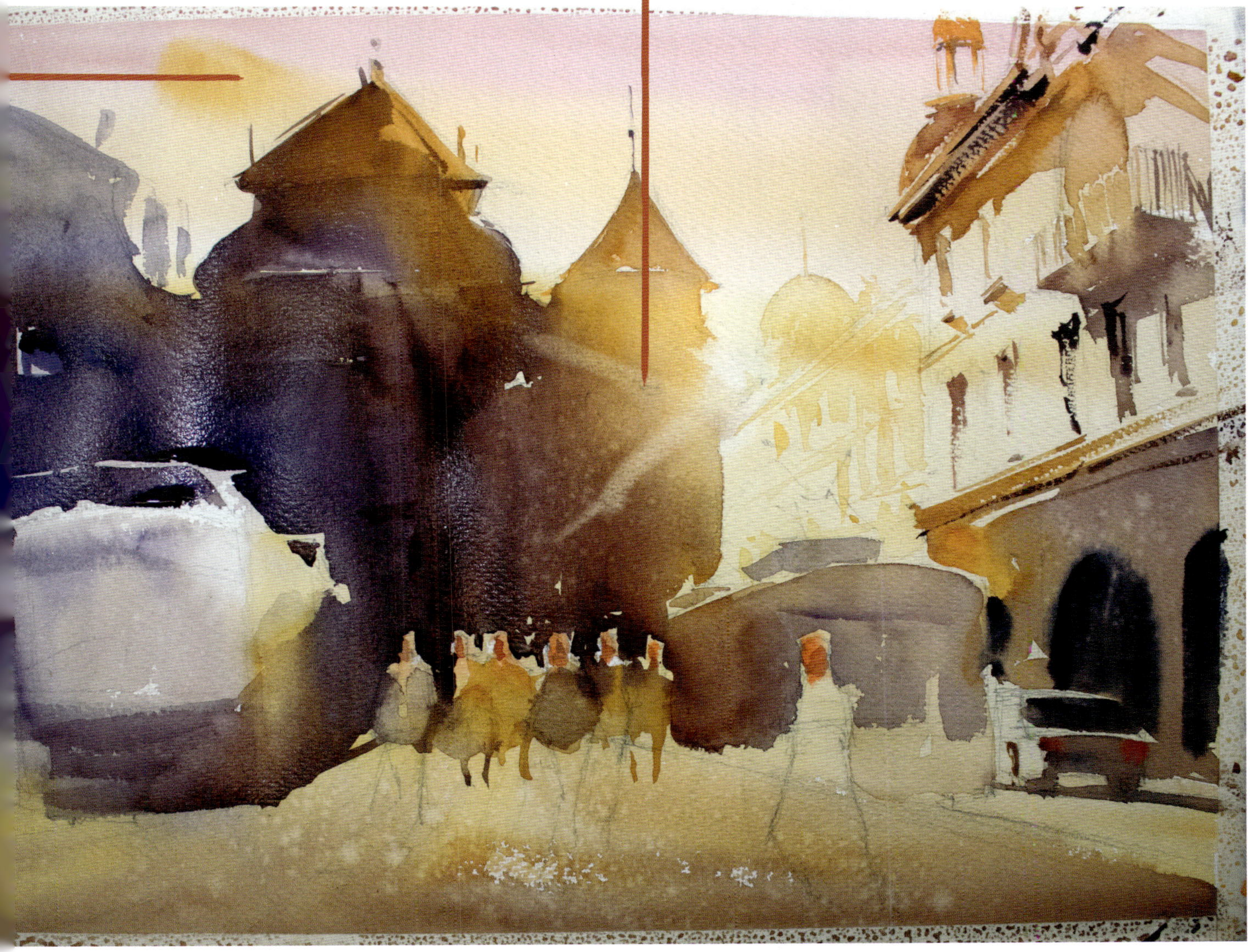

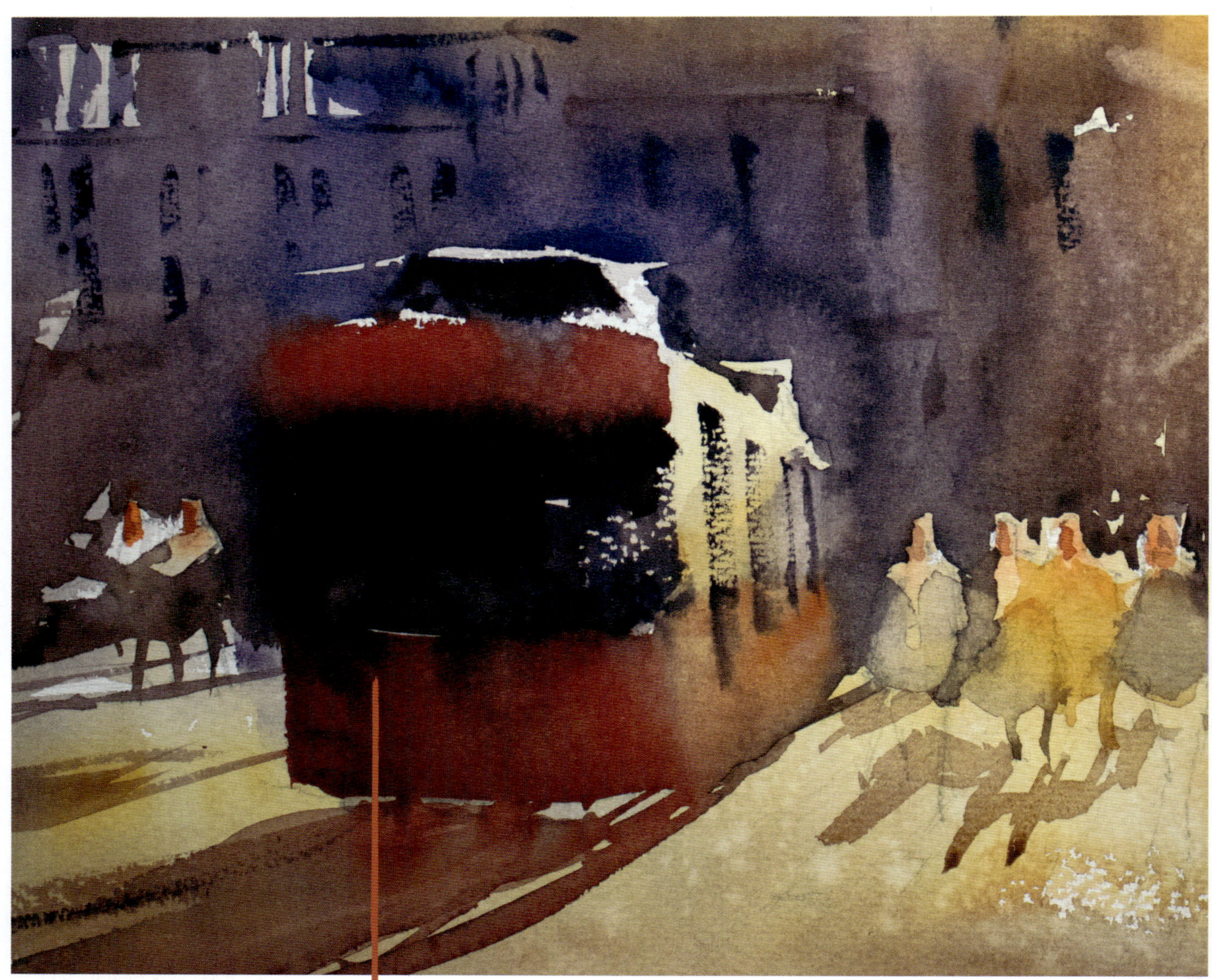

There wasn't a reason to put much detail on the trains, so I allowed my dark mixture to mingle with the cadmium red dark I applied on the top and bottom of the railcars.

At this point, I felt I had enough information to finish the painting back at the studio. Now I'm free to continue the painting unhindered by the details. I finish putting in some of the main figures and with a rigger brush some of the rail lines.

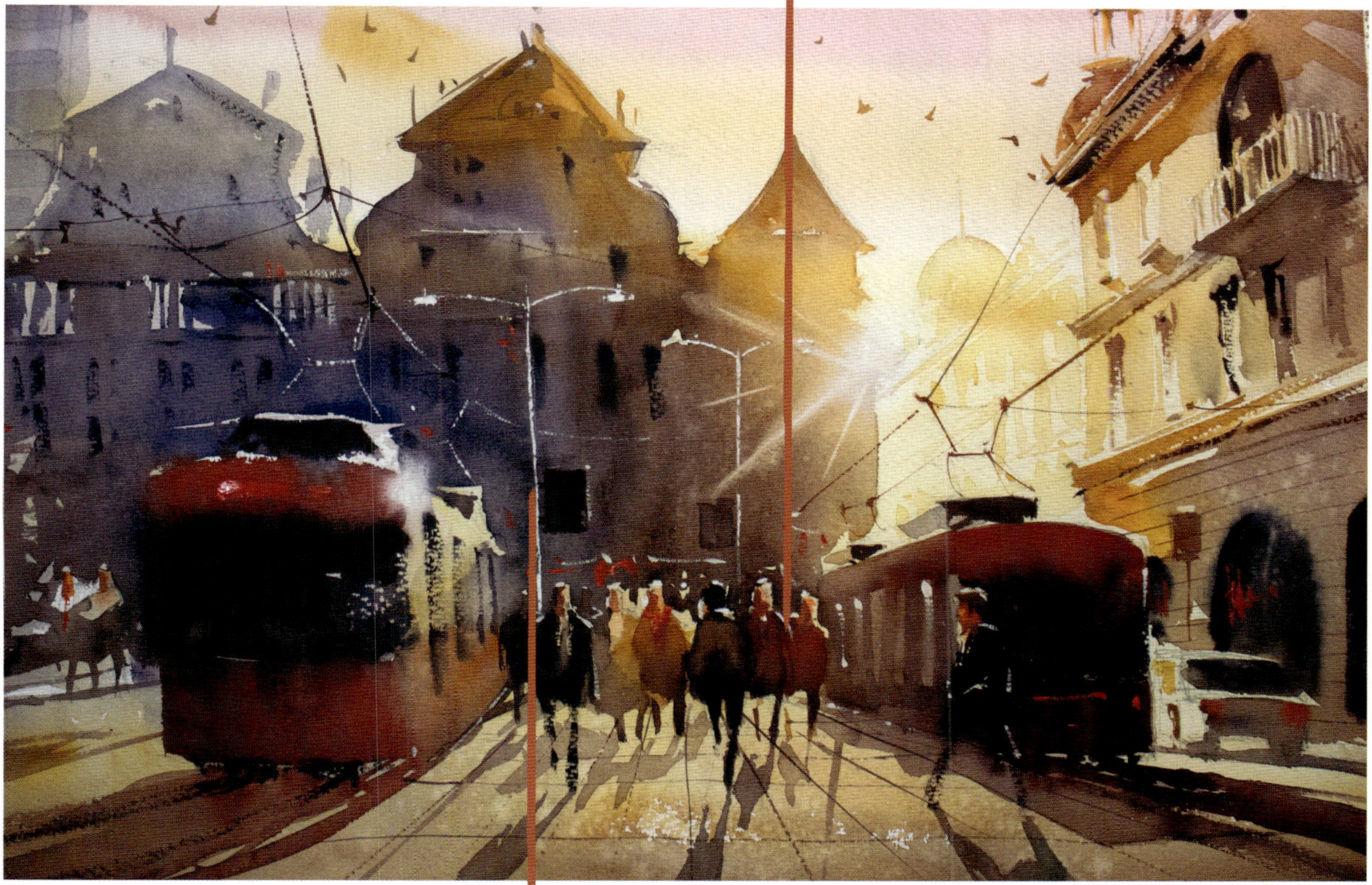

I also scrape into the painting with a razor to establish light poles and more lines.

Individual Style

Each of us have our own unique voice and vision in our work that we should continue to explore as we grow. To show the wide range of styles and possibilities achieved with watercolor media, I am presenting four examples of artists whose work I admire.

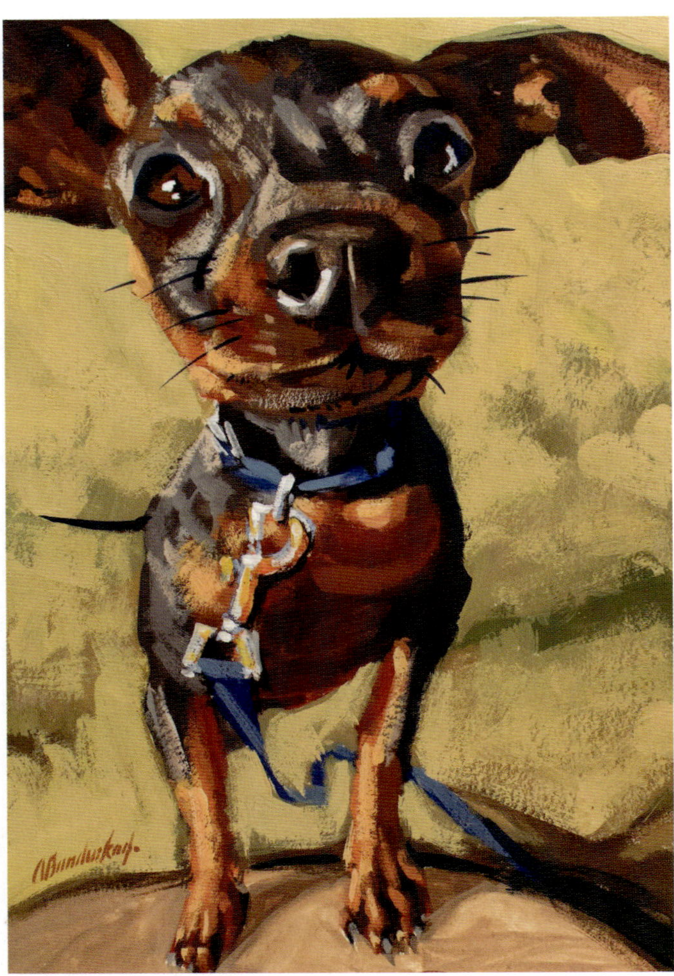

Angela Bandurka, *Ollie*
Gouache, 8 x 5.5 inches

A Canadian artist living in the United States, Angela is best known for her more serious subject matter. However, I chose this gouache painting she did of our dog Ollie, because it shows the artist's fun, whimsical side. Distorted from the foreshortened perspective, see how Angela was able to capture the emotion in Ollie's eyes while working in a very limited palette.

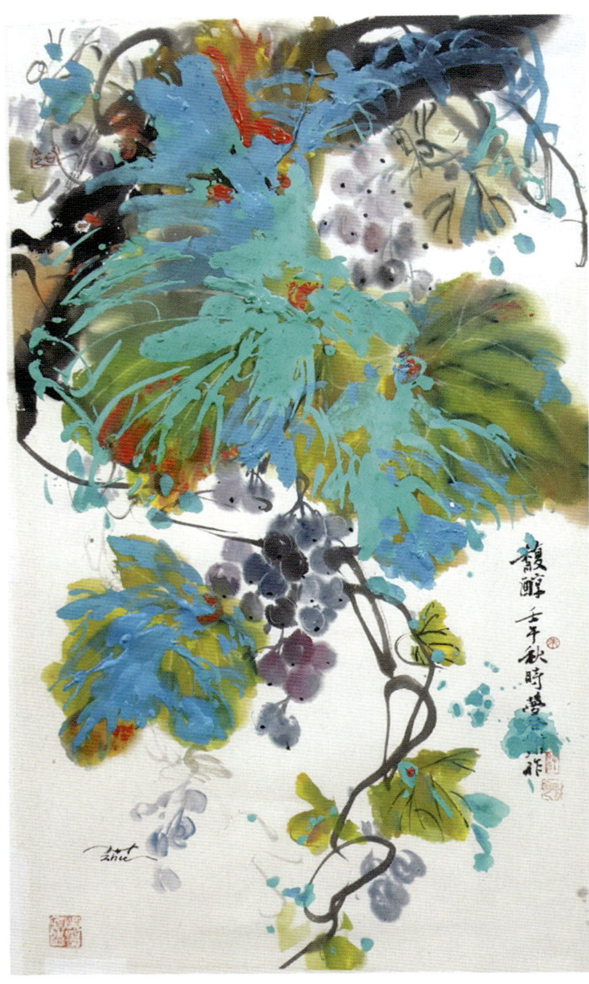

YuMing Zhu, *Lapis Malachite Sumi*
Watercolor and Gouache, 27 x 15 inches

Here YuMing shows how tradition and personal style can combine to make a strong visual. The soft, transparent washes support the more lively brushstrokes of opaque teal and seem to balance this lovely painting of grapevines. Notice how the vine itself connects the entire painting.

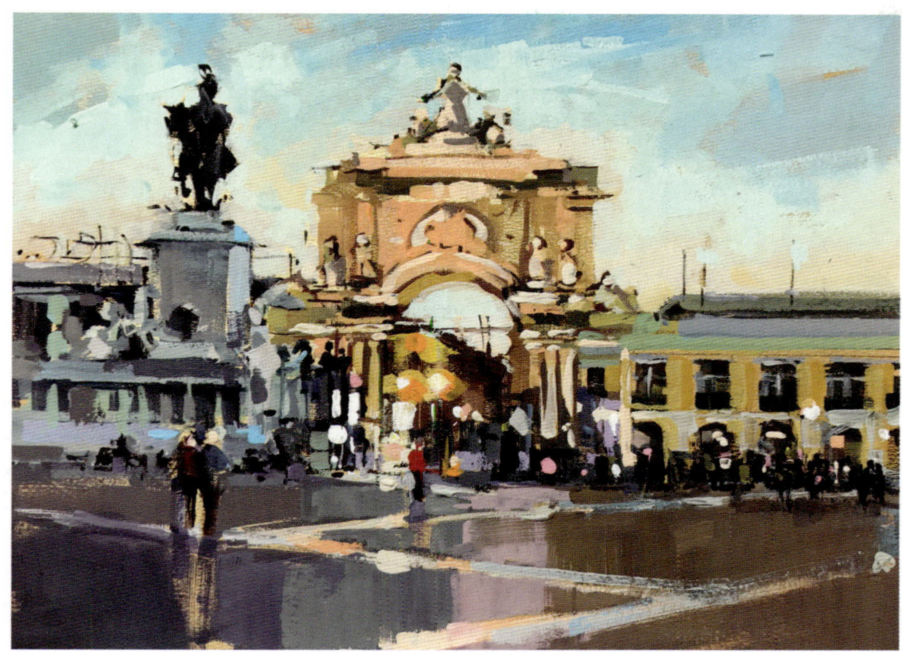

Michele Usibelli, *Lisbon*
Gouache, 9 x 12 inches
Michele's strong use of color and value make her work stand out in any gallery. In this painting, it's easy to see the bold, confident brushstrokes that are indicative of Michele's work. At a second glance, notice the warm and cool notes positioned opposite throughout the painting that tie this piece together.

Bill Hook, *Grain Square Series 10*
Watercolor, 11 x 11 inches
Bill has more than 45 years of experience as an architect/illustrator. You can see the master draftsmanship in all of his work. Small in size, but making a big impression, this painting of a grain elevator works because of the beautiful line and edge quality, good color choices, and simplicity.

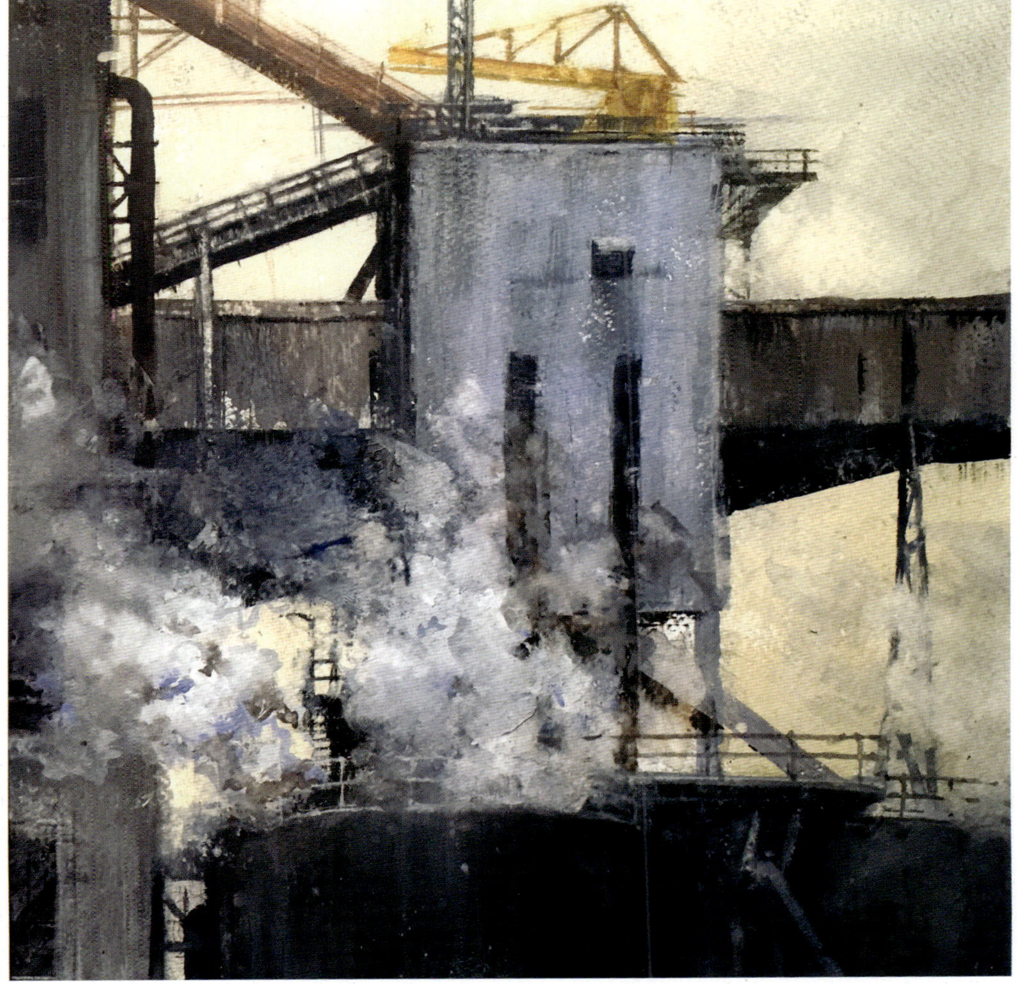

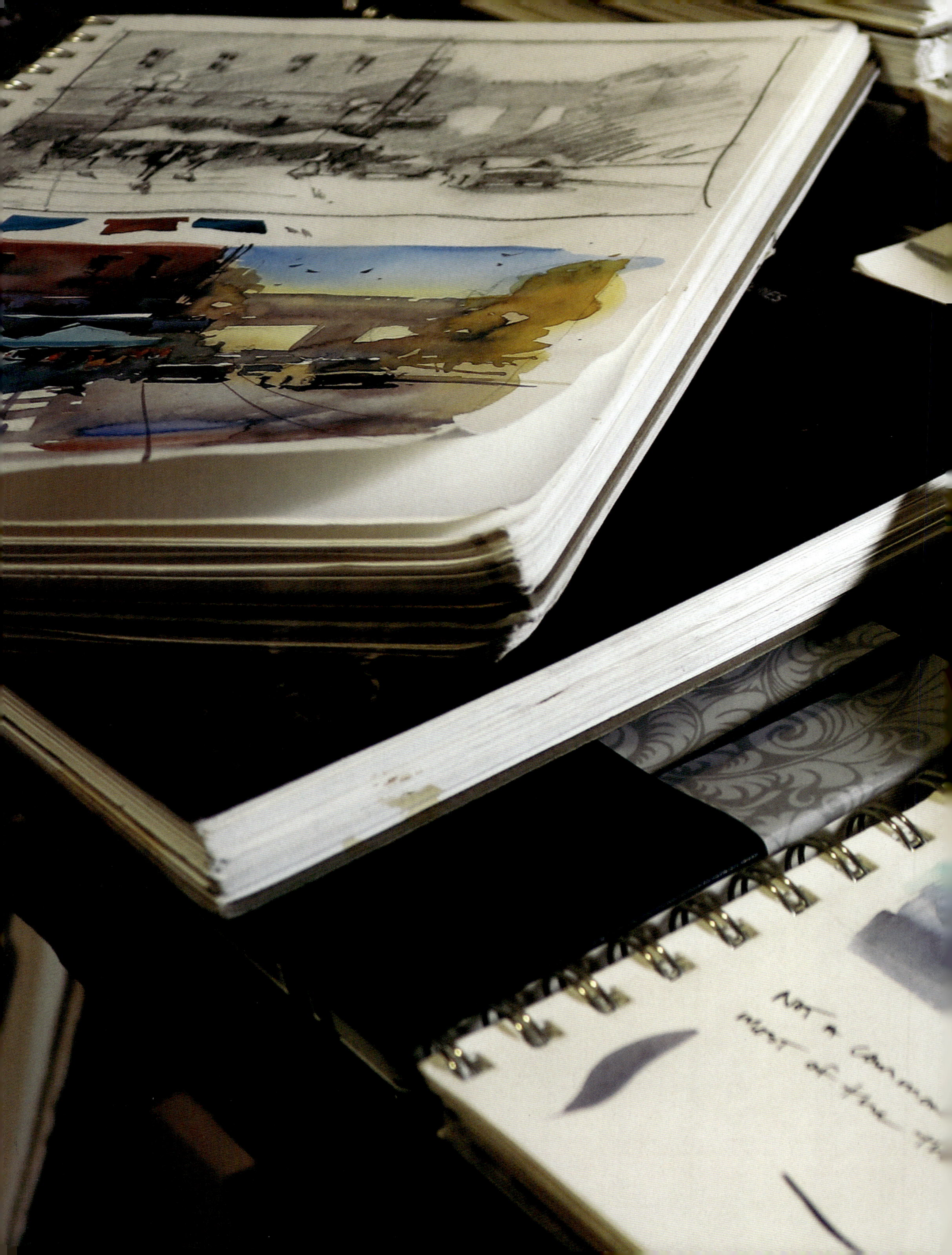

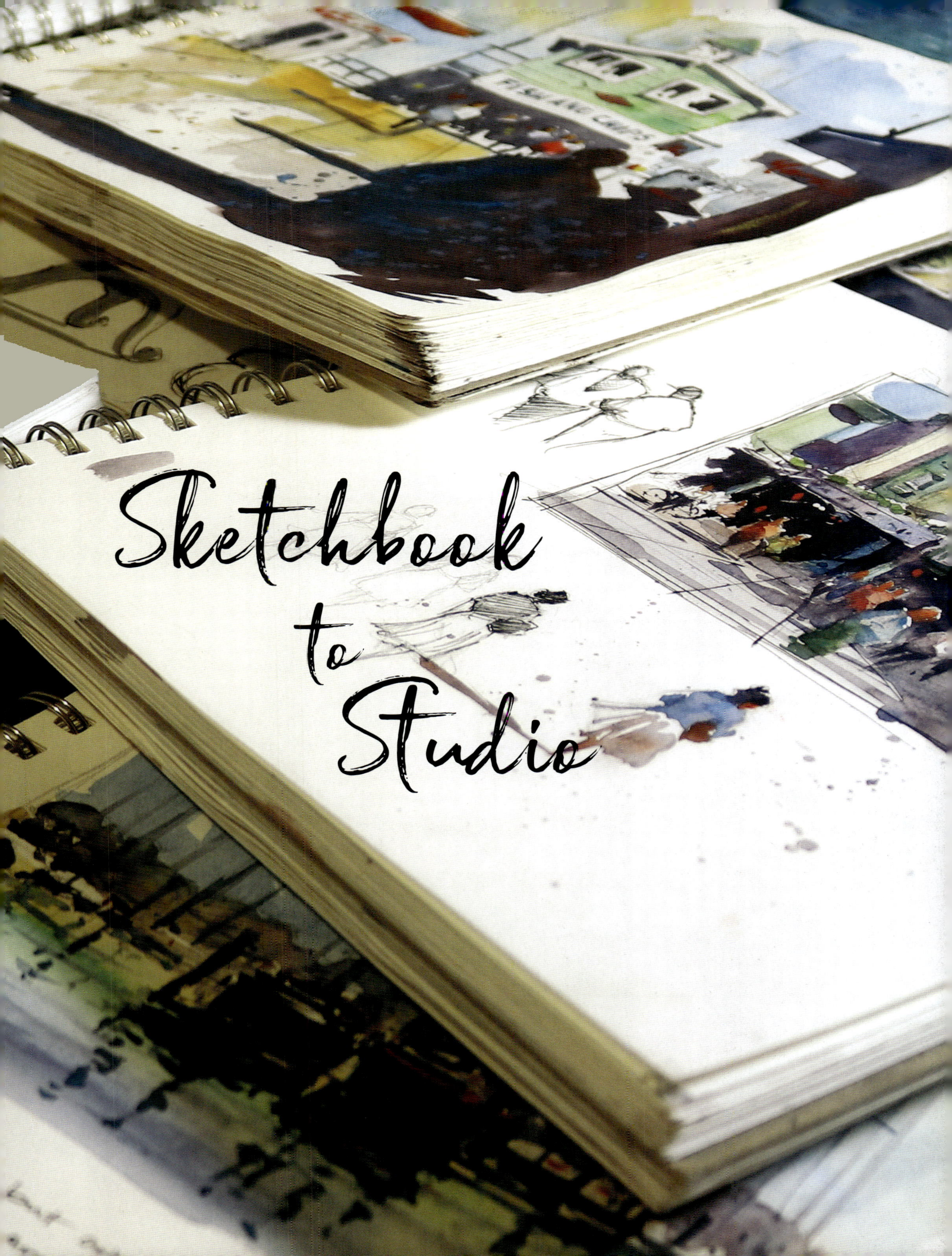

Sketchbook to Studio

Sketching

It's fitting that we are ending this book with the one practice that I started decades ago as a young artist. If there is one item I can't do without, it would be my sketchbook. It has easily become my most valuable artistic tool—a quick, portable resource that has become necessary in my work. Finding the time to paint a finished work every day can sometimes be difficult. Yet it takes no time to open my sketchbook and capture a moment that has sparked my interest or a quick gesture that caught my eye. My sketchbook is a small part of the studio that is always at my side.

When first starting out, my sketchbook was a place filled with fantasy, excitement, and all of the things a young artist dreams about. It is now a classroom, part-time therapist, and yes, the place where some of those dreams have been recorded. The memories captured inside these books are essentially a view of the people, travels, and moments that have made an impression in my life.

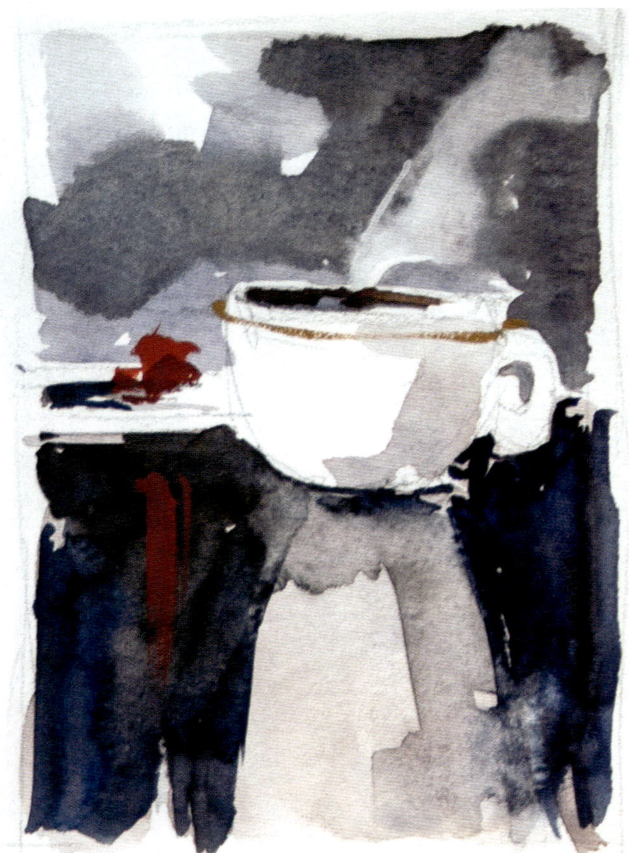

Sketch, *Cappuccino*

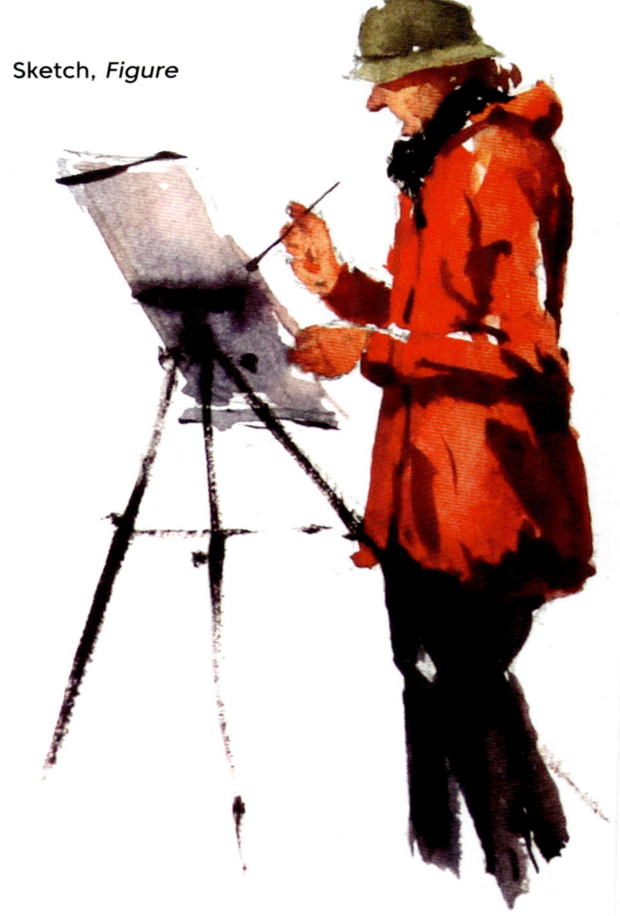

Sketch, *Figure*

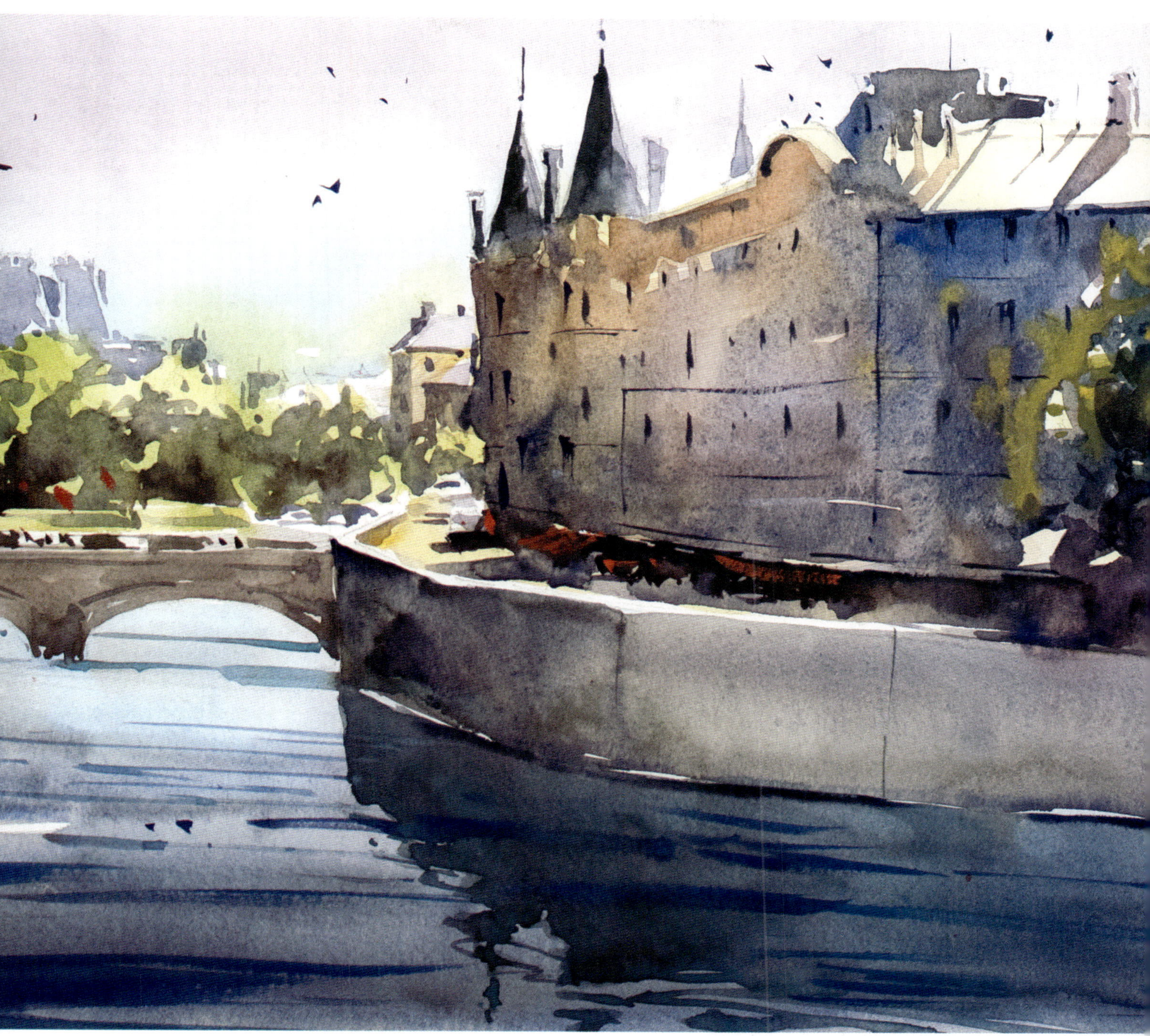

The Conciergerie, Paris

Sketchbooks

My studio is filled with sketchbooks. I always have one at the ready for whenever I need to work out a problem I'm having with a composition, test out a color combination, or when I just need to burn time. I have different sizes, styles, and brands. Some are beautifully crafted, ornate books that I hesitate to draw in because I fear I'll waste a page. Others I'm so familiar with I can't fill them fast enough. A sketchbook is the perfect tool for any level of artist wanting to paint *en plein air*, and it is the first thing I pack when going out.

Today you can find an abundance of sketchbooks in all different sizes, styles, and sheet counts. With all of these choices, it can be challenging to find the one that will work best for you. Like music, every artist has different and unique preferences and needs, so what works for me may not work for you. However, there are some things to consider when selecting the right book.

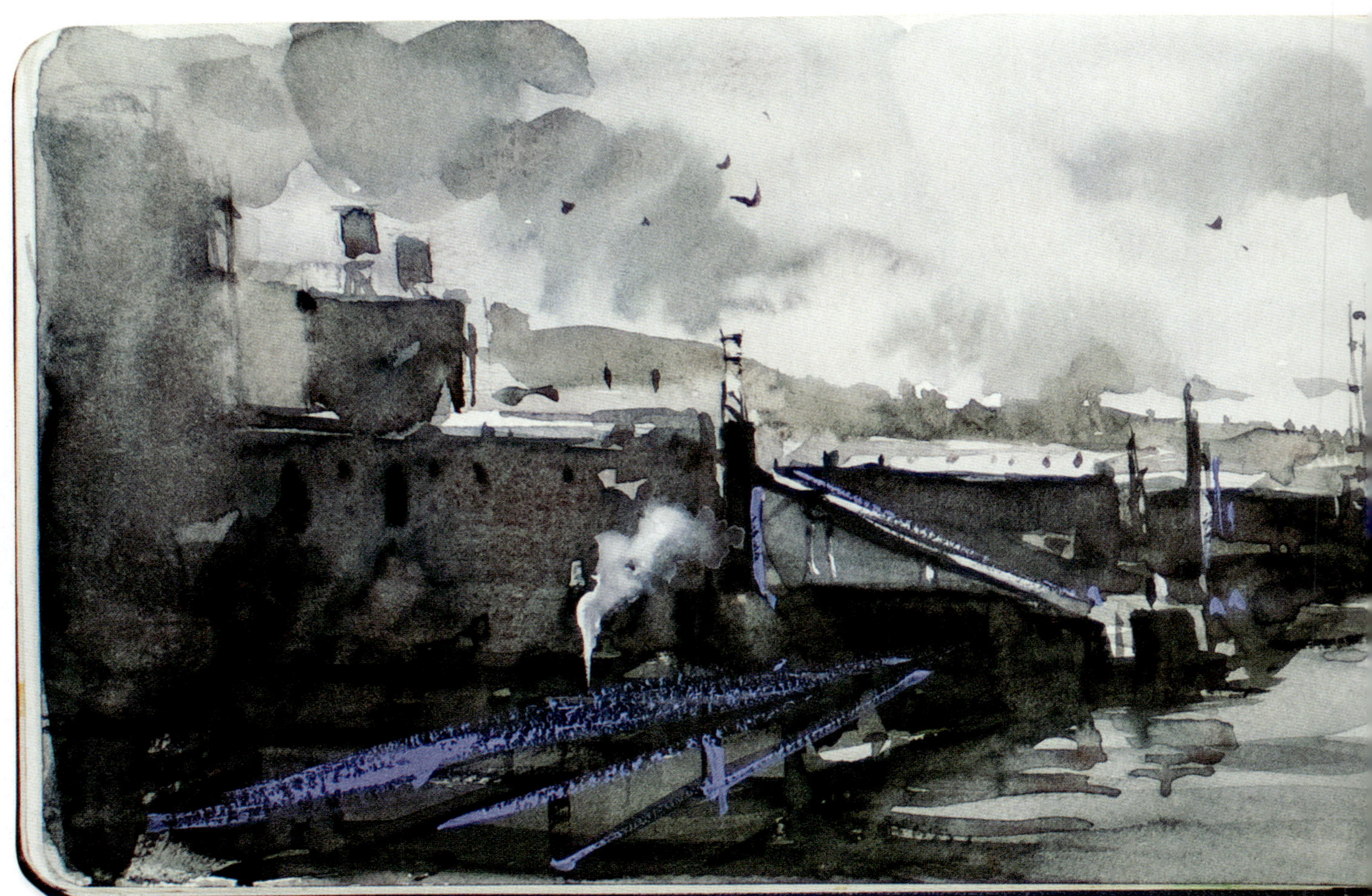

- Look for a sketchbook that can handle multimedia. I try not to pigeonhole myself into specific papers when it comes to sketchbooks. Since you will probably want to work with graphite, ink, and watercolor, look for a book that will accept all of these.
- Pay attention to the page count. I refuse to buy a book with fewer than thirty sheets. The more sheets usually means less cost per sheet.
- I like a firm cover that will protect my pages. Some of the books come with hardcovers that allow you to write on them. Recording your travels or subjects on the front cover is something I do so I can retrieve the sketch easily if needed.

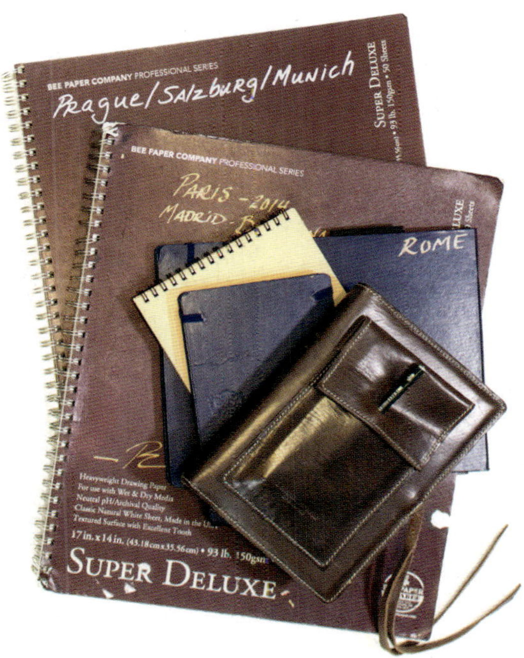

Sketch, *From Harbor Island*

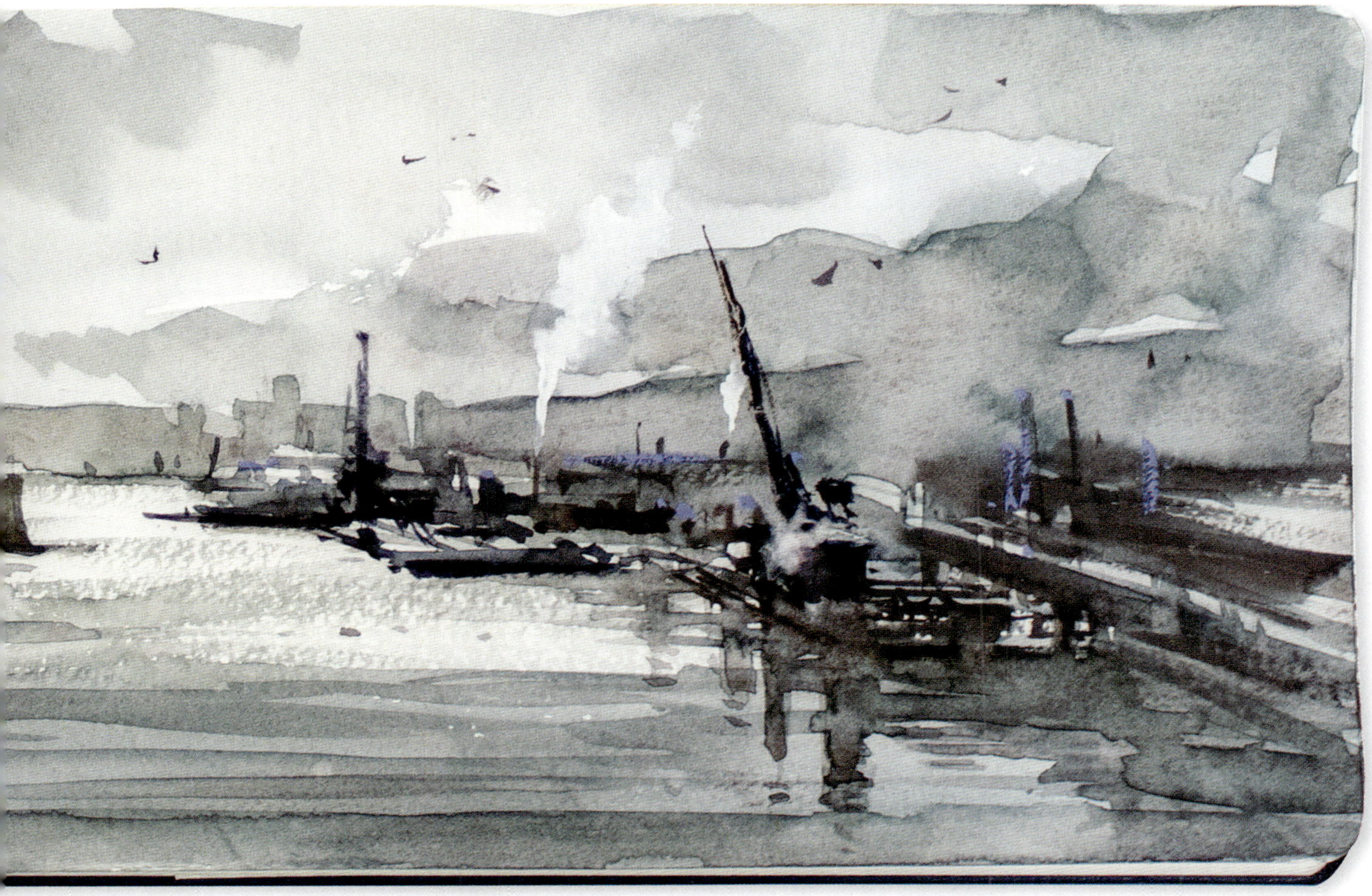

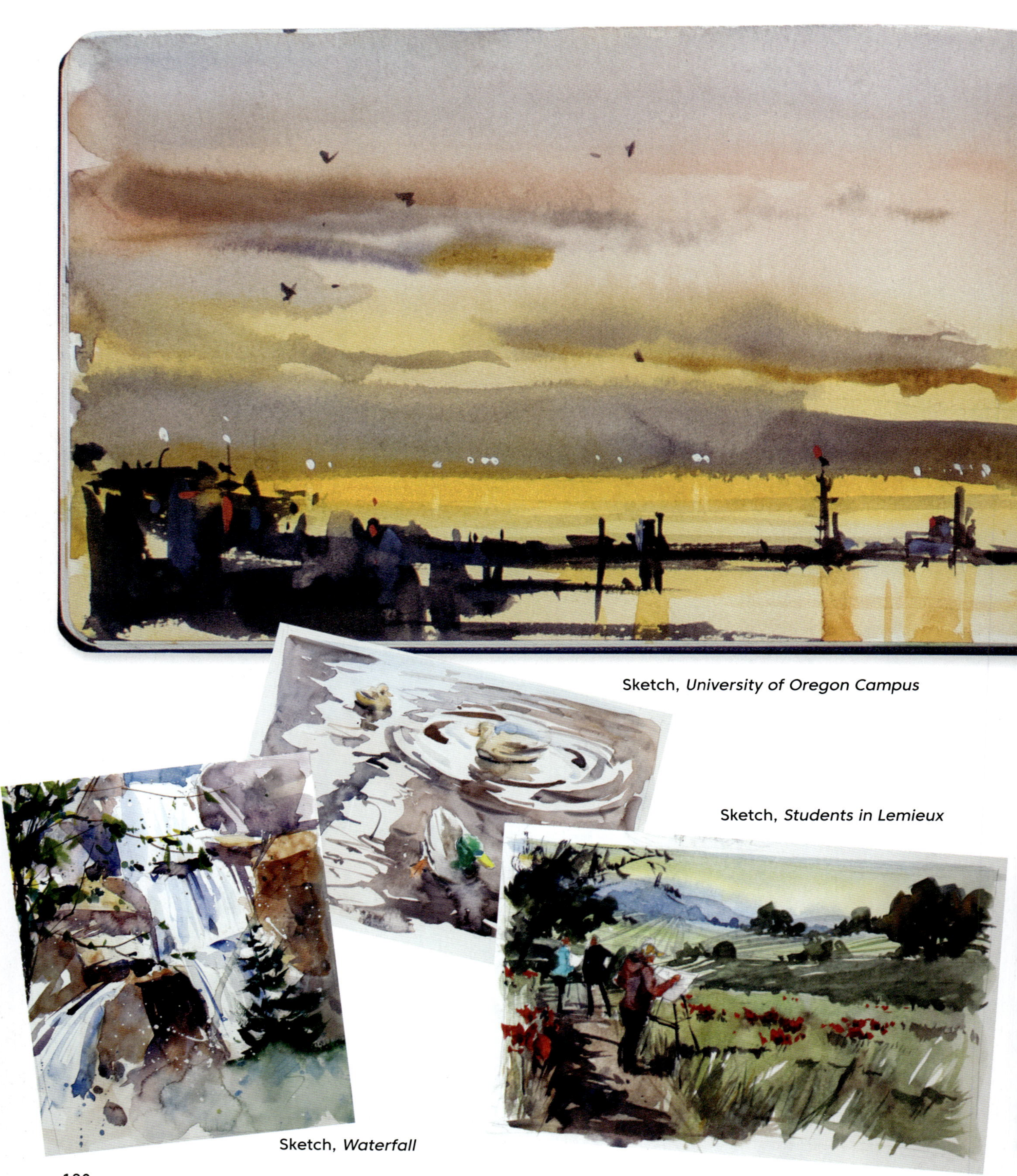

Sketch, *University of Oregon Campus*

Sketch, *Students in Lemieux*

Sketch, *Waterfall*

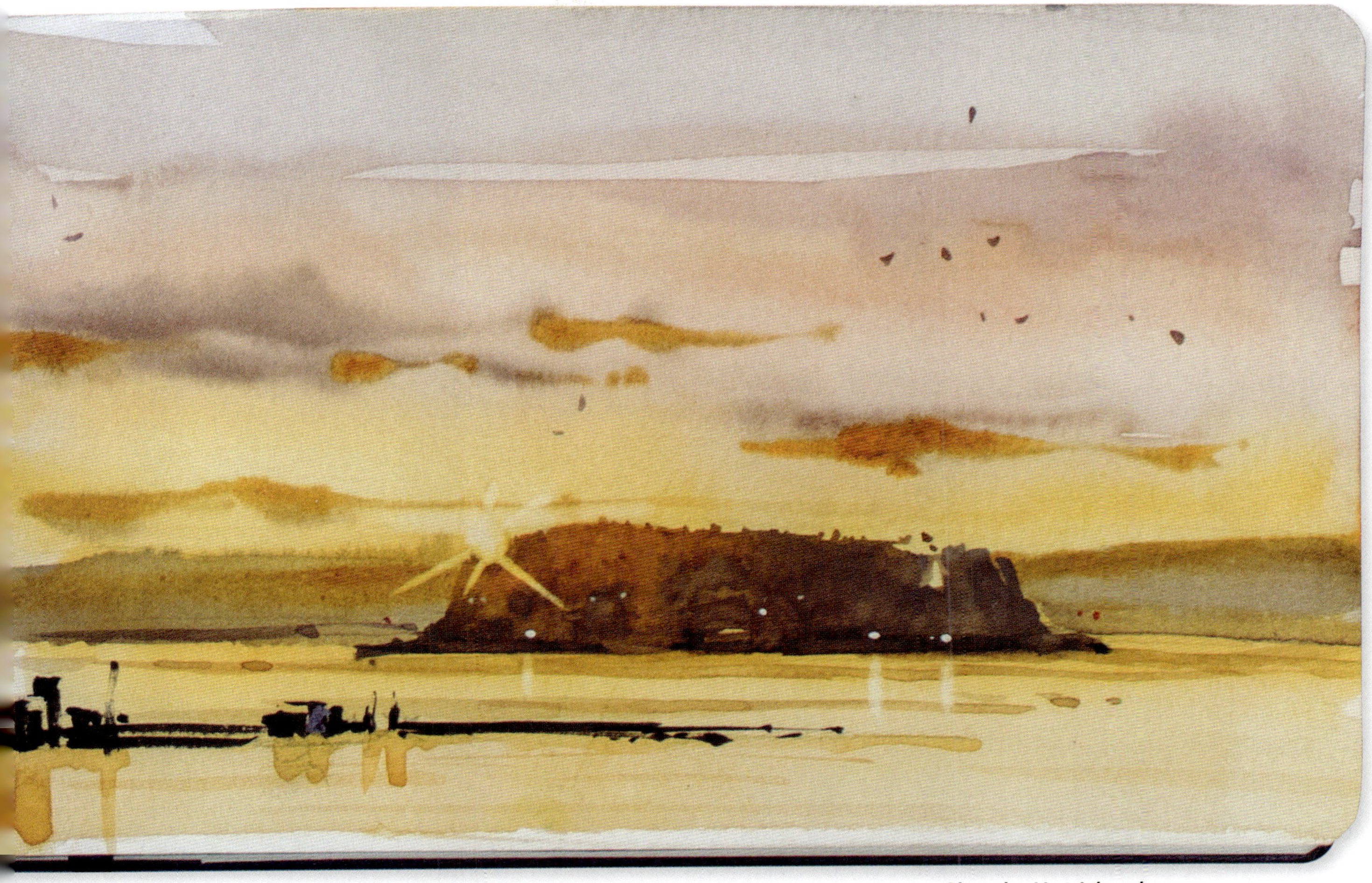

Sketch, *Hat Island*

For practical use, there is a formula I often use when working out a painting in my sketchbook. I start with a value sketch, done in graphite. This is to simplify the shapes and values of my subject, so that I don't hesitate on details when moving through my painting. If I need further information, I do a color study. This is to give me a good idea of the mood or color harmony I want to recreate in the finished painting. After that, I may work on figures or an architectural detail that I particularly want to get right when scaling up to the larger sheet.

Sketch, *Frog*

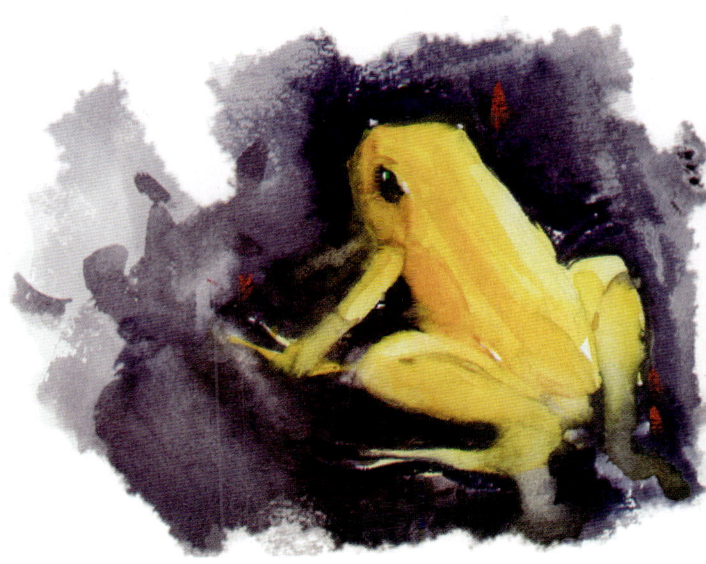

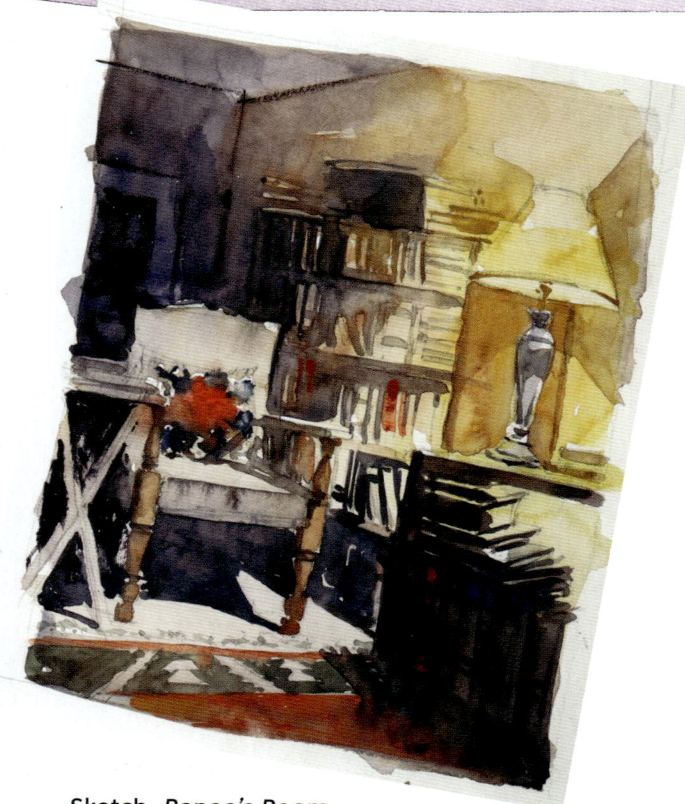

Sketch, *Our Wicker Chair*

The patterns of the chair, area rugs, and old window blinds are what interested me in sketching this subject, but once again, the light stole the show. What you don't see are the shadows cast by the window just out of view to the right. I purposely ignored them so I could simplify the painting.

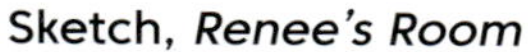

Sketch, *Renee's Room*

This sketch of a room in my sister's home presented a common problem—too many things to paint. My solution was to focus on this one piece of furniture and suggest the many books, record albums, and computers. By reducing these details, I have improved the sketch.

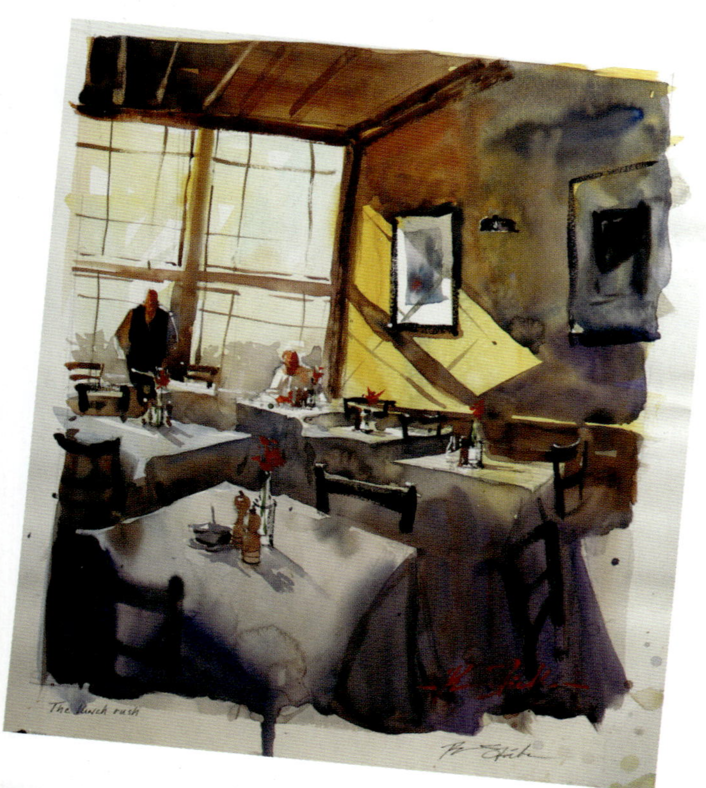

Sketch, *Lunch Rush*

Here is a common example of the interior lighting being overpowered by the light coming through the window. Make sure your values are correct or the important elements such as the figures, tables, and chairs will get lost.

Interiors

Interiors are a favorite subject of mine. Not only do they convey intimacy, but they also present unique challenges. For one, you can usually count on multiple light sources, such as a lamp or chandelier, as well as the light streaming through a nearby window. When dealing with this, I really have two choices: paint multiple shadows, which even when done well can be confusing to the viewer, or choose the dominant light source and direct your shadows from it.

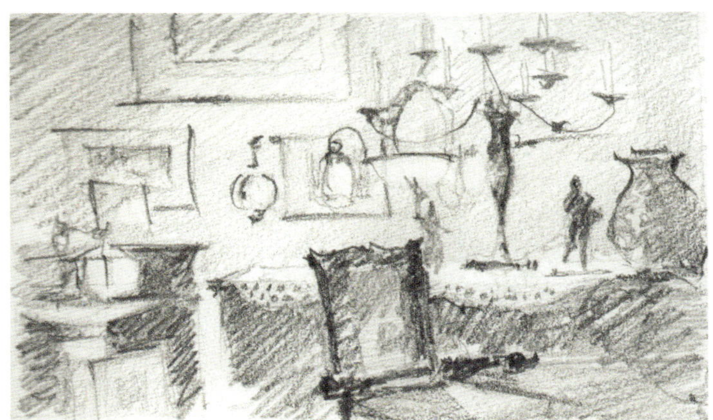

Sketch, *Antique Shop Pencil*

I couldn't set up my painting gear in this small antique shop, but the shop owner allowed me to set up and sketch this quiet corner. The graphite sketch was done quickly using a 4B lead holder. My goal was to capture the values and some of the unique items displayed around the store.

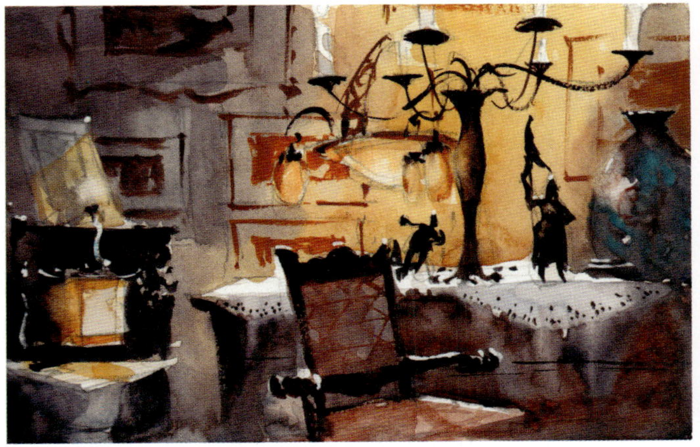

Sketch, *Antique Shop*

The color study above took me a bit longer. The focus here was to capture the intensity of the warm colors cast from the lamps on the sideboard and get enough information to help me when I got back to my studio. The darks were a mixture of ultramarine blue and maroon, the same colors used in the finished painting.

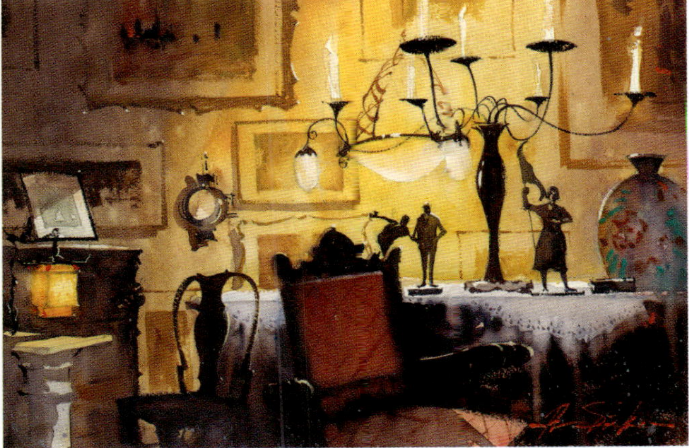

Antique Shop

Back in the studio, I gathered my sketches along with photographs I took on location and painted a more finished piece.

Hotel Negresco Step-by-Step

This studio painting is from a study made *en plein air*. I thought I would tackle two issues in this step-by-step: how to transfer an image I've done on location to a more finished studio painting, and the effect of keeping large areas of white paper exposed in a painting.

After a day out painting, I usually like to take some time to view the work in my studio. This gives me the opportunity to evaluate the pros and cons of the work away from my subject. Along with the painting, I study any notes, sketches, and photographs I may have taken while out that day.

This painting (below) is of one of my favorite landmarks in Nice: the Negresco Hotel. Unlike other paintings where the white of the paper might be concentrated in a small area, about a third of this painting is left almost completely paper white. I wanted to use it to create tension and draw the eye. In this case, It was also perfect for the large, white building at the end of the street.

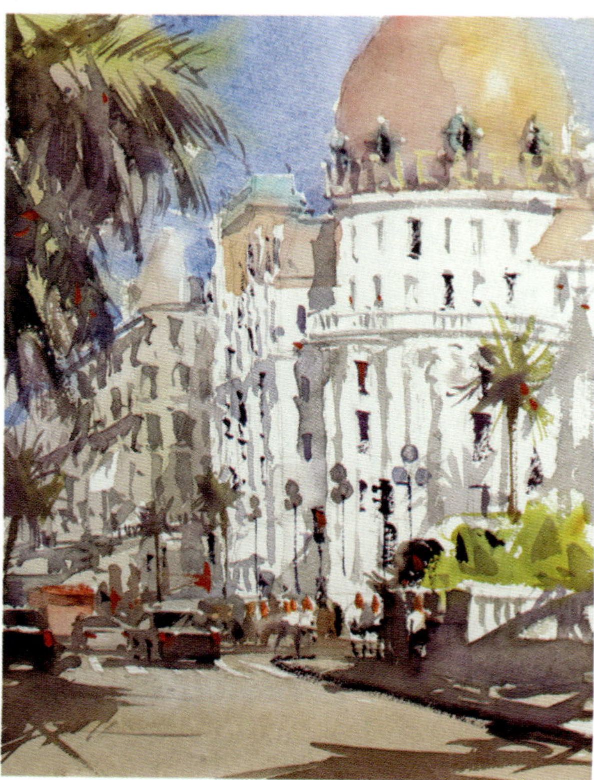

Even though I painted this in the studio, I still wanted to maintain the freshness of the painting I did earlier on location. I also felt that a horizontal format would give the composition a better feel of distance by showing more of the buildings and street. By changing the format, it also presented me with a fresh look at a familiar subject.

Normally I would apply my first wash over the entire sheet, skipping over isolated areas, leaving smaller shapes of the paper exposed. In this case, both buildings and other small shapes were left white. However, I knew that I wanted the top dome of the hotel to stand out against the cobalt blue sky. So I painted it first with a wash of alizarin crimson and added a touch of Indian yellow. The large awning was done quickly with a few bold brushstrokes of cadmium red.

The wash on the foreground building had to be loose and free, allowing the colors to mix on the paper so that they would create an interesting tertiary color. The distant car shapes and a few shadows came next.

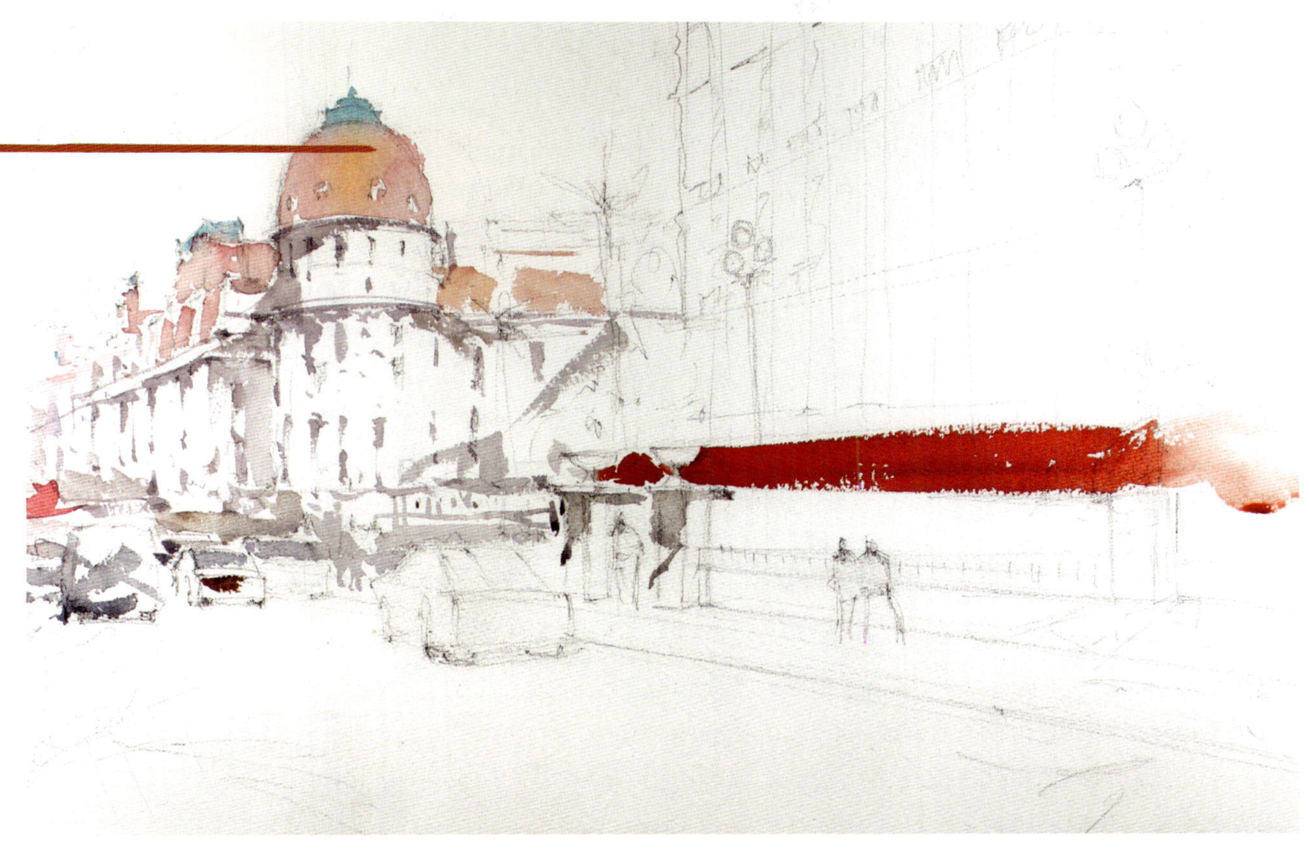

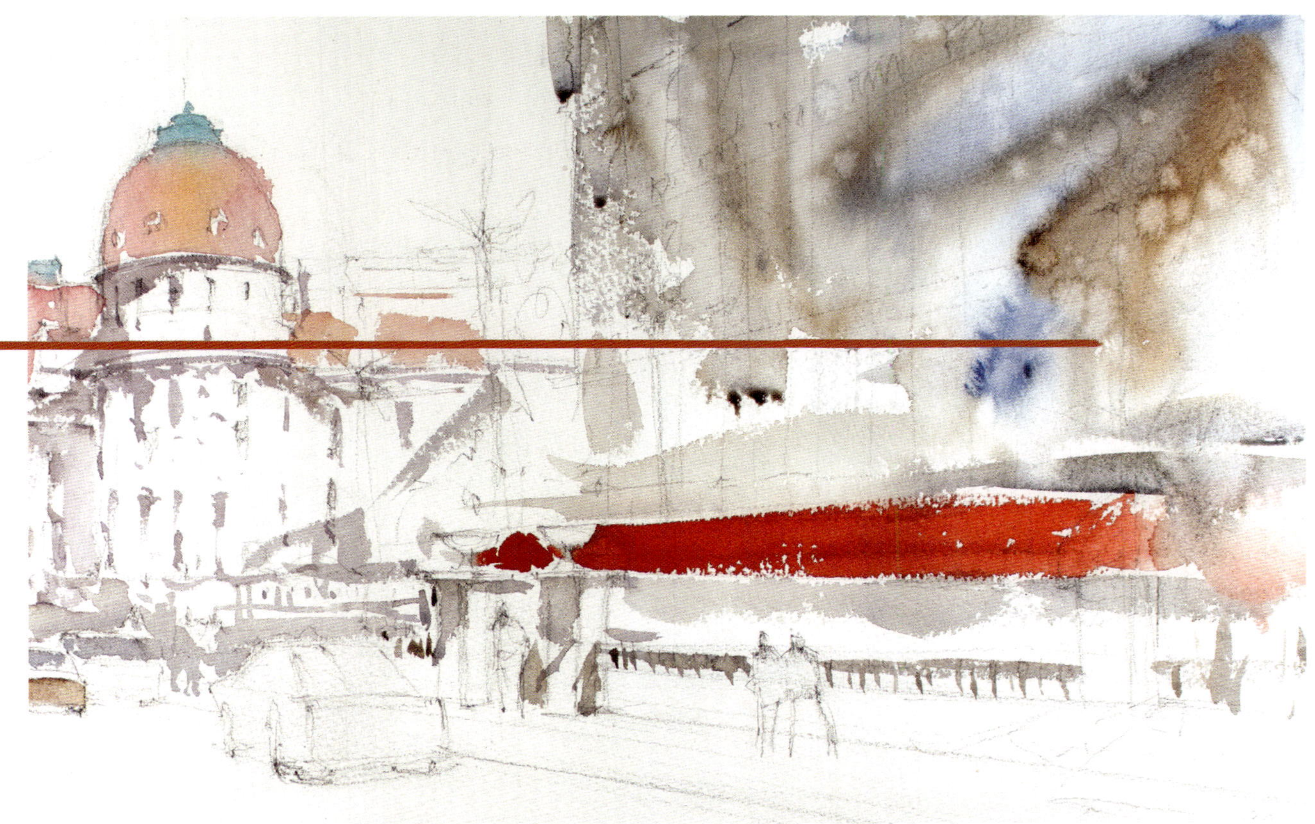

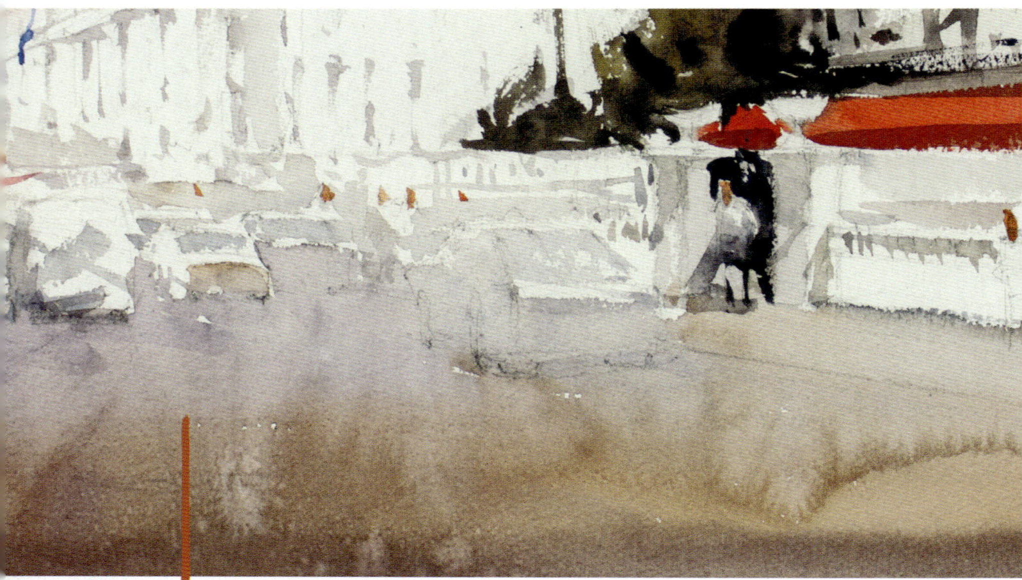

The street needed to be applied quickly before everything dried, so that there would be a smooth transition between mid and foreground. This also helped connect the buildings, vehicles, trees, etc. A powerful wash of cobalt blue was then applied for the sky.

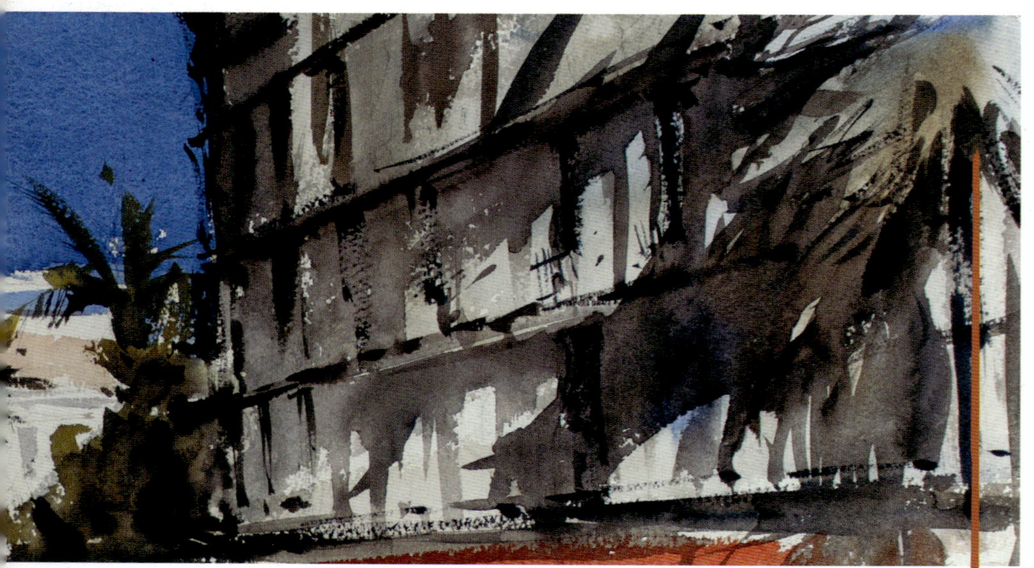

Now came what I feel is the most important part of the painting, the shadows on the buildings. If labored over and controlled, I would have lost the energy of this piece. So I painted the shadows with a large mop brush, using bold positive brushstrokes that represented the broken shadow shapes cast from the balconies, iron work, and palm tress.

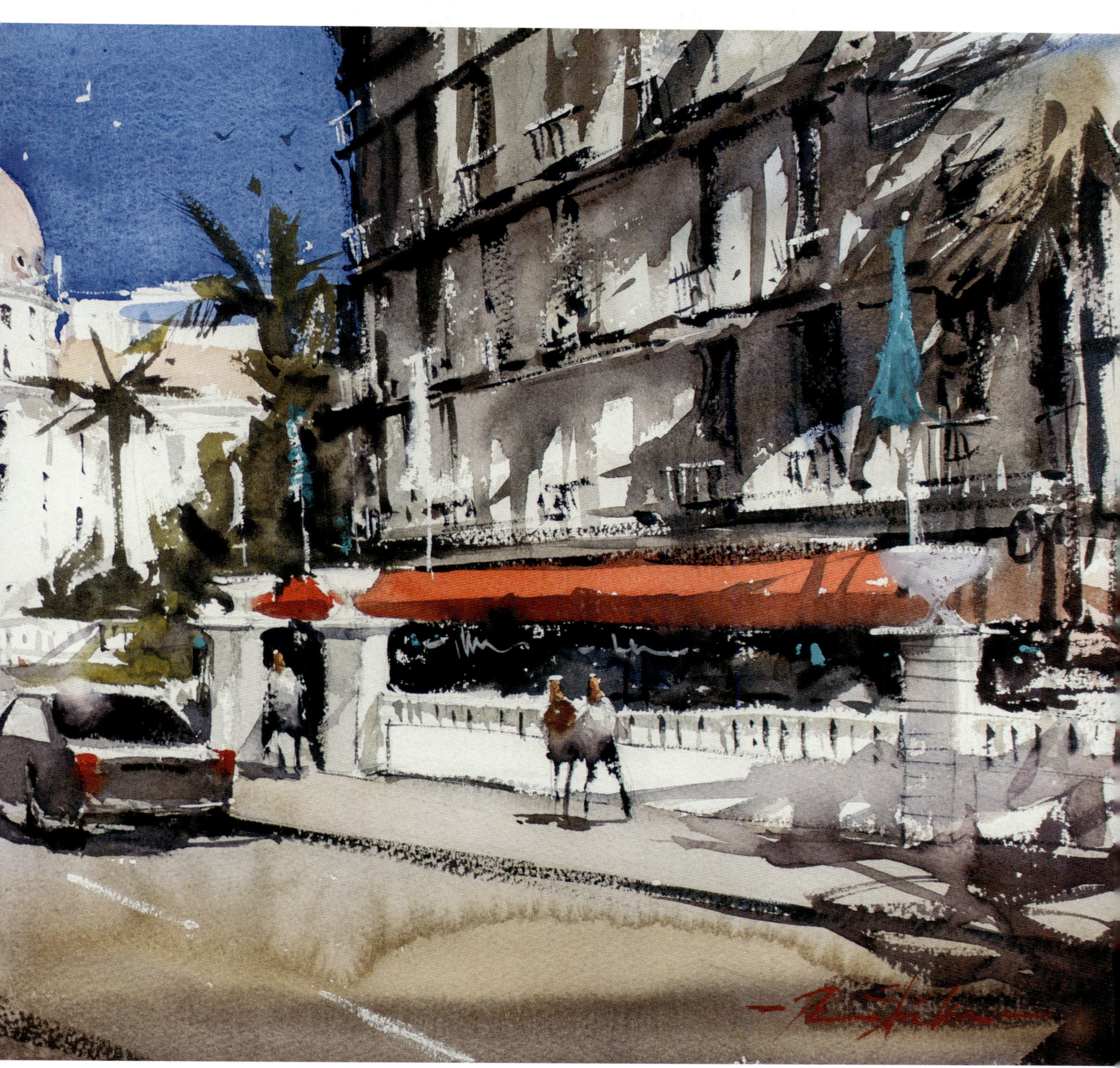

The palm trees, cars, figures, and other details were added for scale and interest.

About the Author

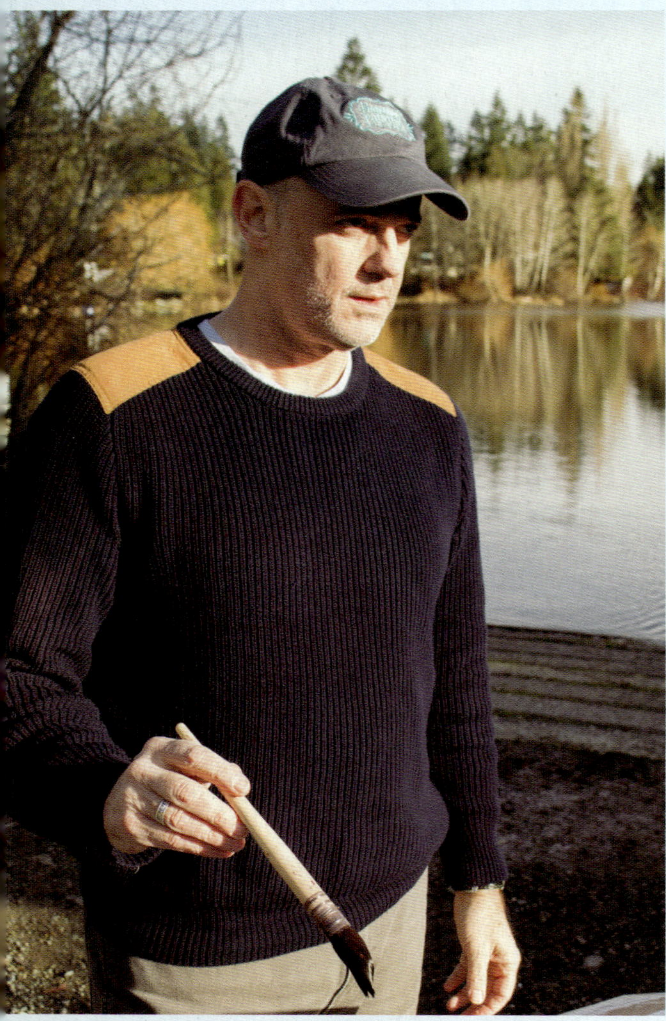

Born in 1966 in Chico, California, Ron Stocke moved to the Pacific Northwest in 1979, where he has remained ever since. Ron's involvement in the art world spans more than three decades.

Ron's award-winning work has received top honors in many international exhibitions, and he holds signature membership in the National Watercolor Society, the American Watercolor Society, and the Northwest Watercolor Society. He is also an elected member of the Canadian Society of Painters in Watercolour, as well as a member of the American Impressionist Society.

His involvement in the art industry extends into the art materials world as well. In 2000, Ron began working with the M. Graham Paint Co. as the face of their watercolor line. Ron regularly does painting demonstrations to show how their honey-based paints lend themselves to his way of working.

Dedication

This book is dedicated to my mother, Pamela, for her love and support; to my two sisters, Rhonda and Renee, who continue to be my best friends; and to my incredible wife, Angela, for her love, patience, support, and sense of humor through this process.
In memory of Ursula Marie Stocke.